THE REASONING AND THE SEASONING OF JEWISH COOKING

MENORAH, BRONZE, SALVADOR DALI

TU B'SHVAT a Variety of Fresh and Dried Fruit is Symbolic.

The Reasoning and the Seasoning of Jewish Cooking

By
UNIVERSITY WOMEN OF
THE UNIVERSITY OF JUDAISM

Joseph Simon   Pangloss Press

MALIBU, CALIFORNIA

Copyright 1994 by
University Women of
The University of Judaism

Library of Congress
Catalog Card Number 94-066029

Mimi Landres, Project Chairperson

Design by Ruth Pordy
Photography by Michael Tov
Food Design by Lorraine Shapiro

All Rights Reserved

FOR ADDITIONAL COPIES OF THIS FINE BOOK WRITE TO:

University Women of the University of Judaism,
15600 Mulholland Drive, Los Angeles, CA 90077.
Proceeds go to the University of Judaism.
Send $24.75 for each copy, plus $2.90 each shipping.
In California add $2.10 sales tax, per copy.

CONTENTS

INTRODUCTION • 6

ACKNOWLEDGEMENTS • 7

WISDOM OF THE SCHOLARS • 9

BREADS • 19

APPETIZERS • 37

SOUP • 55

SALAD • 73

PICKLES AND SAUCES • 91

VEGETABLES • 109

CASSEROLES • 127

FISH • 145

MEAT • 163

POULTRY • 181

COOKIES • 199

DESSERT • 217

PASSOVER • 235

LIST OF CONTRIBUTORS • 255

MENUS • 256

INDEX • 258

INTRODUCTION

DR. DAVID LIEBER
President Emeritus, University of Judaism

One of the most important, but little recognized, ritual objects of Jewish life is the dinner table. Throughout the centuries whenever we recite the blessings over meals, celebrate holidays with special foods or share a Shabbat meal with family and friends, the dinner table has been a central gathering point for the Jewish family. It is during meals that we often share with our children and our families the ideas and traditions of our people. It is a place where we create a warm and intimate sense of Jewish community. And just as our forefather Abraham welcomed the strangers into his tent for a meal, so have Jews throughout time been enjoined to invite the stranger to share the Passover table.

When the University Women suggested the idea of creating a Jewish cookbook, it, therefore, seemed an altogether fitting project. Food has always played an important symbolic role in transmitting Jewish knowledge. From the forbidden fruit of the Garden of Eden to the manna sustaining the Jews in the desert to the rules of kashrut and the ritual foods of the holidays, food is a tool to help us learn about and experience Jewish life.

I hope that when you sit down to enjoy a Jewish meal inspired by this book, that you will also experience a connection to Jewish families throughout history and throughout the world.

DR. ROBERT WEXLER
President, University of Judaism

As any good cook can tell you, the keys to culinary success are imagination and the right basic ingredients. The same is true for a successful institution of higher education. The University of Judaism is well known as a place for innovative programming. Our success is based upon our ability to discern the changing needs of the American Jewish community. The UJ's educational endeavors have already begun to attract a national audience. As we look forward to the 21st century, our collective imagination envisions a university which is known as an institution of academic excellence and an important center of leadership for the Jewish community.

The University can also boast of a "secret spice." In our case that means the University Women who volunteer countless hours in support of the University. Their energy and imagination are a tremendous resource to this institution.

And finally, both good cooks and universities need an audience. Just as the University of Judaism attracts students from all over the country and the world who are tempted by our Jewishly-focused approach to education, we hope you will be tempted by the wonderful recipes collected in this book.

ACKNOWLEDGEMENTS

MIMI LANDRES
Project Chairperson

I have my grandmother's hochmesser. It is not a thing of beauty or intrinsic value, with it's rusting, curved blade and ungainly handle. But, this was touched by my great grandmother, who stayed behind in the village in the Jewish Pale, and handed it as her only legacy to her daughter to bring to America, where she would begin her new life at the age of sixteen. I do not know how many tears went into the fish my grandmother chopped or into the beautifully braided challa, for she never saw her parents again. Her father, a rabbi in their village, taught his daughters, along with his sons. It was all he had to give his children, who would venture into a strange new world. The legacy was a life-long love of learning.

My grandmother adapted to life in America with fervor, and eventually, the hochmesser was put on the shelf and replaced by a hand-operated grinder. But, the memories and the lessons of her youth were passed on to me, and what can I pass on to my daughter and her children besides more and more modern kitchen gadgets? I hope my love of learning, love of Jewish tradition, my dedication to community service, family and friends and as an expression of that love, a creative approach to cooking, utilizing all the modern equipment, but keeping in sight my grandmother's hochmesser. It is out of love and gratitude to my grandmother and the University of Judaism, which has nurtured my love of learning for over 40 years, that I dedicate my efforts to making this cookbook project a lasting source of pride and continuing revenue to the University of Judaism.

The scholarly writings explaining the holidays separates this cookbook from all others. Recipes from Jewish communities around the world have been tested by a comittee led by professional culinary experts. All recipes have been adjusted in terms of our current understanding of health issues regarding food and adapted for use in modern kitchens whose cooks are bound by time limitations. Our recipes have been collected by the members of University Women who have sought out old family treasures. Some of these recipes may be thousands of years old while others were developed yesterday. Jewish holiday specialities are featured. Helpful hints are included. Concern for health in Jewish tradition is as modern as it is ancient. This book utilizes the technology and modern standards of health while preserving Jewish recipes from around the world. As of this writing, in order to avoid Salmonella poisoning, raw eggs are omitted from all recipes, except when treated as per the recipe.

I am certain that every person who contributed a recipe, countless hours of time, professional or lay expertise, love and devotion has a similar memory that has motivated such overwhelming response to our call for help for this project, as well as a love and respect for the University of Judaism which has set before us a standard of excellence unique among academic institutions.

Co-chair, **Betty Kabaker,** with her ready smile and clarity of thought was with me every step of the way and often a few steps ahead—a delight and joy with whom to work. **Kate Geller** originated the idea of the cookbook and followed through with her leadership during her Presidency of University Women, later taking the responsibility for all of the computer work. In that, **Shirley Blumenthal, June Brott** and **Fran Adelman** assisted early on. **Lois Hellman,** current president of U.W. has lent her enthusiastic support and assistance. **Sandy Vorspan, Adele Stogel, Fran Stengel, Harriet Glaser, Ruth Fiske, Marsha Wachtel, Abbie S. Diamond,** responsible for editing the manuscript, were painstaking seekers of perfection in the finished product. The Food Testing Committee was augmented by Kashruth Supervisor, **Miriam Bornstein,** whose articles on Kashruth observance were written with clarity and ease of compliance. The Food Testing Committee consisted of: co-chairs **Sylvia Kaplan** and **Ada Leff** assisted by **Melisa Abehsera, Ruth Fiske, Pat Freedman, Ann Gerber, Ruth Jubelier Greenwold, Charlotte Kamenir, Judy Lamm, Mimi Landres, Sylvia Lawson, Judy Miller, Livia Raskin, Lorraine Shapiro and Judy Wilkin.** These women worked for two and one half years devotedly, diligently and professionally, supplying all of the food and often testing the recipes two and three times. **Michael Engleman,** of Doheny Meats, advised on kosher cuts of meat. **Abbie S. Diamond** generously reviewed each recipe for clarity and accuracy. The Text Writing Team, whose remarkable contributions make this book unique, are humorists **Mell Lazarus, Janet Salter, Frances Myman** and **Rabbi Jacob Pressman;** University of Judaism faculty members, **Dr. Hanan Alexander, Rabbi Ben Zion Bergman, Dr. Gail Dorph, Dr. Elliot Dorff, Dr. Daniel Gordis, Rabbi Jacob Pressman, Dr. Robert Wexler, Dr. Ron Wolfson, Rabbi David Wolpe.** Our appreciation goes out to them as well as to **Drs. David Lieber** and **Robert Wexler,** the University's Presidents who lavished caring approval upon our work. **Dr. Max Vorspan,** Sr. Vice President, was always ready with advice and guidance. The Finance Committee, chaired by **Bunny Diamant,** assisted by **Ida Chester, William Friedland, Lois Hellman, Bel Ostrow, Daisy Schott, Ira Schreck,** and **Julia Weinberg** worked devotedly to find an appropriate publisher and raised the money to start the project. We are eternally grateful to the Treasures of Judaica gift shop and to a few generous members of University Women whose faith in this project was demonstrated by their generous loans offered, interest free, which made the publication of the book possible. The Public Relations Team, led by **Toba Greinetz,** with **Susan Fine, Roslyn Guilis, Lillian Katz, Diane Miller, Marjorie Pressman, Marsha Wachtel, Mimi Sills** and **Rhonda Seaton** mounted an in-house advertising campaign to augment the work of publisher, **Joseph Simon** of Pangloss Press in the marketing of the book. Our thanks and appreciation to **Joseph Simon** of Pangloss Press for his wise counsel and cooperation in getting the book published, and to **Jack Roth** for suggesting him to us. The Art Committee: **Ruth Pordy,** book and cover designer, worked modestly, efficiently and creatively to make the book a thing of beauty. **Lorraine Shapiro,** professional food designer, teacher and columnist, with **Michael Tov,** professional food photographer, designed and contributed all of the photographic work to make this book outstanding—a joy forever. We wish to thank the Treasures of Judaica gift shop and the following people whose personal treasures grace the photographs: **Dr & Mrs. Stephen Geller, Mr. & Mrs. Orrin Kabaker, Dr. & Mrs. Edward Kamenir, Mr. & Mrs. Howard Landres, Mr. & Mrs. Mark C. Levy** and **Mr. & Mrs. Philip Shapiro. Rabbi Jack Schecter,** Department of Continuing Education, gave his generous support.

Over 1000 recipes were submitted by generous cooks who shared old family treasures with wonderful histories. Without them there would be no cookbook. Everyone of you has our eternal thanks and affection. **Betty Carmona,** secretary for University Women, was always ready to help as were other staff members of the University. Our goal is to offer this cookbook as an insight into the past while looking into the future. We hope this book will be treated for years to come as a thing of usefulness and beauty to grace your home.

Working with you and getting to know you better was one great reward for this effort on my part. The other reward will be the continued income to the University of Judaism that *The Reasoning and the Seasoning of Jewish Cooking* will engender for many years to come.

B' Shalom

Miriam D. Landres

WISDOM OF THE SCHOLARS

THE MESSAGE OF THE SABBATH

Dr. Elliot Dorff
Provost, Dean of Graduate Studies

Why is the Sabbath so important? In part it is because of the themes of the day and in part because of the experiences that one has on it. The three major subjects of the Sabbath are expressed in the middle sections of the Amidah (literally, "standing," since it is recited while standing), a central prayer of the Friday evening, Saturday morning and Saturday afternoon services.

On Friday evening they speak primarily of Creation, on Saturday morning of Revelation, and on Saturday afternoon of Redemption. In other words, the holiness of the Sabbath, the special character of the day, is a product of at least three interlocked motifs that constitute its message.

1. Creation
While Jews are allowed—and even commanded—to shape the world for human purpose during six days of the week, we must desist from that every seventh day in recognition of the fact that God owns the world and man enjoys only a borrowed authority to manipulate it.

2. Revelation
This is really not one theme but three: God led us out of slavery from Egypt, gave us the Torah, and created a covenant with us of which the Sabbath is the sign.

3. Redemption
The middle section of the Amidah on Saturday afternoon speaks of the Sabbath rest, "a true and genuine rest that yields peace and tranquillity, serenity and confidence, a perfect rest."

The meaning of the root of the Hebrew word for Sabbath, Shabbat, is "desist": on Shabbat we desist from interfering with nature and the social order and live with the world as it is. There is nothing wrong with the work that we do during the week—on the contrary—God's commandment is "Six days shall you labor and do all your work" as well as "the seventh day is a Sabbath of the Lord your God: you shall not do any work" (Exodus 20: 9-10). The point is, rather, that in doing our work we must not forget the goal for which we strive: a world in which there is no need for changes in nature or the social order because everything is provided and in perfect harmony. That is not the situation in our lives, and hence we must work. However, the Sabbath is, as the liturgy says, "a gift," in that through it we have "a foretaste of the World to Come."

The Sabbath, however, is more than a symbol for the Exodus and for Sinai. It is designated in the Bible as the sign of the ongoing covenant, or agreement, between God and Israel, and most especially of the bond of the People Israel to all of God's laws. The Rabbis therefore declare the Sabbath to be the equivalent of all the other mitzvot, and the prophet Ezekiel (20:10-20) repeatedly singles out the Sabbath as the litmus test of the extent to which Israel was observing God's law and the strength or weakness of the whole relationship between God and Israel.

ROSH HASHANAH

Dr. Hanan Alexander

Unlike the secular New Year which rejoices in the world as it is, the Jewish New Year-Rosh Hashanah beckons to make it better. The traditional liturgy summons us to do so with these words: "On Rosh Hashanah it is written, and Yom Kippur it is sealed, who will live and who will die, who will be raised up and who brought low.... But repentance, prayer, and righteousness can lessen the severity of the decreed birth, death, success, failure and many of life's other vicissitudes that are often out of our control. Each of us is born with limitations. Each is fragile and flawed. But this does not mean that we are powerless. On the contrary, we can make a difference; we can help to heal the world! But to heal the world we must heal ourselves.

The first step is repentance, a deeply personal process that begins up to a month prior to the New Year. In Hebrew it is called, teshuvah, which literally means turning away from sin and toward God. The Hebrew word for sin means missing the mark, like an arrow missing its target. To turn from sin we need first to admit that we have missed the mark. Unless we can accept that we have made mistakes it is impossible to resolve to do better. We miss the mark not because we are evil but because we are human. Indeed, we can improve because we are imperfect. Perfection needs no improvement.

Accepting our imperfections and admitting our mistakes prepares us to pray for forgiveness. The Hebrew word for prayer connotes introspection as much as supplication and the prayer book for Rosh Hashanah, like all Jewish liturgy, teaches us to look inward as well as toward God. It addresses three themes. First, we are reminded that God is ruler of the universe with the power to forgive. Second, we ask God to remember the righteousness of our ancestors. Third, the haunting sound of the shofar, the ram's horn, calls us to return to the good path from which we have strayed and calls God to forgive our sins for the sake of our righteous ancestors if not for our own. God here is the model for human behavior. If God can forgive us, then we can learn to forgive ourselves, our families and our friends.

On Rosh Hashanah, as on all other occasions in Jewish life, prayer is a public as well as a private affair. It leads to acceptance not only of our own frailties but also of the fragility of those around us. This realization is the root of righteousness, or in Hebrew, tsedaka. The word connotes justice tempered by compassion. Justice requires that we accord each person the treatment she or he deserves. When we recognize the profound vulnerability of all human beings, we realize that the imperative to be just calls upon us to be compassionate and caring as well.

Repentance and prayer, then, lead to righteousness, to compassion, to caring. Acceptance and forgiveness of sin should result in a rededication to treat one another with kindness. And if we can learn to do this, then we can indeed heal the world. This is the message of Rosh Hashanah.

YOM KIPPUR

Dr. Robert Wexler

Traditionally, Yom Kippur and Rosh Hashanah share the designation—"Days of Awe". But if popular practice were permitted to be heard on this subject, it would tell us that Yom Kippur, a day of abstinence and liturgical drama, stands virtually alone as the annual focus of Jewish awe and veneration. Thousands of Jews, who routinely avoid the formality of public worship, find themselves drawn to the synagogue to witness the Judaic re-enactment of Kol Nidre or perhaps the closing of the heavenly gates during Neilah. "For on this day atonement will be made for you, to purify you; from all your sins you will be purified before the Lord." (Leviticus 16:30)

Purity and impurity—in the view of the Bible—were terms used to describe the condition of a person's relationship with God and with the community. The pure individual stands in harmony with both his creator and his community, whereas the impure soul endures estrangement. Yom Kippur holds out the yearly promise of reconciliation through the joint mechanisms of personal affliction and public penance.

Normative Judaism adopted a cautious attitude toward asceticism. So a twenty-five hour fast and the other manifestations of abstinence on Yom Kippur are rendered all the more compelling and even attractive because of their relative infrequency during the rest of the year. There is an arguable human need for episodes of self denial—a self-denial which purifies by obliging the distressed and the insouciant alike to retreat from worldly concerns into the realm of the spiritual.

While the Temple still existed, communal and individual penance would be secured through a sacred ceremony whereby a goat—symbolically laden with the sins of Israel—was dispatched into the wilderness. A second goat was sacrificed on the altar as a further expression of the longing for divine forgiveness.

Excited residents and pilgrims within the city of Jerusalem would throng the Temple court to witness the solitary entry of the high priest into the Holy of Holies as he interceded on behalf of his people—a clear Jewish flirtation with the notion of an intermediary between human beings and God. It is told that, when the high priest emerged,"…his face was radiant as the sun when it goes forth in its splendor…," for he was confident that his mission of supplication was successful.

After the destruction of the Temple, participation in the established rites and customs of Yom Kippur, coupled with a sincere desire to repent, became the approved path to atonement. It is a path in which the ancient ritual drama is recalled rather than enacted and it is a path which we are obliged to negotiate almost unassisted.

As night falls, and Yom Kippur draws to a close, we make our final plea for unity with God through the words of the poet:

> Oh keep open for us Your gate of mercy,
> At the time of the closing of the gate,
> Now that the day is waning.
> The day is passing; The sun is setting;
> O let us enter Your gate at last.

SUKKOT
Rabbi David Wolpe

In our lives each of us searches for permanence. We seek stable relationships a secure home, a nation whose political system is orderly and predictable.

Sukkot reminds us that for all of our attempts to be secure, a certain instability is inevitable in life. Sukkot greets us just as we have emerged from the experience of the high holidays, in which we seek the forgiveness of other people, and pray for the forgiveness of God. Having put our spiritual lives in order we return to the rough and tumble of daily life, with all of its challenges, joys and vicissitudes.

On Sukkot we build a temporary structure called a sukkah and are enjoined to eat there, to understand what it is to live in a state of impermanence, what it is to be without a certain home. Still this is a joyous holiday because the challenge of life is to find joy in its instability. We learn how to decorate the sukkah even though we know in a week it will be dismantled until next year.

That is why on Sukkot it is customary to invite guests, "Ushpizin," into the sukkah. The guests we invite, in this folkloric tradition, are our ancestors: Abraham, Isaac, Jacob, Joseph, Moses, Aaron and David. Today a common custom is to expand the list to include Sarah, Rachel, Rebecca, Leah, Miriam, Abigail and Esther. We link our arms with them through the generations and affirm that their teaching and inspiration is part of our bedrock in a world filled with surprises, with gaiety and with tragedy.

Sukkot is also a holiday of harvest. This, too, reflects the theme of impermanence. In an agricultural society nothing is so unsure as the rains and the new crop. The sukkah not only represents the huts in which our ancestors dwelt as they made their way through the wilderness, it represents the harvest booths in which people dwelt during the final ingathering of produce before winter.

On Sukkot we read the book of Ecclesiastes of Koheleth, which summarizes and elaborates many of the themes of the holiday. Koheleth teaches us about the nature of impermanence and change: "I multiplied my possessions. I built myself houses and I planted vineyards. But it was all futile." (2:4) Second, Koheleth speaks about harvest, in a special way—that each person must sow for himself, and seek to achieve: "Send forth your bread upon the water; for after many days you will find it,"(11.1) And Koheleth counsels joy: "Go, eat your bread in gladness, and drink your wine in joy." (9:7)

HANUKKAH
Rabbi Ben Zion Bergman

The Festival of Hanukkah celebrates a unique historical event—the revolt of a people against an occupying power, not primarily to gain political independence but rather to gain cultural and spiritual autonomy.

Antiochus IV, in order to fulfill his ambition to conquer Egypt, set about instituting uniformity of language, dress, and religion among the various peoples that constituted the Seleucid Empire, headquartered in Syria. Since Judea was the province bordering Egypt, it was most important to have a loyal Hellenized population there. While many Jews ardently embraced the Hellenizing program, in order to insure complete Hellenization, Antiochus forbade the observance of the distinctive Jewish rituals of the Sabbath, the holidays and circumcision. The Temple in Jerusalem was transformed into a Temple to Zeus and the crowning abomination was the sacrifice of a pig on the altar on the 25th of Kislev in 168 B.C.E.

The revolt began in the small town of Modin, northwest of Jerusalem. Syrian soldiers came to enforce the royal edict by erecting an altar to Zeus in the marketplace. As the townspeople assembled, aged Mattathias, scion of a priestly family, was ordered to sacrifice a pig on the altar. Upon his refusal, a young Jew seeking to curry favor, stepped forward to volunteer. Suddenly, Mattathias snatched the sword from the captain's hand, slew the apostate Jew and the captain. The sons of Mattathias, together with fellow townsmen, rushed upon the soldiers and succeeding in killing them, demolished the altar.

It is said that Mattathias exclaimed as he took his first step forward, "Whoever is for the Lord, come to me." Thus the banner of revolt was raised and, fleeing into the hills, growing numbers of guerrillas flocked to the banner. Mattathias died in 167 B.C.E. and leadership devolved upon Judah, his son. Some explain the name, Maccabee, as an acronym consisting of the initial Hebrew letters of the Biblical verse: "Who is like unto Thee, O Lord, among the mighty," a motto presumably inscribed on his banner. Others derive it from the word makebet which means 'hammer' indicating that Judah was the hammer with which God smashed the Syrians.

In time, as his forces increased, Judah was successful in defeating the Syrians and liberating Jerusalem. The Temple was cleansed of its pagan worship and rededicated to the worship of the God of Israel on the 25th of Kislev, 165 B.C.E., exactly three years after its desecration.

To rekindle the Temple candelabrum, only one small cruse of uncontaminated oil was found. Although it was sufficient only for one day, it burned miraculously for eight days until new pure oil could be prepared.

Thus, the central ritual of Hanukkah is the lighting of lights for eight days, beginning with one the first night and adding progressively until eight are kindled on the last night.

Hanukkah therefore celebrates the miracle of the oil and the miracle of the victory of the few against the many oppressors in the special Scriptural reading on the Sabbath of Hanukkah from the book of Zechariah: "Not by might nor by power, but by My spirit saith the Lord."

PURIM
Dr. Daniel Gordis

One of the two major Jewish holidays not prescribed by the Torah, Purim is also one of most entertaining and lively of Jewish celebrations. It combines a unique blend of readings from biblical sources, rituals of both fasting and feasting, as well as a host of customs destined to foster social awareness and friendship.

The story upon which Purim is based is found in Megillat Esther or the Scroll of Esther. This well-known story relates that in response to Mordecai's refusal to bow down to Haman, an advisor to King Ahashverosh, Haman set about to destroy all the Jews within the King's land. He succeeded in obtaining the King's assent to this plan, but failed to anticipate that Esther, a Jewish woman who had recently become Queen, would prevail upon the King not only to reverse the decree, but to execute Haman and his sons as well.

The relevance of the Scroll of Esther for Jews today stems from its implications about assimilation. Indeed, the book both demonstrates the ongoing temptations of assimilation and reminds us never to give up on the assimilated Jew. When Mordecai approaches Queen Esther and begs her to intercede with the King on behalf of the Jews, Esther refuses. The mission, she claims, is too dangerous. Mordecai conveys the sense of the author that Esther has lost her sense of self as a Jew by implicitly reminding her of God's role in history, claiming, "if you keep silent in this crisis, relief and deliverance will come to the Jews from another quarter." Ultimately, of course, Esther does intercede, and indeed, masterminds Haman's downfall. The temptations of the "court culture" are great, the Scroll suggests, but one's ties to the Jewish people can always be reawakened.

The story of Megillat Esther also reminds us of the inevitability of what the rabbis called olam hafukh, or a "topsy-turvy world." At every step, the story of Esther takes a turn one could not have imagined. A lowly Jewish woman is made Queen. This assimilated Queen eventually saves the Jewish people. Haman, the most powerful man in the land, is ultimately executed in disgrace. When Haman learns of the King's plan to honor someone, he assumes that it is he who is to be honored. Ironically, of course, he learns that the honoree is Mordecai. And other examples abound. In all, this compelling story reminds us, life always presents us with the eventualities it seems we would least expect.

Jews celebrate this holiday and its important themes in numerous fashions. Traditionally, Jews fast the day before Purim, in keeping with Esther's request that Jews fast in prayer as she approaches the King with her request. On the night of Purim, the Scroll of Esther is read in the synagogue, and the reading is typically followed with dancing, merriment and even some drinking, all in celebration of the Jews' deliverance from what seemed certain doom.

In recognition of the holiday's theme that things are never what they seem, Jews often masquerade on Purim, dressing up either as traditional Purim characters, or even modern figments of their imaginations. The Megillat is read once again on the following morning.

It is also traditional on Purim to give gifts of food or money to the poor of one's community, and to share food baskets with one's friends. The afternoon of Purim is usually marked with a special se'udah, or festive meal, another dimension of the celebration of the good fortune which the holiday marks.

PASSOVER

Dr. Ron Wolfson
Director, Whizen Institute for the Jewish Family

Why is this night different from all other nights?
Because on this night, more that any other night in the Jewish year, Jews come together for a Jewish experience. Although we live in a time and a place where less than 25% of Jews affiliate with a Jewish institution, there is one time and one place when nearly all Jews come together at the Passover Seder.

Why?
Because the Passover holiday celebrates the creation of the Jewish people. On that fateful night before the Exodus from Egypt, God commanded the people to prepare a meal, a very special meal. The menu included the meat of the paschal sacrifice, bitter herbs and the first Jewish fast-food, quick-baked matzah, unleavened bread. In order to commemorate this moment, the meal was re-enacted every year of the anniversary of the night of the Exodus.

What is a Seder?
In the Torah, God commands the people to "tell the story on that very day, saying 'This is what the Lord did for me when I went out from Egypt.'" To help families do this, the rabbis devised a remarkable way to transmit the story from generation to generation: the Seder, a talk-feast filled with ritual, symbol, story and song, all designed for one purpose—to tell the story.

What is the Haggadah?
The word haggadah comes from the Hebrew l'hugid, "to tell." The Haggadah is the text which provides the guidelines for the "order of the Seder." We should not be slaves to the text. The best Seder experiences have elements of improvisation—tangents, observations, reactions, and, above all, questions to help make the meaning of Passover come alive for us today.

How can such an ancient ceremony be meaningful to me?
The goal of the Seder is quite clear: "In each generation, every individual should feel as though she or he had actually been redeemed from Egypt." The Seder is not simply a history lesson. We not only tell the story of the Exodus, we eat the matzah and bitter herbs, we sing the songs of praise to God, just as generations upon generations of our ancestors have done—all with the purpose of simulating the experience of God's redemption.

Why are children so important at the seder?
We are to "tell our children" the story of Passover so they in turn will tell it to their children. When you think about the large majority of Jews who attend a Seder to this day, the Seder must be considered one of the most effective pedagogic experiences ever created!

Why is this night different from all other nights?
The famous translation of Mah Nishtana is not quite correct. A better understanding is: how different this night is from all other nights! The greatest achievement of the Passover holiday is that it transforms our dining rooms into Jewish family classrooms where important lessons of Judaism and Jewish peoplehood are taught by parents to their children in the

place where Jewish identity begins and is fostered—the home. On all other nights, we watch television; tonight, we read out loud together, we sing together, we pray together. On all other nights, we rarely spend twenty minutes at the dinner table; tonight, we relax and take our time, enjoying the conversations, the wonderful foods, the good company. On all other nights, we may not think much about ourselves as Jews; tonight, we take our place in the living chain of tradition which links us to thousands of years of Jewish peoplehood, strengthening our fundamental identity as Jews, and celebrating our Jewishness as individuals, as families and as a community. This is the genius of Passover.

YOM HA'ATZMAUT
Rabbi Jacob Pressman

Israel Independence Day is the newest official holiday in the Jewish calendar. It is celebrated on the fifth day of the month of Iyar, which was the Jewish calendar date on Friday, May 14, 1948 when for the first time in 1878 years an independent Jewish state was established and its Declaration of Independence was signed. The yearning of the Jewish people for a land of its own was emphasized in virtually every aspect of life: over and over again in the daily prayers, in the Kiddush on the Shabbat and holidays, in the wedding blessings, in the placing of soil from the Holyland in every grave when a mourning family was able to secure some of its sacred earth. So significant has been this moment in our long and eventful history, that, for the first time in 2,000 years, a day with special religious significance has been ADDED to the Jewish Calendar. Yom Ha-Atzmaut takes place during the seven weeks of semi-mourning, as we count the days of ingathering of the omers of barley. Weddings and other celebrations were once prohibited on this day, but now they are permitted. Food, of course, is always an important ingredient in making the occasion truly festive.

LAG B'OMER
Rabbi Jacob Pressman

Lag B'Omer, like Tu B'Shvat, is a holiday known by its numerical acronym. The Hebrew letters for 30, Lamed, and 3, Gimel, combine to make "Lag" or 33. They identify the thirty-third day of counting the omer, the Biblical barley offering brought daily to the Sanctuary for seven weeks from the second day of Passover (16 Nisan) to the eve of the Feast of Weeks, Shavuot (Sivan). These seven weeks, originally associated with agriculture, were designated by the Rabbis as a period of semi-mourning during which weddings and celebrations are forbidden, marking the persecutions of the Jews by the Romans under Emperor Hadrian and the later massacres by the Crusaders. The prohibition is lifted on the thirty-third day because tradition holds that a plague which had decimated the ranks of the students of Rabbi Akiba abated on that day. It became known as The Scholars' Festival. The day is also associated with the ruse the students used when they would go out to the countryside where their teachers were holding clandestine classes and, bows and arrows in hand, they would explain to Roman officers that they were going on an outing to hunt. So, today, the day is marked by outings, games with bows and arrows, and foods appropriate for outings and the celebration of nature.

SHAVUOT
Dr. Gail Z. Dorph

As Pesach recalls the quintessential experience of group memory at which we remember, retell and relive our personal redemption from Egypt, Shavuot becomes the day upon which we celebrate the giving of the Torah and accept this gift anew.

This event marks the establishment of the covenant between God and the people, Israel. If other religions can be characterized as relationships between human beings and God, Judaism must be described as a relationship between human beings with Torah and God. It is the Torah which forms the basis of the ongoing relationship of God and Israel, giving that relationship both form and content.

How do we today express our acceptance of the gift of Torah? Through studying it! Each word, each verse, each story which we study becomes ours through the act of study. When we study, it is as though we link ourselves to the Jewish people in a chain going all the way back to Sinai.

Until modern times, one could say that Torah and the study of Torah was the dominant Jewish religious preoccupation. It is the defining document of Jewish identity, somewhat analogous to the United States Constitution. This centrality is communicated in the Mishnaic adage: "Talmud Torah k'neged kulam"—the study of Torah is equal to all (all referring to all other mitzvot). The world according to the rabbis of the Mishnah, rests on three pillars—study, worship and good deeds. Study being the most important of all three, because from study the other two can be derived. It is through our participation in this most sacred of religious pastimes that we come to "own" the most sacred of possessions.

Shavuot, the time of the giving of the Torah, reminds us that Torah has been offered us, but the responsibility of coming to "own" it is ours. When we participate in the custom of Tikkun Layl Shavuot - staying up and studying during the first night of Shavuot - and when we stand and listen attentively to the chanting of the Ten Commandments on the first day of the festival, we are symbolically "owning" Torah.

The dominant motif of Shavuot in the Bible was the agricultural theme. The Torah refers to Shavuot as Hag ha-Katsir (the feast of the harvest) and Yom ha-Bikkurim (the day of first fruits), observed by offerings of the best ripe produce of the fields (Exodus 23:16, Numbers 28:26). Beginning with the second day of Pesach, seven weeks (Shavuot means weeks) or forty-nine days were carefully counted, and the fiftieth day (Pentecost) was celebrated as the beginning of the wheat harvest of the festival of the first fruits.

In traditional French and German Jewish society, it was customary for children to begin their study of Torah on this festival. Other customs include eating dairy foods, especially blintzes and cheesecakes. Some attribute this custom to the verse in Song of Songs which compares Torah to milk and honey. On the second day of the holiday, the book of Ruth is read. In addition to its description of a summer harvest in Israel, Ruth is the story of a convert who is able to join the Jewish people with others who share its values.

TU B'SHVAT
Rabbi Jacob Pressman

Not too many people know that Rosh Hashanah comes four times a year. The Talmud on Rosh Hashanah states, "There are four 'New Years' days: on the 1st of Nisan is the New Year for kings and feasts; on the 1st of Elul is the New Year for the Tithe of Cattle; on the 1st of Tishri is the New Year for the years, of the Years of Release and Jubilee, for the planting and for vegetables; and on the 1st of Shevat is the New Year for trees according to the School of Shammai; and the School of Hillel say: on the 15th thereof."

This "New Year for trees" has come to be celebrated on the 15th of Shevat as Jewish Arbor Day, and is known variously by its date, "Chamisha-Asar Bishevat" (The Fifteenth of Shevat); or, more familiarly, as "Tu Bishvat", the latter because the Hebrew Letters Tet and Vav represent the number 15. It is a one day observance of the beginning of springtime in the Land of Israel. For centuries Jews everywhere marked "The New Year of the Trees" by eating of fruits associated with the land from which they had been exiled. Most times it was deep winter in the places where Jews lived, and so every effort was made to obtain dried carob pods, known as "Bokser" or "St. John's Bread": dried figs, dates, raisins, prunes, apricots and nuts, and give them to the children as a holiday treat. In the Cheder and the Yeshivot little bags of such goodies were distributed and nicknamed "Chamisha Asar". The taste of the Holyland was experienced and reminded them of the land to which they would one day return. Since early in the Twentieth Century the day has been marked by special emphasis on buying trees and planting them, by proxy, in what was then Palestine. The pioneers would go out in festive groups to plant saplings in what became the world's most massive reforestation program. With the establishment of the State of Israel the holiday has achieved a heightened level of importance with tree-planting, the serving of fruits and nuts, and a heightened emphasis upon nature.

TISHAH B'AV
Rabbi Jacob Pressman

There are three weeks in mid-summer which are overlaid with sadness as we recall the destruction of land and people which befell us. Beginning on the 17th day of Tammuz (Shivah Asar Be-Tammuz) which recalls the day on which the walls of Jerusalem were breached in 586 B.C.E. by the armies of Nebechadnezzar, King of Babylon, we observe a period of semi-mourning in which celebration, weddings, etc. are prohibited. The days are climaxed by the Fast of the Ninth of Av, (Tishah B'Av) when the Holy Temple was captured and destroyed. The day of Tishah B'Av is also used to commemorate the destruction of the Second Temple by General Titus of Rome. In later years Tishah B'Av also marked the tragic expulsion of the Jews from Spain by edict of King Ferdinand and Queen Isabella. The day is marked by assembling in the synagogue in an atmosphere of mourning, reading the Book of Lamentations and elegaic poems, called Kinnot, and fasting. It is also known as the Black Fast, as contrasted with Yom Kippur, the White Fast. This time of mourning and fasting makes it very difficult to plan menus.

COMMENTS ON KASHRUT (Jewish Dietary Laws)
Miriam Bornstein

Observing Kashrut is for many of us an integral part of our Jewish way of life. It strengthens our personal sense of Jewish identity, while it helps us feel more connected with the tradition of our people. What are the origins of our dietary laws, and how did they evolve into such an intricate blueprint for the contemporary kosher kitchen?

The laws of Kashrut are of biblical and talmudic origin and are further elaborated and discussed in detail in the Shulchan Arukh. These laws specify what fish, meats and fowl we are allowed to eat and what species are forbidden for human consumption. Fish allowed must have fins and scales. All others, such as shellfish, eel, shark etc., are forbidden. Meats allowed must come from domestic animals that chew their cud and have split hooves, such as cattle and sheep, and from fowl, such as chickens, turkeys, ducks and geese. Furthermore, all meats must derive from ritually slaughtered animals, and, unless broiled, must be kashered; that is soaked in water for half an hour and salted for an hour, then rinsed, before cooking. (Liver can only be kashered by broiling). This process, namely broiling, or soaking and salting, is meant to drain all blood (which symbolizes life) from the meat, and thus ease the conflict we humans have, when satisfying our carniverous need. Kashering is often done routinely now by most kosher butchers. Prepackaged, frozen, kosher chicken has been salted. To remove salt, soak, in cold water, changing water three times in one hour, or remove skin whenever appropriate. Adjust salt in recipes accordingly.

Similarly, the laws decreeing complete separation of meat and dairy foods and dishes stem from the same conflict. They are based on a verse in the Torah, repeated three times, which states: "Thou shalt not seethe a kid in its mother's milk" (Exodus, 23:19, 34:26; Deuteronomy, 14:21). While this is a concession that we need meat for sustenance, it, nevertheless, exhorts us to show some sensitivity in the process: "Don't cook the calf in its mother's milk!" Hence, this injunction has brought about the most visible distinguishing mark of the Jewish home: its kosher kitchen. Here you will find special sections, shelves and drawers, designated "meat" or "dairy". Therefore, the kosher kitchen has, at least, two sets of dishes (often four sets: two for every day and two for special occasions). The same goes for cutlery. It comes equipped with separate meat and dairy pots and pans, utensils, dishpans, sponges, towels, etc. In many a modern kosher kitchen you will find meat and dairy cabinets and drawers labeled or color-coded (such as red for "meat" and blue for "dairy") so that any guest or helper will be able to function in it correctly. Any meal, prepared, cooked and served (no matter how many courses) in the kosher home, will never contain a mixture of meat and dairy ingredients. Strict separation is the rule!

There remains, of course, an immense category of neutral foods, which are neither meat nor dairy. These foods are described as pareve and may be served with either meat or dairy dishes: Note that fish belongs in this category, as well as eggs, fruits, vegetables, flour, grains, nuts, oils, sugar, salt, spices, tea, coffee, and more.

All the above laws and injunctions are indicative of the fact that Judaism takes the matter of food preparation and consumption very seriously. In addition, we have a whole body of proscribed rituals and ceremonies that go with the taking of our meals, such as washing of hands before pronouncing the "Hamotzie" (blessing over bread at the start of a meal), saying special blessings for special foods and reciting grace after a meal, with designated texts for communal meals and special occasions, such as Shabbat, holidays, or weddings.

Our tradition, then, looks at the consumption of food not only as a biological function (to satisfy hunger and sustain our bodies), but also as a social, as well as a religious act. Just think of the beautiful rituals and customs connected with our Sabbath and holiday tables: meals taken in the sukkah or during our symbolically meaningful seder observance, for example, are extraordinary highlights of the Jewish year.

In preparing this cookbook, we have followed the laws of kashrut meticulously. Since the separation of meat and dairy dishes is such an important axiom of our kashrut laws, every recipe is marked by either an "M" (meat or fowl), a "D"(dairy), or a "P"(pareve). All recipes call, of course, for only kosher ingredients; meats, meat cuts (hindquarters of cattle and sheep are forbidden), poultry and fish are allowed.

Furthermore, it is imperative for today's kosher home-maker to read food labels carefully and to check ingredients when buying packaged or prepared food products, such as breads, breadcrumbs, cakes, cookies, crackers, canned or frozen foods, margarine, desserts, so-called "non-dairy" items, etc. Be aware that shortenings, unless marked vegetable, are often derived from animal fats, and that some foods, labeled "non-dairy", may, nonetheless, contain ingredients that are milk derivatives, such as whey and casein. When in doubt, one can either check for kashrut symbols (frequently printed on food packaging), which are usually followed by a "D" for dairy—or by "pareve"; or one can consult a rabbinic authority.

It follows, then, that the observance of kashrut affects not only what we eat and how we prepare, cook and serve our meals, but also how we shop in the markets, at the butcher or at the fish counter.

Kashrut in the kitchen, or kosher cuisine—what a tempting task for the creative kosher cook! It is hoped that this challenge has been well met in the pages of this book.

BREADS

WALL HANGING, PHILIP RATNER

SHABBAT—A Traditional Golden Braided Challah is Symbolic of Shabbat Itself.

BREAD

Frances Myman and Mimi Landres

We begin with bread. It is paramount in Jewish tradition. Bread represents the perfect partnership between God and man in creation—a basic tenet of Jewish belief. Every meal begins with the blessing over bread.

On the Sabbath and holidays, challah is served.

Traditions connected with challah date from the time of Abraham. A small piece of dough is separated and burnt in the oven as a contemporary sacrifice in memory of the destruction of the Temple. Challah is named for this dough. We use two challot to represent the double portion of manna received in the desert on Fridays to provide for Shabbat. There is a tradition not to use a knife on Friday night but rather to break the bread apart as a reflection of Isaiah's prophecy "and they shall beat their swords into ploughshares and their spears into pruning hooks," Is.:2:4. After blessing the bread and before eating, one should salt the bread to recall "by the sweat of your brow you shall get bread to eat", Gen.:3:19. During the blessing over the wine the challah is kept covered. The purpose is to shield the sensitive feelings of the challah lest it be offended by being second to the wine. The bread is passed on a plate rather than handed directly indicating that it is not from man alone that we receive our bread. Seeds may be sprinkled on the loaves to represent the manna that fell from heaven.

No matter if the challah is baked in a simple loaf or in an elaborate six-braided work of art, the wonderful texture and rich taste will call up visions of tranquillity equated with Sabbath and holidays and generations of women kneading and shaping with love.

"Eat thy bread with joy and drink with a merry heart". Ecclesiastes.

CHALLAH [P]

6 cups unbleached flour
1 yeast cake
1/3 cup oil
1-1/2 Tbsp sugar

1 Tbsp salt
2 large eggs, lightly beaten
1-3/4 cups water
1/2 cup flour for kneading, if needed

Egg Glaze:
1 egg yolk
1 tsp honey

1 tsp water or 1 egg
beaten with a little sugar

Put flour into a large bowl. In a small bowl dissolve the yeast in 1 cup lukewarm water. Make a hole in the middle of the flour and pour yeast into it. Mix the yeast liquid into some of the flour from the sides of the hole, covering lightly with flour. Place in warm place, covered with towel. When the batter rises and looks foamy, add remaining oil, sugar, salt, eggs and remaining water, approximately 3/4 cup. Knead into ball. If too sticky, may add the extra 1/2 cup of flour. Cover and let rise. Punch down, shape as desired and place on greased baking sheet or in loaf pans. Let rise until doubled. Before baking, brush with egg glaze. Bake at 350 degrees 45 minutes until brown.

Preparation time: 20 minutes
Rising time: 1-1/2 hours
Baking time: 45 minutes

Makes 2 loaves

SPINACH HERB FILLING FOR CHALLAH [D]

10 oz frozen chopped spinach
1/3 cup Parmesan cheese
8 oz pkg cream cheese
1 to 2 cloves garlic, crushed

1/2 tsp basil
1/2 tsp oregano
pepper to taste
sesame seeds (optional)

Thaw and thoroughly drain spinach. Mix with rest of ingredients to form a smooth mixture.

Roll half of challah dough into 10 x 14 inch rectangle and place on a greased baking sheet. Spread spinach mixture down center. Make diagonal cuts on either side of dough, 2 inches apart and 1 inch from filling. Fold up, alternating right and left strips. Let rise 30 minutes in warm place. Brush with egg glaze and sprinkle with sesame seeds, if desired. Bake according to challah directions. Serve warm, cut into slices.

Preparation time: 10 minutes
Baking time: 40 minutes

WHOLE WHEAT CHALLAH   [P]

2 pkg dry yeast or 1-1/2 oz fresh yeast
1/2 cup warm water
2 Tbsp brown sugar
1/2 cup oil
1/2 cup brown sugar, packed, or honey
1-1/2 cups hot water
2 tsp salt
4 large eggs, beaten
1 cup raisins (optional)
6 to 6-1/2 cups whole wheat flour
1 egg yolk, beaten
1 tsp water
poppy or sesame seeds (optional)

Preheat oven to 350 degrees.
In small bowl, dissolve yeast in warm water and 2 tablespoons brown sugar. Let stand 5 to 10 minutes until foamy.

In a separate bowl, mix oil, brown sugar, hot water and salt. In a third bowl, beat eggs. If using raisins, sprinkle with flour and set aside. Place 4 cups flour in a large mixing bowl. Make a well in the center, add yeast mixture, oil mixture and eggs, stirring with a wooden spoon after each addition. If using raisins, add after eggs. Beat until smooth. Gradually add more flour, working dough until it leaves the sides of bowl. Turn dough onto floured wooden board. Knead 5 to 8 minutes, adding as little flour as possible, until dough is smooth and elastic. Coat a large bowl with oil, place dough in the bowl, turn over to coat other side, cover with a towel and let rise in warm place until doubled.

Punch dough down, let rest 10 minutes. Knead gently until smooth. Form into 2 loaves and place in greased loaf pans.

One quarter of dough can be set aside to braid for decorative top. Place on loaf. Beat 1 egg yolk with 1 tsp water. Brush loaves with egg mixture and sprinkle with seeds, if desired. Cover and let rise until almost doubled.

Bake 40 to 45 minutes, or until loaves are golden brown and sound hollow when tapped.

Preparation time: 15 minutes
Rising time: 1 hour
Baking time: 40 to 45 minutes

Makes 2 loaves
A rich, light and delicious bread. If you add raisins, it is a sweet treat.

BRIOCHE FOR BREAD MACHINE   [D]

1-1/2 tsp active dry yeast
1 tsp salt
2 Tbsp sugar
2-1/2 cups flour
8 to 10 Tbsp unsalted butter
3 large eggs
1/4 cup milk

Have all ingredients at room temperature.
Put ingredients in bread machine according to manufacturer's directions. Set browning time for crust at medium.

The result is a rich, delicious, effortless brioche. Best served warm.

Preparation time: 10 minutes
Baking time: Follow manufacturer's directions
Makes: 1 lb loaf

HOUSKA CHALLAH WITH MILK [D]

1 pkg active dry yeast
1/4 cup lukewarm water
1 tsp sugar
4 cups flour
1 tsp salt
1 tsp grated lemon zest
1 cup scalded milk

7 Tbsp melted butter
1/2 cup sugar
2/3 cup raisins
1 egg plus 2 egg yolks
1-1/2 cup flour
1 egg white, lightly beaten
sliced blanched almonds

Pour yeast into a small bowl containing water and 1 tsp sugar. Let stand for 10 minutes to proof.

In a large bowl, sift together 4 cups flour with salt and lemon zest. In a third bowl, combine scalded milk, butter, sugar, and raisins. Let cool until lukewarm. Stir in 1 egg plus 2 egg yolks, all lightly beaten into the yeast mixture. Pour the mixture all at once into the flour, stirring vigorously. Beat the dough until smooth and let It rise, covered in a warm place for 1-1/2 hours or until double in bulk.

Turn the dough onto a well floured surface. Knead in about 1-1/2 cups more flour and continue to knead until smooth and shiny. Cut off 2/3 of dough and divide in 4 pieces. Roll each piece into a 16 inch rope. Braid ropes; lay braid diagonally on buttered baking sheet and brush with egg white lightly beaten. Halve the remaining dough and divide one piece into thirds. Roll each into 16 inch ropes and braid. Arrange braid on larger braid. Brush with egg white. Halve remaining dough. Roll each into 16 inch rope. Twist and arrange on braids. Tuck ends underneath and let rise covered, for 1 hour or until double in bulk.

Preheat oven to 350 degrees. Brush dough with egg white. Sprinkle with sliced blanched almonds. Bake 35 to 45 minutes until browned. Let cool on rack. This can be made into a round challah. Reserve a small amount (size of a fist) of dough for the top. Make long ropes out of the remainder of the dough and attach them. Make concentric circles getting smaller toward the top. Place the reserved piece of dough on top and proceed according to other recipe.

Preparation time: 20 minutes
Rising time: 1 hour
Baking time: 35 to 45 minutes
Makes: 1 loaf

RAISIN CHALLAH   [P]

Food Processor Method:

3 Tbsp plus 1 tsp sugar
1/2 cup warm water
1 pkg dry yeast
4-1/2 cups all-purpose flour
1 tsp salt

3 eggs
1/2 cup raisins
poppy seeds
1 egg yolk beaten with 1 tsp water
1/8 cup yellow corn meal

Preheat oven to 350 degrees. Grease baking sheets and sprinkle with corn meal.

Dissolve 1 tsp sugar in 1/2 cup water in cup. Sprinkle with yeast and mix. Let stand 10 minutes until bubbles form. Place 4 cups flour, remaining 3 tablespoons sugar and salt in processor with metal blade. Pour in yeast mixture and process 12 seconds. While machine is running, add eggs and oil through feed tube. Process until blended, about 10 seconds. Turn dough onto floured board and knead in remaining 1/2 cup flour and raisins until smooth and elastic, about 5 minutes. Place dough into large greased bowl, turning to grease top of dough. Cover with towel and let rise in warm place until doubled, about 1 hour. Punch down and divide into 4 equal portions. Using three portions, form into thin ropes and braid. Form remaining dough into 3 ropes. Braid and lay on top of lower braided dough. Pinch ends together. Pinch at various points along bread. Brush with egg yolk wash and sprinkle with poppy seeds. Let stand in warm place about 1 hour. Place on prepared baking sheet. Bake for about 45 minutes or until top is golden brown and crusty and tester comes out clean.

Preparation time: 20 minutes
Rising time: 2 hours
Baking time: 45 minutes

RAISIN WALNUT WHEAT BREAD   [D]

1-1/4 cups water or less for bread machine
2-1/2 cups bread flour
3/4 cup wheat flour
2 Tbsp dry milk
1/2 tsp salt
1 tsp cinnamon

2 Tbsp butter
3 Tbsp honey
2 tsp quick rising yeast or
   3 tsp active dry yeast
1/2 cup chopped walnuts
1/2 cup raisins

Conventional Method: Refer to Whole Wheat Challah recipe page 23. Bake 350 degrees for 45 to 60 minutes.

Electric Bread Machine: Add nuts and raisins after mixing is completed and when machine signals, prior to baking. Note: Check bread machine for quantity of water. May vary with machine. Consult machine brochure.

Preparation time: 15 minutes
Baking time: varies with machine
Makes: 1-1/2 lb loaf

WHOLE WHEAT CITRUS BREAD   [D]

Electric Bread Machine Method:

1 tsp orange zest
1 pkg active dry yeast
1/8 tsp lemon zest
1 Tbsp lime juice
1 Tbsp lemon juice
1/3 cup orange marmalade
2 Tbsp butter, melted
1-1/2 tsp salt

2 Tbsp sugar
2 Tbsp dry milk
2 cups bread flour
1 cup whole wheat flour
1 cup lukewarm water (quantity may vary with humidity and individual machine instructions)
1/4 cup raisins (optional)
1/4 cup slivered almonds (optional)

Mix all ingredients in bread machine, except raisins and nuts. Add after second kneading when signal is given by machine.

To make rolls: stop machine before baking cycle. Remove dough. With floured hands, shape into rolls, place on greased baking sheet, and allow to rise 15 minutes. Bake at 350 degrees for 15 to 20 minutes.

Preparation time: 20 minutes
Baking time: as per machine instructions
Makes: 1-1/2 lb loaf

WATER BAGELS   [P]

2 pkgs active dry yeast
1-1/2 cups warm water
3 Tbsp sugar
1 Tbsp salt
3-3/4 cups unbleached flour
2 qts boiling water
1 Tbsp sugar

1 egg white
1 Tbsp water
minced onion
cornmeal
poppy seeds
sesame seeds

Preheat oven to 450 degrees. Grease baking sheet and sprinkle with corn meal.

In large bowl, dissolve yeast in warm water. Let stand 2 to 3 minutes until bubbly. Stir in sugar and salt. Add 2 cups of flour. Beat with mixer on low speed to blend. Beat 3 minutes on high. Gradually add remaining flour, beating until stiff dough forms. Knead 8 to 10 minutes by hand or 6 minutes with dough hook, until smooth and elastic, but firm when pinched.

Place dough in greased bowl, turning to grease top. Cover and let rise until doubled, about 1 hour. Turn out on floured surface, punch down. Shape into ball and divide into quarters. Divide each part into four 3-oz pieces. Shape each into ball. Let rest 3 to 4 minutes, then flatten. Press thumb into center of bagel and tear open. Shape evenly with fingers forming bagel. Cover with waxed paper and let rise 10 minutes. Meanwhile, heat 2 qts water in saucepan with remaining 1 tablespoon sugar. Gently place bagel in water and simmer 30 seconds, turn and simmer 30 seconds longer. Remove with slotted skimmer to towel. Place on prepared baking sheet. Repeat with other bagels. Brush top with

(continued on next page)

egg white lightly beaten with water. Sprinkle with onion and poppy seeds or sesame seeds. Bake 20 to 25 minutes, turning baking sheet halfway through to brown evenly. To serve, split and toast.

Preparation time: 25 minutes
Rising time: 1 hour
Baking time: 20 to 25 minutes
Makes: 12

PECAN ALLIGATOR [D]

1 pkg active dry yeast, mixed with a tsp of sugar	2 Tbsp vegetable shortening
1/4 cup warm water	1/2 cup sugar
1/4 cup half and half or liquid non-dairy creamer, warmed	1 egg
	1/4 tsp salt
2/3 cup bread flour	zest of 1 lemon
1/4 cup unsalted butter or pareve margarine	5 Tbsp firm unsalted butter or margarine
	1-1/4 cups bread flour

Pecan filling:
2/3 cup butter or pareve margarine	2/3 cup finely chopped pecans
3 Tbsp vegetable shortening	1/3 cup flour
2/3 cup dark brown sugar, packed	

Egg Wash:
1 egg
1 Tbsp water
20 pecan halves

Coffee Icing:
1/2 Tbsp instant coffee
2 tsp hot water
1/3 cup confectioners sugar

Preheat oven to 350 degrees.

In mixing bowl, dissolve yeast in warm water and proof.* Add non-dairy creamer or half and half. Stir in flour. Cover and let stand. In another bowl, cream butter, shortening and sugar. Beat in egg, salt and lemon zest. Add to flour mixture. In a large bowl, cut butter into remaining 1 1/4 cups flour. Stir in yeast batter, blending just until flour is moistened. Wrap with plastic wrap. Chill 2 hours.

For filling: Cream butter and shortening until light. Beat in brown sugar. Add pecans and flour, mixing well. Turn dough out onto floured board. Knead lightly, divide in half. Roll each half out on lightly floured board to 10 X 14 inch rectangle. Spread center with pecan filling. Fold over sides. Roll lightly with rolling pin to seal. Place seam down on parchment lined 10 X 15 inch baking pan. Cut 1/2 inch slashes on long sides. Prick top with fork. Beat egg lightly with water and brush over top. Sprinkle with pecans. Let rise 30 minutes, until light. Bake 30 to 35 minutes, until browned.

Dissolve instant coffee in hot water, gradually add confectioners' sugar until syrupy. Drizzle over coffeecake. Cool in pan. Slice to serve.

Preparation time: 30 minutes
Rising time: 30 minutes
Refrigerator time: 2 hours
Baking time: 30 to 35 minutes
Makes: 2 coffeecakes

***Note:** to proof let yeast and water sit for 10 minutes or until bubbles form.

BREAD

HUNGARIAN PULL APART COFFEE CAKE [D]

1 cup scalded milk
1/2 cup sugar
1 tsp salt
2 yeast cakes
2 large eggs, beaten
1/2 cup soft shortening

5 cups sifted all-purpose flour
3/4 cup sugar
1 tsp cinnamon
1/2 cup chopped nuts
1/2 cup pareve margarine or butter, melted
1/4 cup raisins (optional)

Preheat oven to 375 degrees.

Scald milk and cool to lukewarm. Stir in sugar and salt. Add crumbled yeast and stir until dissolved. Stir in eggs and shortening. Add flour gradually. Mix thoroughly. Small lumps may be present in dough.

Mix well until dough is soft and easy to handle. Knead on lightly floured board. Place in lightly greased bowl. Cover and set in warm place to rise for 1-1/2 hours. Punch down and let rise again 35 to 40 minutes.

Cut dough into walnut size pieces and shape into balls. Mix sugar, cinnamon and nuts. To coat each ball, roll into margarine and sugar mixture. Place one layer in greased 10-inch tube pan. Sprinkle with raisins, if desired. Continue to add balls until all are used. Let rise 45 minutes. Bake 35 to 40 minutes. Let cool. Invert onto plate, but do not remove baking pan until cake has cooled completely.

Preparation time: 40 minutes
Rising time: 45 minutes
Baking time: 35 to 40 minutes
Serves: 10 to 12

CINNAMON WALNUT COFFEE CAKE [P]

1 pkg active dry yeast
1/4 cup warm water
4 cups all-purpose flour
1/4 cup sugar

1 tsp salt
1 cup unsalted pareve margarine
1 cup warm non-dairy pareve creamer
3 large egg yolks, well beaten

Filling:
3 egg whites
1 cup sugar
1 Tbsp cinnamon
1 cup finely chopped walnuts

Icing:
3/4 cup sifted powdered sugar
1/2 tsp vanilla
3 to 4 tsp non-dairy pareve creamer
walnut halves

Preheat oven to 350 degrees. Grease baking sheet.

In small bowl, dissolve yeast in warm water. In large bowl, stir flour, sugar and salt. Cut in margarine until mixture resembles coarse crumbs. Add warm creamer and egg yolks. Stir until soft dough forms. Beat in yeast. Cover and refrigerate, 4 hours or overnight.

(continued on next page)

Beat egg whites until soft peaks form. Combine sugar and cinnamon. Divide dough in half. Roll out one part at a time on well floured board to 9 X 15 inch rectangle (refrigerate remainder). Spread with half the beaten egg whites, sprinkle with half the cinnamon, sugar and nuts. Roll up jelly roll fashion. Flip over onto greased baking sheet. Repeat with remaining dough and filling. Let rise until double, about 40 minutes. Bake 35 minutes until golden brown. Remove to wire rack. Combine powdered sugar with vanilla and creamer to icing consistency. Drizzle over coffee cakes. Top with walnuts.

Preparation time: 30 minutes
Rising time: 40 minutes
Baking time: 35 minutes
Makes: 2

HUNGARIAN HORNS [D]

4 cups flour
1/2 tsp salt
1 yeast cake
1 1/4 cups butter or margarine

3 egg yolks, beaten
1 tsp vanilla
1/2 cup sour cream
powdered sugar

Filling:
3 large egg whites
1 cup sugar

1/2 cup nuts, finely chopped
1 tsp vanilla

Preheat oven to 400 degrees.

Combine flour and salt. Crumble yeast cake and butter into flour. Add egg yolks, vanilla and sour cream. Pat together to form dough. Cover cutting board with powdered sugar. Divide dough into 6 equal portions and roll each out to size of 9 inch circle. Cut into 12 wedges. Make filling: Beat egg whites stiff. Gradually add sugar. Fold in nuts, vanilla and cinnamon. Spread 1 tsp filling on each wedge. Roll into crescents, wide end to center and place on ungreased baking sheet. Bake 15 to 20 minutes. Sprinkle cinnamon and sugar on top if desired.

Preparation time: 25 to 30 minutes
Baking time: 15 to 20 minutes
Makes: 72

ENGLISH SCONES [D]

4 cups self-rising flour
1/3 cup sugar
1 Tbsp baking powder plus 1 tsp
1/4 tsp salt

1/4 lb butter, softened
10 oz buttermilk
3/4 cup raisins

Preheat oven to 375 degrees. Grease cookie sheet.
Sift together, flour, sugar, baking powder and salt. Add butter, mixing with a pastry blender or two knives, to form crumb consistency. Add buttermilk, then raisins.

Roll out on a floured board to 1 inch thickness. Cut into 2 inch circles using a floured drinking glass or cookie cutter. Place on a cookie sheet and bake for 15 minutes.

Preparation time: 15 minutes
Baking time: 15 minutes
Makes: 15

SOUR CREAM COFFEE CAKE   [D]

1/2 cup margarine at room temperature
1 cup sugar
2 eggs
1 cup sour cream
1 tsp vanilla
2 cups flour
1 tsp baking powder
1 tsp baking soda

Topping:
1/2 cup chopped nuts
1 Tbsp sugar
1/2 tsp cinnamon

Preheat oven to 350 degrees. Grease 10 inch tube or bundt pan.

Cream margarine and sugar. Add eggs, sour cream and vanilla alternately with the flour that has been mixed with baking powder and baking soda. Mix thoroughly and transfer batter to a greased and floured 10 inch bundt pan. Combine topping and sprinkle over cake. Bake for one hour.

Preparation time: 20 minutes
Baking time: 1 hour
Serves: 10 to 12

Add any of the following: dried chopped cherries, or dried cranberries, chopped dates or chocolate chips.

STICKY CINNAMON BUNS   [D]

2 pkg active dry yeast
1/3 cup warm water
1 cup butter, room temperature
1/3 cup sugar
2 egg yolks
1/4 tsp salt
1 tsp white vinegar or lemon juice
2/3 cup sour cream
3-1/2 cups unbleached flour

Filling:
2/3 cup butter, room temperature
1-1/2 cups light brown sugar, packed
3/4 tsp cinnamon
2 tsp white corn syrup
24 whole pecans
melted butter
1/2 cup chopped nuts
1/2 cup currants or raisins, rinsed in hot water
1/2 tsp cinnamon

In small bowl, dissolve yeast in warm water. Set aside until foamy. In large mixing bowl, cream butter and sugar. Blend in yeast, egg yolks, salt, vinegar and sour cream. Gradually add flour, beating until well combined. Turn out on floured board and knead 7 to 10 minutes, or knead with dough hook 6 minutes, until smooth and elastic. Place in buttered bowl, turning to butter top. Cover with plastic wrap and refrigerate at least 4 hours or overnight.

Cream butter with 3/4 cup brown sugar, cinnamon and corn syrup. Place a rounded teaspoonful on bottom of each muffin cup, then a whole pecan, rounded side down. Remove dough from refrigerator. Divide in half. Return one half to refrigerator. Roll 1/8 inch thick forming 10 x 18 inch rectangle. Brush with melted butter. Sprinkle with remaining brown sugar, chopped pecans, currants and cinnamon. Roll up tightly from long side, jelly-roll fashion. With a sharp knife, cut into 1-1/2 inch slices, place cut side down in prepared muffin cups.

(continued on next page)

Cover with a towel or waxed paper and let rise in a warm place 1 hour, until puffy. Prepare second half of dough as above. Bake at 375 degrees 25 to 30 minutes, until a rich golden brown. Invert muffin tins over large platters immediately. Serve warm.

Preparation time: 30 minutes
Rising time: 1 hour plus 4 hours refrigeration time.
Baking time: 25 to 30 minutes
Makes: 24

ORANGE HAZELNUT BUNS [D]

2 yeast cakes
1/4 cup lukewarm water
1/3 cup butter or margarine
3/4 cup hot scalded milk
1/3 cup sugar
2 tsp salt
2 tsp grated orange zest
2 large eggs
4 to 4-1/2 cups sifted flour

Nut Filling:
1/3 cup margarine at room temperature
1 cup sifted confectioners sugar
1 cup finely chopped hazelnuts (other nuts
 may be used)

Glaze:
1/4 cup orange juice
3 Tbsp sugar

Preheat oven to 375 degrees. Grease baking sheet.

Combine yeast with warm water and set aside to proof for about 10 minutes. Combine butter with hot milk. Stir until butter melts. Add sugar, salt, orange zest and eggs. Add the yeast mixture. Gradually add flour to form a stiff dough. Cover and let stand 30 minutes in a draft-free area. On a floured surface, roll dough into a 22 x 12 inch rectangle.

Cream margarine. Blend in sugar and nuts. Spread filling along 22 inch length of dough but only half of the width. Fold uncovered half over filling.

Cut 1 inch strips across dough. Twist each strip 4 to 5 times. Then hold one end down on baking sheet for center of roll, curl strip around center, tucking other end under. Cover with waxed paper or towel. Let dough rest in a warm place until doubled in size, about 45 minutes. Bake 15 minutes or until light golden brown.

Meanwhile, combine 1/4 cup orange juice with sugar for glaze. Brush tops of buns and bake 5 minutes longer until deep golden brown. Remove from baking sheets immediately.

Preparation time: 30 minutes
Rising time: 45 minutes
Baking time: 15 minutes
Makes: 18 to 24

STRAWBERRY AMBROSIA MUFFINS [P]

2 large eggs
1/2 cup oil
2/3 cup sugar
10 oz pkg frozen sliced strawberries, thawed, not drained
grated zest of 1 orange
1-1/2 cups all-purpose flour
1/2 tsp soda
1/4 tsp salt
2/3 cup flaked coconut

Preheat oven to 400 degrees.

Beat eggs until light. Blend in oil, sugar, strawberries and orange zest. Stir flour, soda and salt in large bowl. Stir in strawberry mixture and coconut just until moistened. Spoon into muffin cups with paper liners. Bake 25 minutes until golden brown. Remove from pans. Serve warm.

Preparation time: 10 minutes
Baking time: 25 minutes
Makes: 13

GLAZED DARK BRAN MUFFINS [D]

1/4 cup butter room temperature
6 Tbsp dark brown sugar
1 cup sugar
6 Tbsp molasses
1 Tbsp water
1/2 cup whole wheat flour
1/2 cup plus 2 Tbsp cake flour
1/2 tsp salt
1/2 tsp soda
1/2 tsp cinnamon
1/2 cup raisins
2 eggs
1/4 cup oil
3 cups all bran cereal*
1-1/2 cups buttermilk

Preheat oven to 400 degrees.

Cream butter until fluffy and gradually beat in brown sugar and 6 Tbsp sugar. Blend in 2 Tbsp molasses and water and whip until fluffy. Coat 18 muffin cups liberally and evenly with molasses mixture using about 2 tsp per cup.

Combine whole wheat and cake flours, remaining 10 Tbsp sugar, salt, soda and cinnamon. Stir in raisins. Add eggs, remaining 1/4 cup molasses and oil and blend. Stir in bran and buttermilk. Mix just until batter is smooth. Fill coated muffin cups 3/4 full. Bake 20 minutes. Remove muffins from cups immediately by turning upside down on racks.

Preparation time: 20 minutes
Baking time: 20 minutes
Makes: 18

The glaze makes these special.

* Do not use high fiber bran cereal.

ISRAELI DOUGHNUTS (SOOFGANIOT) [D]

2 pkgs dry yeast
2 tsp sugar
3/4 cup warm water
1/3 cup sugar
2 egg yolks
1/4 cup butter or pareve margarine, melted
1 tsp vanilla
1/2 tsp brandy extract
grated zest of 1 lemon
3 cups all-purpose flour
jelly
oil for frying
confectioners sugar

In large mixing bowl, stir yeast and 2 tsps sugar into warm water. Let stand 5 minutes, until bubbly. Stir in remaining sugar, egg yolks, butter, vanilla, brandy extract, lemon zest and 1 cup flour. Beat 1 to 2 minutes. Gradually stir in remaining flour to form a soft dough. Knead until smooth and elastic, about 5 minutes.

Place in greased bowl, turning to grease top. Cover with plastic wrap and damp towel. Let rise in warm place until doubled, about 1-1/2 hours. Punch down and shape into two oblongs, 2 inches wide. Cut each into 10. Shape each into a round. Place a spoonful of jelly in center. Shape into a ball, enclosing jelly, and pinch to seal. Set on lightly floured trays or line with parchment. Let rise 45 minutes, until doubled.

Heat oil to 370 degrees. Fry doughnuts, a few at a time, until golden brown, turning once. Drain on paper towels. Sprinkle with confectioner's sugar. Serve warm.

Preparation time: 30 minutes
Rising time: 1 hour 45 minutes
Cooking time: 10 minutes
Makes: 20

SANTA FE CHEESE BREAD [D]

1/2 cup margarine
2 cups flour
2 tsp baking powder
1 cup grated mild white cheese
4 Tbsp grated Parmesan cheese
4 oz diced mild green chiles,
　　canned or fresh, seeds removed
1/2 tsp cayenne pepper
2 large eggs
1/2 cup light sour cream
2 Tbsp oil
2 Tbsp sesame seeds

Preheat oven to 350 degrees.

In a large bowl, cut together margarine, flour and baking powder until it resembles coarse meal. Stir in white cheese, 2 Tbsp Parmesan cheese, chiles and cayenne. Add eggs and sour cream. Stir until soft dough forms. Place 1 Tbsp oil on pizza pan or a 12-inch round pan. Spread dough evenly in pan. Drizzle top with 1 Tbsp oil, 2 Tbsp Parmesan cheese and sesame seeds. Bake for 40 minutes.

Preparation time: 20 minutes
Baking time: 40 minutes
Serves: 10

Hot and spicy with south of the border ingredients.

SWEET & EASY CORNBREAD [D]

1 cup yellow corn meal
1 cup flour
1/2 cup sugar
1 Tbsp baking powder
1/4 tsp salt

1/2 cup margarine cut into pieces
1/2 cup light sour cream
1/2 cup milk
1 large egg

Preheat oven to 375 degrees. Grease an 8 inch square baking pan.

In large mixing bowl mix first 6 ingredients to form coarse meal. Beat in sour cream, milk and egg until just blended. Spread in greased 8 inch square baking pan.

Bake for 30 minutes or until tester inserted in center comes out clean. Cool in pan.

Preparation time: 10 minutes
Baking time: 30 minutes
Serves: 8

Variation: 1 onion sliced thin. 2 Tbsp oil. Brown onions in a skillet. Top cornbread batter with onions and bake as above.

PECAN LEMON BREAD [D]

2-3/4 cups all-purpose flour
1/2 tsp baking soda
1/2 tsp baking powder
1/2 tsp salt
1/3 cup oil
1 cup sugar

3 to 4 Tbsp grated lemon zest
2 large eggs, lightly beaten
1/2 cup lemon juice
1/2 cup water
1/2 cup pecan halves
1/2 cup chopped pecans

Preheat oven to 350 degrees. Grease a loaf pan 5 X 9 inches.

In mixing bowl, sift flour, soda, baking powder and salt. With pastry blender work in oil. Stir in sugar, lemon zest and eggs. Mix lemon juice with water. Add and stir until moist. Lightly mix chopped pecans into batter. Place pecan halves on bottom of greased 9 x 5 x 3 inch loaf pan. Pour batter into prepared pan. Bake 1 hour or until loaf tests done. Turn out of pan when cool.

Preparation time: 10 minutes
Baking time: 1 hour
Makes: 1 loaf

THIN CRUST PIZZA   [P]

Crust:

2 tsp olive oil or vegetable oil
2 tsp corn meal
1 pkg dry yeast
1 tsp sugar

1/2 cup plus 2 Tbsp warm water
1 1/2 cups plus 2 Tbsp flour
3/4 tsp salt

Prepare pan: Use one 14 inch or two 9 inch pizza pans.

Rub 1 tsp oil over pans. Sprinkle pans with corn meal.

Stir yeast and sugar into warm water and let stand until foamy.

Combine flour, salt and remaining oil in food processor bowl fitted with a metal blade. Pour yeast mixture through feed tube. Process until dough forms ball. If dough sticks, add more flour by tablespoons through feed tube, letting each addition work in before adding more. If dough is crumbly, add water by teaspoons through feed tube, letting each addition work in before adding more. Process dough until smooth and elastic. Place dough in an oiled bowl, turning to oil top. Cover with plastic wrap and set in a warm place to rise until doubled, about 45 minutes.

Preheat oven to 450 degrees.

Punch down the dough. On lightly floured board, roll dough to 14 inch circle; or divide dough in half and roll each half to two 9 inch circles. Transfer dough to pan and form a thick rim by doubling dough around edge. When a very moist filling is used, prebake crust 5 to 10 minutes. Cool crust 5 minutes before adding filling. Preparation time: 30 minutes.

WHITE PIZZA FILLING   [D]

1/3 cup olive oil
1 large shallot or a piece of onion
4 garlic cloves
1/2 tsp dried oregano, crumbled
1/2 tsp dried basil, crumbled

1/2 tsp dried parsley, crumbled
1/2 tsp dried thyme, crumbled
1/2 tsp dried crushed, red pepper flakes
1/4 tsp freshly ground pepper
1 lb Fontina or Gruyere cheese, grated

In food processor with metal blade, mix all ingredients, except cheese, until smooth, about 1 minute, stopping to scrape down the sides of bowl. Using medium shredding disc with light pressure, shred Fontina cheese.

Preheat oven to 450 degrees. Spread with herb mixture. Sprinkle with cheese. Bake until edges of pizza are lightly browned and crust is done, about 10 minutes. Serve pizza immediately.

Preparation time: 10 minutes

NEW METHOD POPOVERS   [D]

1 cup sifted bread flour
1/4 tsp salt
2 large slightly beaten eggs
1 cup milk
1 tsp melted butter or margarine
4 custard cups

Combine flour and salt and set aside. Mix eggs, milk and butter. Stir in flour until well mixed and smooth. Fill cold, well greased custard cups a little more than half full. Place on cookie sheet and put in a cold oven. Turn on oven to 425 degrees and bake 1 hour.

Preparation time: 10 minutes
Baking time: 1 hour
Serves: 4

ONION PLETZL   [P]

1/4 cup oil
3 large onions, coarsely chopped
1/2 cup oil
4 large eggs
1/2 cup cold water
4 cups all-purpose flour
1 tsp salt
1/2 tsp pepper
1/4 cup poppy seeds
1 Tbsp baking powder
2 Tbsp sugar

Preheat oven to 350 degrees. Grease two baking sheets.

In large skillet, heat 1/4 cup oil, add onions and saute 5 minutes until tender. Let cool. In mixing bowl, beat eggs with remaining oil and cold water until mixed. Combine dry ingredients and add to egg mixture, stirring until blended. Roll out dough on floured board into two large rectangles about 1/2 inch thick. Place on baking sheets and top with onion mixture. Bake for 30 minutes. Cut into slices and serve warm.

Preparation time: 15 minutes
Baking time: 30 minutes
Serves: 12 to 14

GREEK FLATBREAD   [D]

1/8 cup olive oil
1 large egg
1-1/2 cup buttermilk
1 Tbsp sugar
1/2 cup chopped green onion
1 Tbsp grated lemon zest
3 cups flour
4 tsp baking powder
1/4 lb feta cheese, crumbled
1 Tbsp oil
1 Tbsp sesame seeds
1/4 cup Greek olives chopped (optional)

Preheat oven to 350 degrees.

Place oil in 12 inch round pizza pan or 10 x 15 jelly roll pan. Beat all ingredients except seeds and olives until just blended. Pour into pan. Brush top with oil and sprinkle with seeds and olives. Bake for 45 minutes or until brown. Cool in pan.

Preparation time: 15 minutes
Baking time: 45 minutes
Serves: 10

APPETIZERS

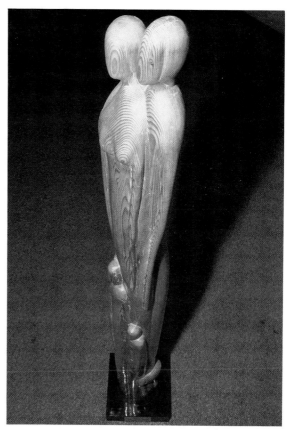

THE FAMILY, WOOD SCULPTURE
GIFT OF RUTH AND GEORGE WELLINGTON

WEDDINGS, BAR and BAT MITZVOT, BRIT MILAH—Simple and Sophisticated Appetizers are a Prelude to Festive Occasions.

APPETIZERS
Janet Salter

The newest addition to the Hebrew dictionary is hors d' oeuvres. Nothing, but nothing ever begins—not a Bar or Bat Mitzvah, not a wedding or a Bris, without those delightful morsels called appetizers. Why are they called appetizers? Because they are appetizing and also kill your appetite!

The hors d' oeuvres or appetizers have now become firmly fixed in the mores of modern Jewry. Their variety is as broad as the earth is round. They are eclectic. They range from the ubiquitous bagel, cream cheese and lox, herring and sour cream, to the colorful cuts of vegetables called crudites, from cold-cuts and cole slaw, to the tiny cucumbers, olives and green tomatoes of the Near East. What follows the hors d' oeuvres? Who cares?

CAVIAR DIP IN PUMPERNICKEL BOWL [D]

4 cups sour cream
3 to 4 oz salmon or white fish caviar
7 cloves garlic, minced
1 medium red onion, finely chopped

juice of 1 small lemon
pepper to taste
parsley to garnish
  2 lb large round pumpernickel

Mix all ingredients except bread. Cut off top of bread and carefully scoop out pumpernickel with serrated knife, so that side and bottom remain intact. Save inside of bread, cut into cubes and use for dipping.

Place dip inside bread and refrigerate till ready to serve. Garnish with parsley.

Preparation time: 15 minutes
Serves: 8-10 as an appetizer

White fish caviar will produce a mauve color. Salmon caviar will produce pink color.

DIPSY DAISY [D]

1/4 cup chopped green onions
1/2 cup low fat cottage cheese
1/2 cup low fat cream cheese

1/4 cup minced parsley
2 tsp capers, drained
1/4 tsp white pepper

In food processor, fitted with metal blade, combine all ingredients. Blend until completely smooth. Chill. Serve with crudites or crackers.

Preparation time: 5 minutes
Makes: 1-1/2 cups

It will keep one week in refrigerator.

CHILIED BEAN DIP [P]

16 oz can kidney or pinto beans,
    drained and rinsed, reserve liquid
2 Tbsp fresh, finely chopped green chile,
    seeds removed (use rubber gloves
    when handling chile)

1 Tbsp wine vinegar
1 tsp chili powder
1/8 tsp cumin
2 tsp minced onion
2 tsp minced fresh parsley

In food processor, fitted with metal blade, blend beans, chiles, vinegar, chili powder and cumin until smooth. Transfer to a bowl and stir in onion and parsley.

If desired, mixture may be thinned slightly with bean liquid. Serve with tostada chips.

Preparation time: 10 minutes
Serves: 10-12

HORSERADISH AND CHIVE DIP [D]

2 cups low fat cottage cheese
1/3 cup freshly grated horseradish
1/4 cup minced chives
1/2 cup minced parsley
1/2 tsp salt (optional)
1 tsp freshly ground pepper

Combine all ingredients in food processor, fitted with metal blade or blender. Turn into a glass bowl. Refrigerate until ready to serve.

Preparation time: 5 minutes
Serves: 12

Serve with crudites or crackers. May also be used as an accompaniment to smoked fish.

TARAMASALATA (GREEK COD ROE DIP) [P]

3 slices (3 oz) rye or firm white bread, crusts removed
1/4 cup cold water
1 clove garlic, minced
1/4 cup finely minced onion
6 oz (2/3 cup) tarama (smoked cod's roe)
1 small lemon, juiced
1/4 cup olive oil
chopped parsley

In a small bowl, soak bread in water several minutes, then squeeze dry with hands. In food processor, fitted with metal blade, combine garlic, onion, bread and tarama, blend well. Add lemon juice, then gradually add olive oil. Taste and add more lemon juice or olive oil if needed (mixture should be thick and creamy with a slightly salty flavor) Turn into serving dish, sprinkle with parsley. Serve with hot pita bread or fresh vegetables.

Preparation time: 15 minutes
Makes: 2 cups

For caviar lovers. Smoked cod roe may be found in a Greek specialty store.

FRESH GARDEN BRUSCHETTA [D]

7 large tomatoes, cored and quartered
1 large yellow bell pepper, cored, seeded and quartered
3 cloves garlic, peeled
1/4 cup chopped Italian parsley
2-3 Tbsp chopped cilantro (optional)
2 Tbsp fresh basil leaves
3 Tbsp chopped chives
1 Tbsp fresh thyme
8 olives, pitted, Greek or Kalamati
4 Tbsp capers, drained
1/2 cup olive oil
freshly grated Parmesan cheese (optional)
salt and pepper to taste

In food processor, fitted with metal blade, coarsely chop first 10 ingredients. Mix in olive oil, Parmesan cheese, if desired, salt and pepper to taste.

Serve on small pieces of toasted French bread rubbed with garlic clove. The bread should be toasted under the broiler until golden brown on both sides.

Preparation time: 15 minutes
Serves: 10

EGGPLANT RELISH (ITALIAN STYLE) [P]

1 large firm eggplant
1 green bell pepper
1 clove garlic, chopped fine
1 medium tomato, diced
1 small onion, chopped
2 Tbsp chopped parsley
1/2 tsp dry oregano
1 tsp salt
1/2 tsp pepper
1/2 tsp sugar
1/2 cup olive oil
2 Tbsp wine vinegar

Preheat oven to 350 degrees.
Pierce eggplant and green pepper several times and roast for 1 hour. Cool, peel and drain in colander. Cut into pieces 1/2 to 1 inch. Place in food processor with steel blade along with garlic, tomato, onion and parsley. Add rest of ingredients. Process to count of 5. Mix well and adjust seasonings to taste. Refrigerate.

Preparation time: 10 minutes
Cooking time: 1 hour
Serves: 8 for salad or 12 as appetizer

Tastes better if allowed to marinate overnight. Keeps well for one week in refrigerator. Serve with pita bread.

FETA STUFFED TOMATOES [D]

1 basket cherry tomatoes
1 bunch parsley
1 oz fresh basil leaves
1/4 cup sun-dried tomato
2 oz feta cheese
2 cloves garlic
1 Tbsp olive oil

Wash tomatoes, core with a melon ball scooper and turn upside down to drain. In food processor, chop remaining ingredients coarsely. Stuff mixture into tomatoes.

Preparation time: 20 minutes
Makes: 20

An attractive and healthy appetizer. Note: If you do not have a food processor chop each ingredient finely and mix well, then add to tomatoes.

SPICY MARINATED MUSHROOMS [D]

1 lb mushrooms
1/4 cup water
1 bay leaf, crumbled
1/4 tsp salt or to taste
1 Tbsp grated Parmesan cheese (optional)
1 Tbsp chopped chives
1/2 cup olive oil
3/4 cup red wine vinegar
1 tsp tarragon
1 clove garlic, crushed
1/2 tsp sugar

Wipe mushrooms with damp towel. Put in bowl. Mix remaining ingredients and pour over mushrooms. Cover and let marinate at least one hour or longer.

Preparation time: 10 minutes
Serves: 8-10 as an appetizer

KOSHER DILL PICKLES [P]

For 1 Quart:
Medium, firm pickling cucumbers
  (about 3/4 lbs) or green tomatoes
3 3 inch pieces celery
2 sprigs dill or 1 Tbsp dill weed
1 tsp mixed pickling spice
1 small dried red hot pepper

1/4 tsp coarse black pepper
3 cloves garlic, crushed
1 Tbsp sugar
4 tsp salt
2 cups water
celery leaves
pinch rye bread crust

Soak cucumbers or tomatoes in cold water 2 hours. Scrub and rinse. Pack cucumbers and celery tightly in clean 1 quart jar so cucumbers don't float. Add spices, garlic and sugar. Dissolve salt in water. Add brine to cover. Top with celery leaves. Add rye bread crust.

Cover lightly and place on paper towels on plate to catch any brine that runs over during fermentation. Pickles are ready to eat when gas stops forming and a pickle when cut in half is half or fully pickled and becomes translucent. Allow 3 to 4 days for pickles, longer for tomatoes. Place jar of pickles in refrigerator. Chill well. Keeps several weeks.

Preparation time: 5 minutes
Processing time: 3 to 4 days

Traditional family favorite that's crunchy, garlicky and hot.

ROAST PEPPERS ISRAELI STYLE [P]

6 large green or red bell peppers
  (best to mix for color)
2 Tbsp olive oil

2 large cloves garlic, minced or pressed
2 Tbsp chopped cilantro
salt and pepper to taste

Preheat oven to broil.

Wash peppers and slice in half. Remove seeds and dry with paper towel. Place cut side down on a lightly greased baking sheet. Roast under broiler until peppers are blistered and charred. Remove from broiler. Place in paper bag for 15 minutes. Remove skin and slice.

While peppers are still warm, add rest of ingredients and serve at room temperature.

Preparation time: 5 minutes
Cooking time: 10 minutes
Serves: 6 to 8

Variations: Add toasted pine nuts or pistachios. Add lemon juice if desired. Note: For a milder taste add Italian parsley instead of cilantro.

CAPONATA [P]

3 Tbsp olive oil
1 lb eggplant, cut in 1 inch cubes
1 medium onion, sliced
3 medium tomatoes, peeled, seeded, cut in chunks
1 tsp salt
1/8 tsp freshly ground pepper

1/4 tsp red pepper flakes
2 Tbsp sun-dried tomatoes in oil
1 stalk celery, chopped
1 Tbsp capers, drained
6 large green cracked olives, chopped
1/4 cup red wine vinegar
1 Tbsp sugar

In large skillet, heat 2 Tbsp of the olive oil over medium heat. Add eggplant and saute 10 minutes, until golden brown and slightly limp. Remove from pan. Saute onion in remaining 1 Tbsp olive oil until wilted. Add fresh tomatoes, salt, pepper and red pepper. Simmer 5 minutes. Add sun-dried tomatoes, celery, capers and olives. Bring to a boil, return eggplant to skillet. Add vinegar and sugar and cook 5 minutes until vinegar has evaporated. *Do not overcook.* Vegetables should be tender-crisp. Turn into dish. Cover and refrigerate. Serve cold.

Preparation time: 15 minutes
Cooking time: 20 minutes
Serves: 6

Note: To peel tomatoes, plunge in boiling water for 10 to 30 seconds. Remove to cold water and peel skin.

CLASSIC HUMOUS [P]

2 cups chickpeas, canned, drained with liquid reserved
4 to 6 medium lemons, juiced as needed
4 to 6 cloves garlic, pressed
3/4 cup sesame paste, (tahini)

1/2 tsp salt
1/2 tsp cumin to taste
2 Tbsp olive oil
chopped parsley
paprika, toasted pine nuts, to garnish

Place 1/2 the amount of chickpeas in a food processor. Add garlic and lemon juice to taste and blend. Add remaining chickpeas. Add sesame paste, seasoning and olive oil. Blend till mixture is smooth or slightly chunky, depending on personal preference.

Using a spatula, spread the mixture on two or more plates. Sprinkle chopped Italian parsley around the edges. Make a thin circle of olive oil parallel to the parsley, or pour a small amount in the center. Sprinkle with paprika and toasted pine nuts and serve.

Preparation time: 10 minutes
Makes: 3 cups.
Serves: 20 for appetizer

TAPANADE [P]

4 ounces Greek olives, pitted
2 anchovy fillets
1 Tbsp capers

2 tsp Dijon mustard
3 to 4 Tbsp extra-virgin olive oil

In a blender or food processosr, fitted with a metal blade, place olives, anchovies, capers and mustard. Pulse on and off until finely chopped. Gradually pour in olive oil and process until smooth. Turn into small crock and serve with toasted French bread or crudites.

Preparation time: 5 minutes
Makes: about 2/3 cup.

For a less salty mixture use 2 oz ripe olives and 2 oz Greek olives.
A traditional provencal appetizer.

DOLMATHES [P]

3 Tbsp olive oil
1-1/2 cup chopped onion
1 cup long grain rice
2 cups minus 2 Tbsp hot water
1 Tbsp tomato paste
1 tsp salt
1/4 tsp pepper
1/4 cup currants

1/4 cup toasted pine nuts
1-1/2 tsp minced mint
1 Tbsp minced parsley
1 lb jar grape leaves
juice of 1 medium lemon
1/2 cup cold water
1 Tbsp olive oil
lemon wedges

Heat olive oil in large saucepan. Add onion and saute until tender, but not brown. Add rice and heat, stirring occasionally, until all grains are coated with oil. Add hot water, tomato paste, salt, pepper and currants. Cover and cook over low heat until liquid is absorbed about 15-20 minutes. Remove from heat and stir in pine nuts, mint and parsley. Let cool.

Unroll grape leaves, separate and place in colander. Rinse with water. Line casserole with small or broken grape leaves. On a flat surface lay leaf with vein side up.

Place a heaping spoonful of stuffing in center of leaf, varying amount of stuffing with size of leaf. Fold the stem end, then the two sides, rolling up firmly. Place rolls, seams downward, side by side in layers in casserole or in pot on top of stove.

Combine lemon juice and cold water and pour over stuffed rolls. Sprinkle with olive oil. Bring liquid to a boil, reduce heat and simmer 30 to 40 minutes. Serve warm or chilled. Garnish with lemon wedges.

Preparation time: 1 hour
Cooking time: 30 to 40 minutes
Makes: about 40

TZATZIKI [D]

Greek Cucumber and Yogurt Spread

1 unpeeled hot house cucumber, seeded, finely chopped and drained
1 clove garlic, crushed
1/4 cup olive oil
juice of 1/2 lemon
2 cups whole milk unflavored yogurt
1 tsp salt
3 Tbsp chopped parsley

In a food processor, add all ingredients and blend well. Refrigerate. Sprinkle parsley on top before serving. Serve with melba toast or as a dip with raw vegetables.

Preparation time: 10 minutes
Makes: about 2-1/2 cups

In Greece this is served as a spread for bread. May be used as a dip or salad topping.

GERMAN HERRING SALAD [P]

1 large jar pickled herring, drained
1 large apple
1 large onion
8 oz can beets, drained with liquid reserved
1/2 cup chopped walnuts

In food processor, fitted with metal blade, finely chop herring, apple, onion and beets. Add nuts and enough beet juice to color it red. Refrigerate 8 hours or overnight.

Preparation time: 10 minutes
Serves: 8-12

An old family recipe similar to Scandinavian salad.

SMOKED WHITEFISH SPREAD [D]

1 lb smoked whitefish, skin and bones removed
1/4 cup mayonnaise
1/4 cup sour cream
1/4 cup lemon juice
1/8 tsp cayenne pepper
1/4 tsp Worcestershire sauce
1/4 tsp fresh dill
dash paprika or parsley, chopped for garnish

In food processor, fitted with metal blade, chop fish finely. Add remaining ingredients, except paprika or parsley, and process for 30 seconds. Taste for seasoning. Garnish with paprika or chopped parsley and serve with crackers or toast.

Serve cold.

Preparation time: 10 minutes
Makes: about 3 cups

SMOKED SALMON WITH ENDIVE [P]

2 lbs smoked salmon fillet
1 medium red onion, finely minced
3 Tbsp capers, drained
1/2 cup fresh mint, chopped
3 Tbsp aquavit or vodka

2 Tbsp olive oil
1/4 lemon, juiced
1/4 tsp ground black pepper
Belgian endive

Place all ingredients, except endive, in food processor, fitted with metal blade, and process until finely minced, but not pureed. Serve on individual leaves of Belgian endive.

Preparatione time: 10 minutes
Serves: 8-10

VODKA HERRING [P]

1-1/2 lbs fresh or schmaltz herring
1-1/2 cup white vinegar
1 cup water
1 cup sugar
8 whole black peppercorns
8 whole allspice

8 juniper berries
1 medium carrot, sliced thin
1 medium onion, sliced thin
1/4 cup vodka
1/4 cup red onion, chopped
3 Tbsp fresh dill, chopped

Wash herring. If using schmaltz herring, wash several times to remove salt. Cut into 1/2 inch slices. Place in large glass jar. Make marinade of vinegar, water, sugar, peppercorns, allspice and juniper berries. Place onion and carrots in jar with fish. Pour marinade over all. Cover and refrigerate for 2 weeks. Two or three days before serving, add vodka. Return to refrigerator. When ready to serve, drain liquid and reserve. Garnish with chopped red onion and fresh dill. If you have leftovers, return to marinade.

Preparation time: 10 minutes
Refrigeration time: 2 weeks
Serves: 12 to 16 as an appetizer. Serve with black bread.

MISO SEASONED FISH [P]

6 2 oz cubes firm white fish
1 tsp salt
7 oz white miso (soy bean paste)
1/2 cup sake

2 Tbsp sugar
1/4 cup soy sauce
pickled ginger

Sprinkle fish with salt. Refrigerate 4 hours. Rinse fish and place in marinade of miso, sake, sugar and soy sauce. Refrigerate overnight. Drain fish and broil on skewers 5 to 6 minutes or until browned and fish is just cooked. Dip in additional soy sauce. Decorate with pickled ginger.

Preparation time: 15 minutes
Processing time: 4 hours plus overnight
Cooking time: 5 to 6 minutes
Serves: 3 to 4

Miso, sake, soy sauce, pickled ginger are available in Asian markets or most supermarkets.

SALMON GRAVLOX [P]

2 lb salmon, 3/4 to 1 inch thick
1/4 cup salt
1/2 cup sugar

2 tsp white pepper, crushed
1 bunch fresh dill, coarsely chopped

Take center cut salmon, remove bones with tweezers. Wipe dry. Mix salt, sugar and pepper together. Rub on fish, under and over it. Add dill. Place fish skin side down in glass dish. Cover with plastic wrap and weigh it down with a heavy bowl or cans. Refrigerate 48 hours, turning it every 12 hours. After first 6 hours, liquid may be removed. Slice thin to serve.

Preparation time: 30 minutes
Refrigeration time: 48 hours

DILL SAUCE [P]

3 Tbsp minced fresh dill
3 Tbsp vegetable oil
1 Tbsp red wine vinegar
1 Tbsp sugar

1/4 tsp salt
pinch of white pepper
3 Tbsp mustard

In food processor, fitted with metal blade, combine all ingredients. Refrigerate. Serve with Salmon Gravlox on pumpernickel bread squares.

Preparation time: 5 minutes

TRADITIONAL CHOPPED LIVER [M]

1-1/4 lbs chicken livers
2 Tbsp chicken fat
1 small onion, sliced
1 to 1-1/2 tsp salt
1/4 to 1/2 tsp pepper
3 eggs, hard cooked

Trim chicken livers. Broil 5 to 6 minutes, turning once, set aside. Heat 2 Tbsp fat in large skillet. Add onion, saute 5 minutes until onion is tender. Add chicken livers to pan and continue cooking until livers are no longer pink.

In food processor, add liver, onion, remaining fat and eggs, using "pulse" on and off, to chop to right consistency. Do not over process. Add salt and pepper to taste. Refrigerate.

Preparation time: 5 minutes
Cooking time: 15 minutes
Serves: 6 to 8 as appetizers

"NOUVELLE" CHOPPED LIVER [M]

1/2 lb beef liver
1/2 lb chicken liver
1 medium Spanish onion or
    other sweet variety
1 Tbsp oil (use less if using coated pan)
3 large eggs, hardcooked, chopped
1/4 cup chicken broth
1/4 tsp sugar
1/2 tsp salt
1/4 tsp pepper

Preheat oven to broil.

Broil liver until it is just cooked. Do not overcook. Chop onion and saute in a little oil, until translucent. Place onions, cooked liver, eggs, soup, sugar and seasonings into the food processor, fitted with metal blade. Process until just mixed. Refrigerate.

Preparation time: 10 minutes
Cooking time: 10 minutes
Serves: 6 to 8 as appetizer

May be made with all chicken livers.

Note: Be careful not to over process or chopped liver will liquify.

ISRAELI SECRET CHOPPED LIVER [M]

2 Tbsp oil
1 eggplant, peeled and sliced
1 onion, chopped
salt and pepper
6 large hard cooked eggs, chopped

In a large skillet heat oil. Saute eggplant with onion. Cool.

In food processor, fitted with metal blade, puree eggplant and onions, add salt and pepper to taste. Add chopped hard cooked eggs. Refrigerate at least two hours. Serve cold with crackers.

Preparation time: 20 minutes
Cooking time: 20 minutes
Serves: 6-8

You'll never guess the secret!

TIROPETES [D]

4 oz feta cheese
4 oz cream cheese
2 Tbsp beaten egg

8 filo sheets
1/2 cup sweet butter, melted
1/4 cup fine dry bread crumbs

Preheat oven to 400 degrees.

In electric mixer bowl, combine feta and cream cheese. Add egg and blend well. Chill.

On counter place waxed paper. Unfold filo and place on waxed paper. Cover with damp towel. Keep covered as you work, removing only one sheet at a time. Place sheet on clean surface and cut width-wise into thirds. Brush both sides lightly with butter and sprinkle with bread crumbs.

Fold each section lengthwise in thirds to form section 2 inches wide.

Place a spoonful of filling on top corner of one section. Fold corner to cover cheese and make a triangle. Fold flag fashion left to right and right to left. Brush with butter as needed. Repeat.

Place on buttered baking sheet. Bake at 400 degrees for 20 minutes, until golden brown. Serve at once.

Preparation time: 20 minutes
Baking time: 20 minutes
Makes: 3 dozen

If you prefer your tiropetes less salty, you can use more cream cheese and less feta cheese. Can be frozen.

STUFFED MUSHROOMS [D]

12 fresh mushrooms, 2 inches in diameter
3 Tbsp butter or margarine
2 Tbsp pine nuts
1 small onion, finely minced
1 slice white bread, crumbled
1 Tbsp chopped parsley
3 Tbsp dry white wine

1 clove garlic, finely minced
1/4 tsp dried tarragon, crumbled, soaked in white wine
1 egg yolk
3 Tbsp nonfat milk
3 Tbsp grated cheese, Parmesan or Romano

Preheat oven to 350 degrees.

Wipe mushrooms, remove stems and chop stems finely. In a skillet, melt butter and saute pine nuts for one minute. Add onions and continue cooking one minute more. Add chopped mushroom stems. Add the bread crumbs, parsley, wine, tarragon and garlic. Cook a few minutes longer until all is blended. Beat egg yolk and add the milk. Stir into hot stuffing mixture. Butter an oven-to-table shallow dish, and arrange the mushrooms. Mound the filling in the hollow of the mushroom and sprinkle with grated cheese. Can be refrigerated at this point, a day ahead, and then baked. Bake for 30 minutes.

Preparation time: 20 minutes
Baking time: 30 minutes
Serves: 12 as appetizer

A pareve variation: Omit milk and cheese, substitute 3 Tbsp water or vegetable broth for milk and use pareve margarine.

SPANAKOPITA [D]

1 Tbsp sweet butter
1/2 cup onion, minced
10 oz pkg frozen chopped spinach, thawed & drained
3 large eggs, lightly beaten
1/2 cup sliced green onions
1/4 cup minced dill
1/4 cup minced parsley
4 oz feta cheese, crumbled
4 oz hoop or dry cottage cheese, crumbled
3/4 cup dry bread crumbs
1/4 tsp pepper
1/4 tsp nutmeg
salt to taste
1/2 cup sweet butter, melted
10 filo sheets

Preheat oven to 350 degrees.

In skillet, heat 1 Tbsp butter. Add onion and saute until tender. Cook and drain spinach, pressing out excess moisture. Combine sauteed onion, spinach, green onions, dill, parsley, eggs, cheese, 1/4 cup bread crumbs, pepper and nutmeg. Mix well. Taste and add salt, if needed.

Place damp towel on counter and cover with waxed paper. Unfold filo and place on waxed paper. Fold damp towel over to keep dough from drying. Brush a 9 inch pie pan with butter. Fit one sheet of filo into pie pan. Brush with butter and sprinkle lighly with bread crumbs. Continue to layer filo sheets into pan, buttering and crumbing each layer. Use six filo sheets for pie shell. Turn spinach mixture into filo lined pan. Place 3 more sheets over filling, brushing each with butter and crumbing lightly. Trim edges to edge of pan. Place trimmed pieces on top of pie. Cover with last filo sheet and tuck edges underneath. Turn pie pan upside down on cookie sheet and bake for 40 to 45 minutes until filling is set and pastry is golden brown. Invert on serving platter. Let stand 5 minutes before serving. Serve warm or at room temperature.

Preparation time: 40 minutes
Baking time: 40 to 45 minutes
Serves: 10 to 12 for appetizers

For 9 x 13 inch baking dish, double ingredients and use 12 sheets of filo. Bake for 40 to 50 minutes until golden brown. Serves 12 to 15 for appetizers

GOLDEN CHEESE AND ONION CRACKERS [D]

1/2 lb sharp cheddar cheese, grated
1/2 cup sweet butter, or margarine
1 egg
1-1/4 cups flour
1/2 tsp salt
1/8 tsp cayenne pepper
1 cup chopped scallions

Preheat oven to 350 degrees.
In a food processor, fitted with metal blade, mix ingredients. Shape into walnut sized balls. Bake for 18-20 minutes. Serve warm. May be frozen.

Preparation time: 5 minutes
Baking time: 18 to 20 minutes
Serves: 12 as appetizer

KREPLACH [M]

Noodle Dough:
3 large eggs, slightly beaten
2 Tbsp water
2 cups all-purpose flour
3/4 tsp salt

Meat filling:
1 large onion
3/4 lb ground veal or ground beef, cooked
1 large egg
2 cloves garlic, minced
1/2 tsp salt
1/4 tsp white pepper
2 Tbsp oil

To make dough: mix all ingredients. Using hands, knead dough until elastic. If using food processor, mix to form ball. Divide dough into two balls. Cover while preparing filling.

To make filling: saute onion, garlic, and meat in 2 Tbsp of oil. Drain. Cool then combine with egg and seasoning.

Working with one ball at a time, roll dough to rectangle on floured board. Cut into squares about 1-1/2 x 1-1/2 inches.

Place 1/2 tsp of meat mixture on each square and fold into a triangle by folding over one corner to opposite corner. Allow to rest 30 minutes. May be frozen at this point.

To cook: Fill a large pot 3/4 full with water. Bring to boil. Drop in kreplach and cook covered until they rise to top of pot 20 to 30 minutes.

Kreplach are often served in soup. They can also be baked, after boiling, for 10 to 15 minutes in a 350 degree oven. Serve warm as an appetizer.

Preparation time: 20 minutes
Cooking time: 30 minutes
Makes: 3 dozen

At Shavuoth time, they are filled with a cheese mixture as might be used for blintzes, cooked in water and then browned in the oven and served with a mixture of sugar and cinnamon.

LACHMAJENE (MIDDLE EASTERN PIZZA) [M]

1 lb ground lamb or beef
1/3 cup tomato juice or sauce
1/3 cup pomegranate juice
1/2 tsp salt
1/4 cup sugar
2 Tbsp pine nuts, toasted
1 pkg frozen pareve bread dough (3 loaf pkg), thawed or prepared pizza dough, cut into wedges

Preheat oven to 350 degrees.

In a large bowl, combine and mix all ingredients thoroughly, except dough. Lightly grease baking sheets. On floured board roll out dough, having cut each into 4 pieces (12 pieces). Cut with cookie cutter into 2 1/2 inch rounds. Spread meat mixture dough. Place on baking sheets and bake for 25 minutes.

Preparation time: 20 minutes
Baking time: 25 minutes
Makes: about 20 portions for appetizers

KNISH ROLL UPS [M]

1 lb beef, ground
1 large onion, chopped
1 tsp seasoned salt
pepper to taste
2 medium potatoes,
    peeled, cooked and mashed
1 large egg
1 pkg frozen puff pastry (pareve)
1/4 cup flour
1/2 tsp paprika

Defrost puff pastry (4 sheets). Preheat oven to 425 degrees

Brown meat. Brown onion separately. Add seasoned salt and pepper to taste. Put potatoes through grinder, then grind onion. Mix meat, potato, onion, seasonings and egg. Place 1 sheet of dough on waxed paper dusted with flour and paprika. Roll out to 13 X 7 inches. Place 1/4 of meat filling on pastry. Roll up with the help of the waxed paper. Cut roll into 1 inch slices. Repeat with rest of sheets. Place on greased cookie sheet cut side down. Bake for 15 to 20 minutes. This may be frozen and reheated in hot oven for 8 to 10 minutes.

Preparation time: 30 minutes
Baking time: 15 to 20 minutes
Makes: 25 to 30 slices

CRANBERRY MEATBALLS [M]

1 lb ground beef
1 lb ground turkey
1 medium onion, chopped finely
1 egg
2 Tbsp crumbs, bread or matzo meal
1 tsp salt
1/2 tsp pepper
1 tsp garlic powder
1 can whole cranberries
2 8 oz cans tomato sauce
1 large onion, chopped

Prepare meatballs using first eight ingredients. Form into 1 inch balls. Set aside. Place cranberries, tomato sauce and chopped onion in large pot. Bring to a boil. Add meatballs. Reduce heat to low and cook 1-1/2 hours. Serve as an appetizer

Preparation time: 30 minutes
Cooking time: 1-1/2 hours
Serves: 12

HORSERADISH MEATBALLS [M]

1/2 cup water
1 egg
1/2 cup bread crumbs
2 Tbsp prepared horseradish (pareve)
1 cup water chestnuts, finely chopped
1 lb ground beef
1/4 cup chopped green onions
1 large clove garlic, minced

Preheat oven to 400 degrees.

In medium bowl beat water with egg. Add bread crumbs, horseradish, water chestnuts, meat, green onions and garlic. Stir well. Shape into 1 inch balls. Place on a baking sheet and bake 24 minutes. Serve with hot marmalade sauce.

Preparation time: 20 minutes
Baking time: 24 minutes
Makes: 16

HOT MARMALADE SAUCE [P]

1/3 cup orange marmalade
1 clove garlic, minced
1/4 cup soy sauce
2 Tbsp fresh lemon juice
1/4 cup water

Mix and boil together for 1 minute. Serve hot as a dip for meatballs.

Delicious as a glaze for chicken.

Preparation time: 5 minutes
Cooking time: 3 minutes

SOUP

"UNDETERMINED LINE", **METAL, BENAR VENET, 1990, VISION OF CREATION OF THE WORLD**

ROSH HASHANAH—At Rosh Hashanah a Festive Meal Features Chicken Soup.

LET'S TALK SOUP, DR. KOOP

Mell Lazarus

C. Everett Koop was our most distinguished Surgeon General, the one who really defined the job for the rest of us, but he never seemed to talk about chicken soup. Maybe it was because the world's four leading proponents of chicken soup, my mother and her three sisters, never got excited about his medical insights.

I believe Dr. Koop would like to know that these four estimable women did believe in doctors, but not in medicine, if he can see the distinction. They respected doctors because no boy or girl could become a doctor unless they were devoted to their mother. But medicine? Medicine was expensive, it was prescribed in a foreign language and it never worked. They practiced their own folk medicine, brought over from the old country. It involved things like sachets of camphor around the kid's neck, mustard plasters on his or her chest, and little suction cups, bankas, wherever there was room. They never even considered thermometers to be diagnostically useful, because everyone knew that body temperature was more accurately gauged by kissing the patient's forehead. If a fever was detected, a thermometer might then be inserted in an appropriate orifice, but only for show.

The closest thing to anything pharmacological that my mother and aunts ever administered was, in fact, chicken soup. With it they quietly effected many brilliant cures. Each of the four sisters was a specialist in that she made a soup that would cure specific ailments. For example, my mother's soup—"Chicken Soup Flatbush"—cured all respiratory conditions, from the simple cold to double pneumonia. Aunt Helen's "Chicken Soup Bensonhurst" treated the liver and kidneys, Aunt Sophie's "Chicken Soup Borough Park" took care of whooping cough, scarlet fever and nagging backaches, while Aunt Anna's variety, "Chicken Soup Coney Island", was effective against rashes, hives and all psycho-neurotic disorders.

It should be noted that my mother and aunts never really became known as terrific cooks, but rather as a Jewish pharmaceutical cartel—a sort of Ciba of Brooklyn. They shunned publicity, however, and always gave the credit to the true discoverer of chicken soup, Jonas Salk's grandmother. A small (and belated) nod in their direction wouldn't hurt, Dr. Koop, now would it?

WATERCRESS SOUP [D]

1 lb new potatoes, cubed
1 medium onion, cubed
2 bunches fresh watercress
1/4 cup margarine
2 Tbsp flour

1/2 tsp salt
1 sprig fresh dill or 1/2 tsp dried
6 to 7 cups vegetable broth
1 cup yogurt

In saucepan, saute potatoes, onions, and watercress in margarine. Add flour, salt and seasoning. Add broth. Bring to a boil. Simmer 30 minutes. Cool for 10 minutes. Process in food processor until smooth. Add yogurt. Stir well. When serving swirl a little yogurt in each bowl in center. Add a sprig of watercress. Serve cold or hot.

Preparation time: 10 minutes
Cooking time: 45 minutes
Serves: 8 to 10

GAZPACHO [P]

1 clove garlic
1/2 onion
1/2 large cucumber, peeled in chunks
3 ripe tomatoes, peeled and seeded
1 1/2 cups tomato juice
1/4 cup red wine vinegar
1 Tbsp olive oil
1 tsp salt (optional)

1/2 tsp cumin
1/2 tsp Worcestershire sauce
1/4 tsp black pepper
1/4 tsp hot pepper sauce or to taste
croutons to taste
1 cup diced avocado
1 cup diced green pepper
1 cup diced green onion

In food processor fitted with metal blade, mince garlic. Add onion, cucumber, tomatoes and half of tomato juice. Process until coarsely chopped. Turn into serving bowl. Stir in remaining tomato juice, vinegar, oil, salt and seasonings. Cover and chill several hours. To serve, top with croutons and diced vegetables.

Preparation time: 10 minutes
Serves: 4 to 6

PEACH AND APPLE GAZPACHO [P]

- 1/2 cup orange juice
- 1/4 cup lemon juice
- 3 Tbsp sugar
- 1 medium banana, peeled, cubed
- 3/4 cup peaches, skinned, pitted and cubed
- 1 medium tart green apple, skinned, pitted and cubed
- 1/2 cup dry white wine, chilled
- 1 cup ice water
- 1 large kiwi fruit, peeled and cubed
- 1/2 pint strawberries, sliced
- 1 medium cantaloupe, peeled, seeded and cut in chunks

In small non-aluminum saucepan, heat juices and sugar. Cover and simmer until sugar dissolves, about 5 minutes. Transfer to bowl and refrigerate.

In a food processor, puree the banana, peaches and apple, then add chilled juice. Continue processing, adding wine and water, working rapidly. Return to juice bowl, stir and refrigerate until serving time. At serving time, pour into bowls and pass bowl with remaining fruit.

Preparation time: 20 minutes
Cooking time: 5 minutes
Serves: 4

PEACH SOUP [P]

- 4 cups peaches, peeled and diced
- 2 cups sweet white wine
- 3 cups water
- 1/3 to 1/2 cup sugar
- 1 cinnamon stick
- 2 Tbsp lemon juice
- 1/8 tsp almond extract
- lemon slices for garnish

In 3 quart saucepan, combine peaches, wine, water, sugar and cinnamon. Cover and simmer 30 minutes. Discard cinnamon stick. Pour half the mixture at a time into blender. Puree until smooth. Repeat with remaining half. Return puree to pan, add lemon juice and almond extract. Heat to boiling, stirring frequently. Add more sugar if needed. Cover and refrigerate. Serve cold, topped with lemon slices.

Preparation time: 10 minutes
Cooking time: 45 minutes
Serves: 8

CUCUMBER SOUP [M/P]

4 to 5 cups cucumber, peeled and cubed
1/2 cup minced shallots or
    1 medium onion, minced
3 Tbsp pareve margarine
6 cups chicken broth or water
1-1/2 tsp wine vinegar
3/4 tsp tarragon or dill
4 Tbsp quick-cooking farina (cream of wheat)
salt and white pepper to taste
minced fresh tarragon, dill or
    parsley for garnish

Saute minced shallots in margarine until tender but not browned. Add cucumbers, broth, vinegar and herbs. Bring to a boil, stir in farina. Simmer, partially covered, 25 to 30 minutes until cucumbers are cooked. In food processor, puree and return soup to pot. Thin with more broth if necesssary. Season to taste with salt and pepper.

Preparation time: 15 minutes
Cooking time: 40 minutes
Serves: 6

POTATO LEEK SOUP [M]

2 large leeks
1/4 cup oil
2 large onions, chopped
2 stalks celery, chopped
2 quarts chicken broth
1 tsp salt
1/2 tsp pepper
1/2 tsp marjoram
1/2 tsp thyme
1-1/4 lbs russset potatoes,
    peeled and diced
hard salami, diced (optional)

Split leeks and wash well. Cut crosswise into 3/4 inch pieces, including tender green part. In pot, heat oil and onion. Saute until tender, about 5 minutes. Add leek and celery and cook over low heat 10 minutes.

Add broth, salt, pepper, marjoram and thyme. Cover and cook 15 minutes. Add potatoes to soup. Cook 20 minutes longer or until potatoes are soft. Mash potatoes slightly with back of spoon. Add salami, if used, and heat thoroughly.

Dairy Chilled Potato Leek Soup: Prepare potato leek soup, omitting salami and using vegetable instead of chicken broth. Refrigerate until cold. Stir in one cup non-dairy creamer. Sprinkle top with chopped chives.

Preparation time: 10 minutes
Cooking time: 45 to 50 minutes
Serves: 6 to 8

SORRELL SOUP [D]
Schav

1 lb (bunch) spinach
1-2/3 oz pkg sorrel (may use all spinach)
1 large onion, chopped
1 quart water
2 tsp salt

6 Tbsp lemon juice
1 Tbsp sugar
sour cream for garnish
chives, minced, for garnish

Wash spinach and sorrel thoroughly. Drain and coarsely chop. In large saucepan, combine spinach, sorrel, onion, water and salt. Bring to a boil, cover, reduce heat and simmer 15 minutes. Add lemon juice and sugar. Cook 5 to 10 minutes longer. Cool for 10 minutes. Puree in food processor until smooth. Refrigerate. To serve, beat in or top with sour cream, sprinkle with chives.

Preparation time: 20 minutes
Cooking time: 40 minutes
Serves: 6

COLD RHUBARB SOUP [P]

1 lb rhubarb, diced
1-1/2 cups water
3/4 cup sugar
1 cinnamon stick or 1 tsp ground
1 Tbsp cornstarch

1 Tbsp water
1/2 cup dry red wine
2 Tbsp lemon juice
6 Tbsp toasted sliced almonds

In a 3 quart saucepan, combine rhubarb, water, sugar and cinnamon. Bring to boil over high heat. Reduce heat and simmer 15 minutes. Blend cornstarch and water together. Add and bring to boil, stirring until clear and thickened. Remove from heat, add wine and lemon juice. Cover and refrigerate until thoroughly chilled, at least 3 hours. To serve, sprinkle almonds over each portion.

Preparation time: 10 minutes
Cooking time: 25 minutes
Serves: 6

EASY BEET BORSCHT [D]

2 15 oz cans sliced beets, with juice
1 quart buttermilk
1 bunch green onions, chopped
1/2 tsp citric acid crystals (sour salt)
1/2 tsp white pepper

Combine all ingredients in a blender or food processor and puree until smooth. Chill until serving time.

Preparation time: 10 minutes
Serves: 8

VEGETARIAN BARLEY SOUP [P]

1 medium green pepper, chopped
1/2 cup chopped onion
1 clove garlic, minced
2 Tbsp olive oil or salad oil
6 cups water
3 medium tomatoes, peeled and chopped
2 tsp salt
1/2 tsp dried basil
1/2 tsp dried oregano
1/2 tsp pepper
1/2 cup barley
2 cups broccoli pieces
2 medium carrots, cut julienne
1 cup celery, sliced
1 cup green beans

In a 4-1/2 quart Dutch oven, saute green pepper, onion and garlic in oil. Add water, tomatoes, salt, basil, oregano and pepper. Bring to a boil and stir in barley. Cover and simmer about 40 minutes. Add broccoli, carrots, celery and green beans. Return to a boil and simmer about 20 minutes or until vegetables are tender.

Preparation time: 15 minutes
Cooking time: 1-1/4 hours
Serves: 12

MINESTRONE [P]

- 1 cup diced onions
- 1 cup diced carrots
- 1 cup diced celery
- 6 cloves garlic, crushed
- 1 bay leaf
- 4 bouillon cubes, vegetarian
- 8 cups boiling water
- 1/2 tsp salt
- 1/4 tsp pepper
- 1/4 tsp oregano
- 1/4 tsp thyme
- 1/4 tsp basil
- 1 Tbsp Worcestershire sauce
- 1 14 oz can tomatoes
- 1 cup peeled and diced potatoes
- 1/2 cup small tubular pasta
- 1 lb can cannellini white beans or kidney beans with juice
- 1/4 cup parsley
- 10 oz pkg frozen mixed vegetables, thawed or equal amount fresh
- 10 oz pkg frozen chopped spinach, thawed or 1 lb fresh spinach, washed thoroughly and chopped

In a large pot with 1/2 inch of water, add onions, carrots, celery and garlic with bay leaf and cook until tender, about 10 minutes. Dissolve bouillon cubes in boiling water and add to pot containing vegetables. Add seasonings and tomatoes. Bring to boil. Reduce heat and simmer 5 minutes. Add potatoes and pasta. Simmer 5 minutes. Add beans, mixed vegetables and spinach. Bring to boil, reduce heat and simmer 5 minutes or until vegetables are thoroughly cooked.

Preparation time: 30 minutes
Cooking time: 1 hour
Serves: 10

CORN CHOWDER [D]

- 2 cups raw, peeled and diced potatoes
- 1-1/2 cups water
- 1-1/2 cups canned cream style corn or 1-1/2 cups fresh corn cut from cob
- 1-1/2 cups milk (non or low fat)
- pepper to taste
- 1 onion, diced
- 2 Tbsp butter or margarine
- minced parsley for garnish

In saucepan, boil potatoes in water until tender. Mash in water. Add corn, milk and pepper. Cook 5 minutes if fresh corn is used or 3 minutes if using canned. Cook onion in butter or margarine until light brown. Add to corn. Top with parsley. Serve hot.

Preparation time: 20 minutes
Cooking time: 30 minutes
Serves: 4

MUSHROOM SOUP [M/P]

1 Tbsp pareve margarine
1 Tbsp olive oil
1 medium onion, chopped
1 garlic clove, split, placed on toothpick
1 lb mushroom caps, sliced thin
3 Tbsp tomato paste
3 cups chicken broth or vegetable broth
3 Tbsp sweet Italian vermouth
1/2 tsp salt
1/4 tsp pepper
4 thick-cut slices Italian bread, spread with pareve margarine

In a large pot, heat margarine and oil. Saute onion and garlic. Let brown slightly. Discard garlic. Stir in mushrooms and saute 5 minutes. Add tomato paste. Mix well, then add 3 cups chicken broth. Stir and add vermouth with seasoning. Let simmer for 10 minutes.

At serving time: spread bread slices with margarine, grill under broiler on one side. Place a slice in each bowl and pour soup over.

Preparation time: 10 minutes
Cooking time: 25 to 30 minutes
Serves: 4

SQUASH SOUP [M/P]

1 large (1-3/4 lb) acorn squash
1 medium (1-1/4 lb) butternut squash
1 medium (2 lb) spaghetti squash
3 Tbsp hazelnut oil or light olive oil
1 cup chopped onion
1-1/2 Tbsp minced garlic
1 Tbsp fresh chopped thyme or
   1 tsp dried
1 Tbsp fresh chopped rosemary or
   1 tsp dried
1/2 tsp freshly grated nutmeg
4 to 5 cups chicken broth or
   vegetable broth
salt
pepper
cayenne pepper

Preheat oven to 350 degrees.

Cut each squash in half. Use large spoon to remove seeds and fibers from cavities. Rub cut surfaces with 1 Tbsp oil. Place cut side down on jellyroll pan. Bake until tender, about 45 minutes.

In 3 quart pot over medium heat, place remaining oil, add onions and garlic. Saute until tender but not browned, about 5 minutes, stirring often. Add thyme, rosemary, nutmeg and 4 cups broth. When cool enough to handle, scoop flesh from squash shells and measure 5-1/2 cups, solid packed. Add to pot and simmer, covered, about 30 minutes, stirring often. Puree soup in batches in blender or food processor until smooth. If soup is too thick, thin with remaining broth. Season to taste with salt, pepper and cayenne.

Preparation time: 50 minutes
Cooking time: 30 minutes
Serves: 8 to 10

Serve hot or chilled. Can be made 3 days ahead and refrigerated or frozen up to 6 months. If you're in a hurry, microwave squash for 8 minutes or until tender.

HEARTY HERB LENTIL SOUP   [D]

1-1/2 cups lentils
8 cups water or vegetable broth
2 bay leaves
1/4 cup butter or margarine
1 Tbsp olive oil
3 cloves garlic, minced
1 large onion, finely chopped
1 parsnip, peeled and finely chopped
4 medium carrots, peeled and finely chopped
2 stalks celery, finely sliced
1/2 cup minced parsley
1 Tbsp fresh rosemary or 1 tsp dried
4 tomatoes, peeled, finely diced
salt and pepper
2 Tbsp minced parsley
2 Tbsp minced green onions
2 Tbsp minced basil leaves or 1 tsp dried

Soak lentils in 4 cups water, 6 hours or overnight. Drain lentils and place in large pot with 8 cups warm water and bay leaves. Bring to a boil. Reduce heat and simmer 20 to 25 minutes or until tender.

Heat butter and olive oil in large saucepan. Add garlic, onion, parsnip, carrots, celery and parsley. Saute 10 minutes or until vegetables are tender. Add rosemary and tomatoes. Simmer 10 minutes.

Drain lentils, returning liquid to large pot. Remove bay leaves. Add 2 cups drained lentils to garlic mixture and mix well.

Place remaining drained lentils in food processor or blender with 1/2 cup reserved liquid and puree. Add pureed lentils and lentils with garlic mixture to pot with reserved liquid. Mix well. Season to taste with salt and pepper. Bring to a boil and simmer until soup thickens, about 30 to 40 minutes. Sprinkle parsley, green onions and basil on top.

Preparation time: 20 minutes after lentils have soaked
Cooking time: 1-1/2 hours
Serves: 10

SPLIT PEA SOUP   [M/P]

2 quarts chicken broth or vegetable broth
1 cup water
1 large onion, chopped
2 medium carrots, chopped
1 lb dried green split peas, rinsed
1/2 tsp chopped garlic
1 tsp thyme
salt and pepper to taste

Put all ingredients into a large pot. Mix well. Bring to a boil and reduce heat to simmer for 2 to 2-1/2 hours, stirring frequently. Adjust seasoning. Puree in food processor or blender. Add more water if soup is too thick.

Preparation time: 5 minutes
Cooking time: 2-3/4 hours
Serves: 8

GOLDEN CARROT AND CORN SOUP [M/P]

1 Tbsp pareve margarine
1 medium onion, chopped
6 cups chicken broth or vegetable broth
2 stalks celery, cut into pieces
1 lb carrots, cut into chunks
10 oz corn frozen or 3 ears fresh corn, scraped (save 1/2 cup for garnish)
1/2 tsp thyme
1/2 tsp salt (optional)
1/4 tsp white pepper

In a large soup pot, melt margarine. Saute onion until limp. Add remaining ingredients. Cook about 20 minutes or until carrots test very tender. Puree in batches in food processor. Season with thyme, salt and pepper.

Preparation time: 15 minutes
Cooking time: 20 to 30 minutes
Serves: 4 to 6

If soup seems too thick, thin with a little extra broth. This has a glorious color and is delicious hot or cold.

CARROT AND LEEK SOUP [M/P]

1 Tbsp oil
3 medium leeks, rinsed and thinly sliced (white part only)
1 lb carrots, thinly sliced
1/2 lb small long white potatoes, quartered
1 large stalk celery, thinly sliced
6 cups chicken broth or vegetable broth
1-1/2 tsp dried tarragon, crushed
salt to taste
1/4 tsp white pepper
1/4 cup finely chopped watercress or a few additional flecks dried tarragon to garnish

In a large heavy soup pot, heat oil, saute leeks 2 minutes. Add carrots, potatoes, celery, broth, tarragon, salt and pepper. Bring to a boil. Cover and cook over medium heat until carrots are very soft, about 20 minutes. In blender or food processor, puree soup in batches. Return soup to reheat before serving. Garnish with watercress or tarragon.

Preparation time: 25 minutes
Cooking time: 30 minutes
Serves: 4

This elegant soup uses no cream. Potatoes are the thickening secret.

ASPARAGUS SOUP [D]

1/2 cup margarine, melted
4 cups coarsely chopped onions
4 large cloves garlic, minced
8 cups vegetable broth
2 to 3 lbs asparagus, stems removed and tips reserved
2 medium carrots, cut into 1 inch pieces
8 to 10 fresh basil leaves or 2 tsp dried
1 Tbsp dried tarragon
dash of cayenne pepper
salt and pepper to taste
1/2 cup sour cream, heavy cream or buttermilk

In a large soup pot, melt margarine, add onions and garlic. Simmer 25 minutes, stirring 3 to 4 times, until soft. Add broth and bring to a boil. Add asparagus (reserve tips), carrots and seasoning. Cover and simmer 45 minutes or until vegetables are tender. Remove from heat. Puree in batches in food processor until smooth. Strain if woody fibers remain. Return to pot, add asparagus tips and simmer 10 minutes longer over medium heat. Add sour cream and heat gently to serving temperature.

Preparation time: 10 minutes
Cooking time: 1-1/4 hours
Serves: 12

Can be served hot or cold.

LEMON CHICKEN SOUP [M]

8 cups unsalted, defatted chicken broth
4 Tbsp fresh lemon juice
1-1/2 Tbsp hoison sauce
1/2 cup fresh basil, chopped
1 Tbsp Dijon mustard
1 cup (scant) couscous

Bring broth to boil. Stir in lemon juice, sauce, basil and mustard. Stir in couscous. Remove from heat and cover for 5 minutes. Serve. If made ahead, add more broth and reheat.

Preparation time: 10 minutes
Cooking time: 10 minutes
Serves: 6

GINGER CHICKEN SOUP [M]

1-1/2 lbs chicken breasts, boned and skinned
6 cups water
1 tsp salt
3 Tbsp ginger root, peeled and grated
3 green onions, sliced diagonally
1 cup sliced mushrooms
1 cup canned water chestnuts, drained and sliced
1 tsp soy sauce (optional)
1/2 head shredded lettuce

In saucepan, simmer chicken in salted water for 10 minutes. When chicken is tender remove from soup and slice. Return to soup. Add all other ingredients except lettuce. Heat soup for 5 minutes. Place lettuce into individual soup bowls. Ladle soup into bowls.

Preparation time: 35 minutes
Cooking time: 15 minutes
Serves: 6

CHICKEN OKRA SOUP [M]

1 medium onion, chopped
1 medium green pepper, chopped
1 clove garlic, minced
1 Tbsp oil
4 cups chicken broth
1 8 oz can tomatoes
1 16 oz pkg frozen okra
2 cups corn, fresh or canned
1 bay leaf
1/2 tsp dried thyme or 1 tsp fresh thyme
2 cups boned, cooked chicken, cubed
salt and pepper to taste

In a large pot, saute onion, green pepper and garlic in hot oil until tender. Add broth, tomatoes, okra, corn and seasoning. Simmer for 20 minutes, covered. Add chicken and simmer 10 minutes more.

Preparation time: 10 minutes
Cooking time: 35 minutes
Serves: 8

HOT AND SOUR SOUP [M]

- 1/2 cup cooked chicken or turkey, cut in match stick pieces
- 1 tsp dry sherry
- 1 Tbsp plus 1 tsp soy sauce
- 3 Tbsp cornstarch
- 1/4 cup dried wood ears or other Chinese mushrooms or 1 cup sliced fresh mushrooms
- 5-1/2 cups chicken broth
- 1/2 tsp salt or to taste
- 1/2 cup carrots, sliced julienne
- 1/2 cup bamboo shoots, sliced julienne
- 1/2 cup extra firm bean curd (tofu), cut in small cubes
- 1/2 cup cold water or chicken broth
- 2 large eggs, beaten
- 2 Tbsp red wine vinegar or malt vinegar
- 1/4 tsp white pepper
- 1/4 tsp hot pepper sauce
- sesame seed oil
- 2 Tbsp green onions, chopped

In small bowl, combine chicken with sherry, 1 tsp soy sauce and 1 tsp of the cornstarch. If using wood ears, soak in separate bowl, in boiling water to cover about 30 minutes. Cut off woody pieces and slice julienne.

In large saucepan, combine chicken broth, salt and remaining soy sauce. Bring to a boil. Stir in marinated chicken. Bring to a simmer and cook 1 minute. Add mushrooms, carrots and bamboo shoots. Bring to a simmer. Add bean curd. When soup returns to a simmer, combine and add remaining cornstarch and water. Cook and stir until thickened. Remove from heat and stir in eggs. Stir in vinegar, pepper and hot pepper sauce. Ladle into serving bowl and garnish top with sesame oil and green onions. Serve at once.

Preparation time: 15 minutes
Cooking time: 10 minutes
Serves: 4 to 6

SWEET AND SOUR CABBAGE BORSCHT WITH SHORT RIBS [M]

- 6 lbs short ribs
- 4 brown onions, chopped
- 6 cloves garlic, minced
- water to cover
- 1 cabbage, chopped
- 2 beets, peeled and sliced
- 2 14-oz cans stewed tomatoes
- 1 tsp dried basil
- 1 Tbsp paprika
- 1/2 cup brown sugar, packed
- 2/3 cup lemon juice
- salt and pepper to taste

In large pot, combine ribs, onions and garlic. Cover with water. Bring to a boil and skim off foam. Add rest of ingredients. Reduce heat and simmer 2 hours. Cool, cover and refrigerate. Remove fat that has solidified on top and reheat before serving. Add more sugar and/or lemon juice if needed.

Preparation time: 30 minutes
Cooking time: 2 hours
Serves: 4 to 6

HOT BEET BORSCHT [M]

2 to 2-1/2 lbs flanken or short ribs, trimmed
6 cups water
1 large onion
1 medium carrot, cut in thirds
2 stalks celery, tied
1 Tbsp salt
1/4 tsp pepper
1 bunch fresh beets or
    1 lb can sliced beets, undrained
3 Tbsp lemon juice
3 Tbsp sugar

In large pot, place meat, water, onion, carrot and celery. Bring to a boil, reduce heat and simmer 2 hours, until meat is almost tender. Skim off fat and foam. Add salt and pepper.

Meanwhile, wash beets and trim their greens, leaving 1 inch of tops. Do not peel. Bring a large saucepan of water to a boil. Add beets. Simmer, covered until tender when pierced with a fork, about 20 to 30 minutes. Plunge beets into cold water. When they are cool enough to handle, slip off their skins, trim and slice. Add 1 cup of cooking liquid, strained through cheese cloth to remove grit. Add beets, lemon juice and sugar. Cook 1 hour longer until meat is tender and flavors blended. If using canned beets, add 15 minutes before end of cooking time. Taste and adjust seasoning, adding more salt, lemon juice and sugar as needed.

Preparation time: 30 minutes
Cooking time: 3 hours
Serves: 6 to 8

OXTAIL SOUP [M]

1 oxtail, cut into joint sections
7 cups cold water
2 Tbsp dried mushrooms
1 cup boiling water
3 Tbsp barley
1/4 cup dried baby lima beans
2 medium carrots, sliced
1 large onion, chopped
3 stalks celery with leaves, chopped
1 clove garlic, minced
1 tsp beef stock concentrate
1 tsp chicken stock concentrate
2 tsp salt (optional)
1/4 tsp pepper
2 tsp Worcestershire sauce
1 Tbsp soy sauce

Trim excess fat from oxtail. Place in large saucepan. Add cold water. Bring to a boil, reduce heat and simmer 1 hour.

Meanwhile, wash mushrooms to remove grit. Soak in boiling water 1 hour. Add to saucepan. Add barley and lima beans. Simmer 1 hour.

Add vegetables, stock concentrates and seasonings. Simmer at least 1 hour until meat is tender and flavors blend.

Preparation time: 10 minutes
Cooking time: 3 hours
Serves: 8

VEGETABLE BEEF SOUP [M]

6 lbs flanken (short ribs)
2 medium onions, cut up
4 beef bouillon cubes
water to cover
8 oz can tomato sauce
1/2 red cabbage, sliced
1/2 green cabbage, sliced
1 medium red pepper, cubed
1 medium yellow pepper, cubed
1 small head cauliflower, sliced
2 large tomatoes, seeded and cubed
1 lb green beans
1 lb wax beans
3 celery stalks, sliced
3 turnips, cut into 1/4 inch cubes
3 zucchini, sliced
2 tsp salt
1/2 tsp pepper

In large pot, cover the flanken, onion and bouillon cubes with water. Bring to boil and simmer 2 hours. Skim 2 or 3 times during cooking. Strain, cool and refrigerate soup. Remove fat that solidifies on top. Add tomato sauce and all vegetables except zucchini. Simmer 1 hour. Add zucchini last 20 minutes. Season with salt and pepper.

Preparation time: 25 minutes
Cooking time: 3 hours
Serves: 24

SPANISH FISH SOUP

1/4 cup olive oil or salad oil
1 lb thin skinned potatoes, diced
1 large red bell pepper, seeded and diced
1 medium onion, finely chopped
3/4 cup celery tops, chopped
1 quart vegetable broth
14-1/2-oz can stewed tomatoes
1/2 cup pitted green olives
2 lbs skinless halibut fillets
1 Tbsp lime juice
1 Tbsp fresh dill, chopped or 1 tsp dried
4 cloves garlic, minced

In a 5 to 6 quart pan, heat oil over medium heat. Add potatoes, bell pepper, onion and celery. Cook, stirring often, until vegetables are lightly brown, 15 to 20 minutes. Add broth, reduce heat, cover and simmer until potatoes are tender when pierced, about 15 minutes. Meanwhile, rinse fish, pat dry and cut into 6 to 8 equal pieces, removing any bones. Add to soup, along with lime juice, dill and garlic. Cover and simmer until fish is slightly translucent, about 5 minutes.

Preparation time: 15 minutes
Cooking time: 40 to 45 minutes
Serves: 6 to 8

RED SNAPPER CHOWDER [P]

3 cups leeks, white part only, washed and chopped
1 cup onion, chopped
1/2 cup olive oil
2 cups water or vegetable broth
4 cups white potatoes, peeled and cubed
28 oz can Italian plum tomatoes
2 cups carrots, washed and cubed
1-1/2 tsp dried marjoram
1 bay leaf
1 tsp salt
1/4 tsp pepper
1 clove garlic, (optional) on a toothpick
6 fillets red snapper, cut in chunks

In a large soup pot, saute onions and leeks in olive oil over medium heat, until transparent. Add water, potatoes, tomatoes, carrots and seasoning. Bring to boil. Reduce heat and simmer covered until vegetables are tender, about 30 minutes. Add fish. Allow to cook 10 minutes. Correct seasoning. The garlic may be added during cooking of vegetables, if desired. Remove garlic.

Preparation time: 30 minutes
Cooking time: 50 minutes
Serves: 6

POTAGE D'AGNEAU PROVENCALE [M]

2 Tbsp olive oil
2 lbs lamb, cubed
1 large white onion, chopped
3 cloves garlic, minced
4 shallots, minced
2 quarts water
1 cup rice, preferably brown
2 bay leaves
1-1/2 cups chopped apples
5 medium carrots, sliced
3 stalks celery, diced
1 cup fresh parsley or 1/2 cup dried
1 Tbsp fresh rosemary or 1 tsp dried
1/2 tsp nutmeg
1/8 tsp cayenne pepper
2 cups frozen peas
1 tsp salt (optional)

In large soup pot, heat oil. Saute lamb over high heat until browned on all sides. Add onion, garlic and shallots. Cook until onion is translucent. Add water, rice and bay leaves. Stir. Bring to boil, cover, reduce heat and cook 30 minutes or until meat tests done. Add remaining ingredients except peas. Simmer 20 minutes. Add peas 10 minutes before serving. Add salt to taste.

Preparation time: 15 minutes
Cooking time: 60 to 70 minutes
Serves: 6 to 8

SALAD

***MOBILE*, STAINLESS STEEL, GEORGE RICKEY**

YOM HA'ATZMAOT—Fresh Salads Set the Tone for Israel Independence Day.

YOM HA'ATZMAUT

Janet Salter

Israel Independence Day is the newest official holiday in the Jewish calendar. It is marked by formal and informal parades through the streets, throngs singing and dancing, watching entertainers perform, enjoying fireworks and fellow citizens reveling.

When the liberated Israelite slaves were following Moses in the wilderness and being fed miraculously with "manna," they still complained: (Numbers: 11:5) "We remember the fish which we ate in Egypt for naught; the cucumbers and the melons and the leeks and the onions and the garlic." They also longed for other food (Numbers: 20:5) "the nuts, figs, vine leaves and pomegranates" and also (Numbers: 13:27) the dressing made with "milk and honey." Toss any, and all, of the above with an assortment of fresh greens and...**Behold! YOU HAVE CREATED A SALAD!**

MINTED YOGURT SALAD [D]

1 cup plain yogurt, drained in cloth lined sieve overnight
1/2 cup sour cream
1/2 tsp sugar
1/4 tsp salt
seasoned garlic pepper
3 cucumbers, cubed
2 bunches radishes, sliced
3 tomatoes, cubed
1 bunch green onions, sliced
1/2 cup parsley, minced
1/4 cup fresh minced mint

Mix all ingredients together. Refrigerate and serve cold.

Preparation time: 10 minutes plus preparation time for yogurt: 8 hours
Serves: 4 to 6

SPINACH SALAD WITH MANDARIN ORANGES [P]

Salad:
1 bunch red leaf lettuce
1 cup fresh spinach leaves
11 oz can mandarin oranges, drained
1/2 cup slivered almonds, toasted

Dressing:
1/2 cup oil
1/3 cup white wine vinegar
1/2 tsp garlic powder
1/2 tsp curry powder
1 tsp soy sauce

Wash lettuce and spinach thoroughly. Spin dry. Add mandarin oranges and almonds. Combine oil, vinegar, garlic powder, curry powder and soy sauce.
Toss with greens.

Preparation time: 20 minutes
Serves: 4 to 6

FRENCH WHITE BEAN SALAD [P]

Salad:
1-1/2 cups dried small white beans
2 quarts water
1 tsp dried basil
1/2 tsp dried thyme
1 tsp salt
1/4 tsp pepper

bouquet garni:
bay leaf, celery tops, parsley sprigs,
3 garlic cloves all tied in cheesecloth

Dressing:
3 Tbsp olive oil
3 Tbsp lemon juice
1 tsp salt (optional)
1/4 tsp pepper
1/4 cup finely chopped onion
1/4 cup parsley sprigs

Soak beans overnight in water to cover. Drain. Cook slowly about 1 hour, until just tender, in 2 quarts of water with spices and bouquet garni. Drain thoroughly and chill several hours. Mix dressing. A half-hour before serving, toss beans with dressing. Trim with parsley.

Preparation time: 10 minutes plus soaking time
Cooking time: 1 hour
Serves: 6 to 8

ISRAELI CARROT SALAD [P]

3 medium large carrots, peeled,
    sliced diagonally and cooked
1/8 bunch parsley, leaves only
2 cloves garlic
2 Tbsp olive oil

1-1/2 Tbsp lemon juice
1-1/2 tsp white vinegar
1/2 tsp salt
2-1/2 tsp paprika
1/4 tsp cumin

Combine carrots with all other ingredients. Toss well. Refrigerate 3 to 4 hours before serving.

Preparation time: 5 minutes plus 3 to 4 hours to marinate
Cooking time: 15 minutes
Serves: 3 to 4

EGGPLANT SALAD   [P]

Salad:
2 (1 lb) eggplants
1 large tomato, peeled, seeded, chopped
1 small onion, finely chopped
2 cloves garlic, minced
3 Tbsp chopped parsley

Dressing:
1/4 cup olive oil
2 Tbsp lemon juice
1 tsp salt or to taste
1/4 tsp freshly ground pepper
1/8 tsp cayenne pepper (optional)

Preheat oven to 400 degrees.

Prick eggplants with fork in several places. Place on baking sheet and bake about 45 minutes until soft. Remove from oven and let cool. Peel and cut into small cubes. Place cubed eggplant in large salad bowl. Add tomato, onion, garlic and 2 Tbsp of the parsley. Mix dressing. Sprinkle top with remaining parsley. Cover and refrigerate.

Preparation time: 30 minutes
Cooking time: 45 minutes
Serves: 8

For Moroccan style add 1/2 tsp ground cumin, roasted red pepper strips, and 1 tsp paprika

SWISS GREEN PEA SALAD   [P]

Salad:
10 oz pkg frozen petite green peas, thawed
1/2 cup finely chopped green onions
1/2 cup finely chopped celery
1 cup green goddess dressing
8 red peppers, halved, steamed

Green Goddess Dressing:
2 Tbsp chopped white part green onion
2 Tbsp chopped green part green onion
2 Tbsp parsley
1 Tbsp tarragon vinegar or 1 tsp tarragon and 1 Tbsp cider vinegar
juice of 1 lemon
2 oz anchovy filets, drained
1 cup mayonnaise

Blend all dressing ingredients in blender or food processor.
Mix salad ingredients with dressing and fill red pepper halves. Serve chilled.

Preparation time: 10 minutes
Serves: 8

CAULIFLOWER AND OLIVE SALAD   [P]

1 large head of cauliflower
6 Tbsp olive oil
6 Tbsp wine vinegar
2 Tbsp chopped capers
2 Tbsp minced parsley
2 Tbsp chopped pimiento
2 green onions, chopped
1/2 tsp salt (optional)
1/8 tsp dry mustard
1/8 tsp black pepper
1/2 cup sliced black olives

Wash cauliflower, separate into flowerets and cut into bite-size pieces. Blanch in boiling water for 4 minutes or microwave for 2 to 3 minutes. Drain and cool.

Combine all remaining ingredients except olives. Place cauliflower in serving bowl. Cover with dressing. May be refrigerated overnight. Drain cauliflower, reserving marinade, add olives and then spoon marinade over mixture.

Preparation time: 15 minutes
Cooking time: 4 minutes
Serves: 4 to 6

Variations: Add Chinese peapods, sugar snap peas or carrots.

MOROCCAN PEPPER AND TOMATO SALAD   [P]

2 sweet red or green peppers
4 large ripe tomatoes
1/3 cup minced parsley
2 cloves garlic, minced
2 Tbsp lemon juice
2 Tbsp olive oil
1 tsp salt
1/4 tsp freshly ground pepper
1/2 tsp cumin (optional)

Grill peppers under broiler, turning until charred. Place blackened peppers in paper bag and set aside to cool about 10 minutes. Remove skin and seeds and cut peppers into cubes. Scald, peel, seed and chop tomatoes. Combine peppers and tomatoes with parsley, garlic, lemon juice, olive oil, salt, pepper and cumin. Cover and chill.

Preparation time: 30 minutes
Cooking time: 15 minutes
Serves: 4 to 6

SUMI SALAD [P]

Salad:
1/4 cup sliced almonds
1/4 cup black or white sesame seeds
1/4 cup sunflower seeds
8 green onions, sliced
1 large head cabbage, finely sliced
2 3 oz pkg soba noodles, broken
1 small carrot, shredded

Dressing:
1/4 cup sugar
1/2 cup oil
6 Tbsp rice vinegar
1 tsp salt
1 tsp coarse black pepper
1/2 tsp allspice (optional)

Toast almonds, sesame seeds and sunflower seeds in 325 degree oven just until lightly browned. Watch closely to prevent burning seeds and nuts.

In a large bowl, combine onions, cabbage, noodles, carrot, toasted seeds and nuts. For dressing, combine sugar, oil, vinegar, salt, pepper and allspice. Toss with cabbage mixture. Cover and refrigerate several hours, stirring several times.

Preparation time: 15 minutes
Serves: 6 to 8

ORIENTAL VEGETABLE SALAD [P]

Salad:
1/2 lb green beans or asparagus
1/4 lb snow peas
1 small head Chinese cabbage, coarsely shredded
1 pkg enoki mushrooms
1 Tbsp sesame seeds, toasted

Dressing:
1/2 tsp dry mustard
2 Tbsp sugar
2 tsp soy sauce
1 Tbsp sesame oil
1/4 cup salad oil
3 Tbsp rice vinegar

In a medium saucepan cook green beans or asparagus in 2 inches boiling water until crisp-tender, about 3 minutes. Remove with slotted spoon to colander. Rinse with cold water to stop cooking.

Return water in saucepan to boiling. Add snow peas and cook until crisp-tender, about 1 minute. Drain and rinse with cold water. Mix dressing. Layer vegetables on large platter, as follows: cabbage on bottom, then peas, then enoki mushrooms. Finish with beans or asparagus in center of top. Sprinkle all over with sesame seeds. Just before serving, drizzle dressing on top.

Preparation time: 10 minutes
Cooking time: 5 mintues
Serves: 4

PERSIAN CHOPPED SALAD   [P]

Salad:
1 cucumber, chopped
2 tomatoes, chopped
1 small "sweet" brown onion, chopped
1/2 bunch parsley, chopped
4 leaves butter lettuce

Dressing:
2 limes juiced
2 Tbsp olive oil
salt and pepper to taste

In a large bowl, combine vegetables. In a small bowl, mix dressing and add to vegetables. Toss well. Serve in lettuce cups.

Preparation time: 10 minutes
Serves: 4

ISRAELI TUNA SALAD   [P]

Salad:
12 oz water-packed tuna, drained and flaked
1 cup canned corn, drained
1 cucumber, diced finely
1 green onion, sliced finely
1 small carrot, diced finely
1 small dill pickle, diced finely
4 stuffed green olives, sliced finely
4 sprigs parsley, chopped finely

Dressing:
1/2 lemon, juiced
1/2 cup mayonnaise
1/4 tsp white pepper
1/4 tsp salt
4 lettuce leaves (optional)
parsley to garnish

In bowl place tuna and vegetables. Mix dressing ingredients and reserve. When ready to serve, toss dressing with tuna and vegetables. Place tuna salad on lettuce leaves and garnish with parsley. May be used as sandwich filling.

Preparation time: 10 minutes
Serves: 6 to 8

SALAD WITH CHICKEN LIVERS [M]

Salad:
1 lb chicken livers

Dressing:
1 Tbsp walnut oil
6 Tbsp wine vinegar
4 Tbsp shallots, crushed
3 Tbsp olive oil

1 tsp kosher salt (optional)
1/2 tsp fresh ground pepper

1 bunch spinach, washed,
2 green onions
    stems removed and dried
4 oz mushrooms, sliced

Broil livers until cooked thoroughly. Season with half of salt and pepper. Mix oil, vinegar, shallots and remaining salt and pepper. Toss spinach, onions, mushrooms and livers with dressing.

Preparation time: 15 minutes
Serves: 6

ZESTY CHICKEN SALAD [M]

Salad:
3 chicken breasts, cooked, skinned,
    boned and cubed
3/4 cup diced celery
3/4 cup diced green or red pepper
1/2 cup diced apple tossed with
    1/2 tsp lemon juice
1/2 cup seedless green grapes

Dressing:
1/4 tsp salt
1/8 tsp pepper
2/3 cup mayonnaise
1 tsp soy sauce
1 tsp curry powder
1/3 cup toasted slivered almonds or cashews

Mix first six ingredients. In another bowl, mix dressing. Toss with chicken mixture. Add almonds last.

Preparation time: 30 minutes
Serves: 3

SALAD TOSCA [M]

2 boneless chicken breasts, cooked
10 oz pickled or fresh tongue, cooked
2 hard cooked eggs, white only
1 pkg frozen artichokes, cooked

1/2 cup mayonnaise
2 Tbsp currant jelly
1/2 head lettuce
1 truffle, peeled (optional)

Cut meats and egg whites into julienne pieces. Add artichokes, mayonnnaise and jelly. Toss. Serve on lettuce. Garnish with truffle.

Preparation time: 10 minutes
Serves: 8

FAR EASTERN CHICKEN SALAD [M]

2 to 3 large chicken breasts, boned and skinned
1/2 cup light soy sauce
2 pkg fresh Shitake mushrooms, sliced in 1/2" slices
2 Tbsp vegetable oil
1 Tbsp garlic oil or 1 clove chopped garlic and 1 Tbsp oil
8 stalks of asparagus sliced diagonally
1 pkg fresh herb salad or baby lettuce mixture or spinach and butter lettuce
1 cup bite size jicama
4 green onions, sliced
2 Tbsp olive oil
3/4 cup seasoned rice vinegar
1 mango, sliced, for garnish
1/4 cup sesame seeds, toasted

Marinate chicken breasts in light soy sauce or any favorite oriental marinade for 4 hours. Grill breasts just until done, do not overcook. Slice on the diagonal and then cut into bite size pieces, not too small. In large skillet, saute mushrooms in both vegetable and garlic oils. Remove mushrooms and put into a salad bowl. Saute asparagus for a few minutes, covered. Add to mushrooms. Add chicken. Toss all with greens, jicama and green onions. Mix olive oil and vinegar and toss with salad. Place slices of mango on salad and sprinkle with sesame seeds.

Preparation time: 40 minutes plus 4 hours to marinate
Cooking time: 25 minutes
Serves: 6

CHINESE CHICKEN SALAD [M]

Salad:
14 oz chicken broth
1-1/2 lb chicken breasts
3 Tbsp sesame seeds
1 head iceberg lettuce or Chinese cabbage, shredded
4 green onions, sliced
1 bunch cilantro (optional)
2 oz rice sticks, deep fried
4 oz can sliced water chestnuts (optional)
1 to 2 Tbsp minced preserved red ginger

Dressing:
1/4 cup rice vinegar or to taste
1/4 cup sugar
3 Tbsp sesame oil
1 tsp soy sauce

In a frying pan with a lid, bring chicken broth to simmering. Add chicken breasts, cover and poach 15 to 20 minutes. Remove chicken and let cool. Remove skin and bones from chicken breasts and cut chicken into julienne. (Reserve chicken broth for another use.) Toast sesame seeds at 350 degrees for 15 minutes until golden. Combine chicken, lettuce, green onion, cilantro, rice sticks and water chestnuts in a large bowl. Sprinkle with sesame seeds and ginger. Mix dressing and drizzle over salad. Toss well.

Preparation time: 30 minutes
Cooking time: 15 to 20 minutes
Serves: 4 to 5

Note: Use only sweet Chinese preseved red ginger. Japanese ginger is too vinegary.

CURRIED RICE SALAD [M/P]

1-1/3 cups cooked rice
3 Tbsp finely chopped green onion
1 tsp wine vinegar
2 Tbsp oil
1/2 tsp curry powder
1/2 tsp salt (optional)

1-1/2 cups cooked chicken,
    turkey or salmon
10 oz frozen or fresh peas
1 cup chopped celery
3/4 cup mayonnaise
red pepper rings

While rice is still hot, stir in onion, vinegar, oil, curry powder and salt. Add chicken, turkey or salmon, peas and celery. Toss with mayonnaise. Garnish with red peppers.

Preparation time: 20 minutes
Serves: 4

RYE APPLE SALAD [P]

Salad:
2 large red apples, unpeeled,
    chopped, cored
juice of 1 lemon
2 cups cooked rye grains
1 cup parsley, chopped
1 large tomato, diced
1/2 cup walnuts, chopped

Dressing:
1 to 2 Tbsp wine vinegar
1/8 tsp salt
1/4 tsp dry mustard
6 to 8 Tbsp olive oil
freshly ground pepper
1/2 Tbsp shallots, minced (optional)
1/4 tsp dried herbs
1/2 Tbsp green onion (optional)

Place apples in salad bowl and drizzle with lemon juice. Add rye, parsley, tomato and walnuts. Combine dressing ingredients and mix vigorously. Toss with salad.

Preparation time: 25 minutes
Serves: 8

TABOULI SALAD [P]

3/4 cup cracked wheat or bulgur
water
2 medium tomatoes, diced
1/2 cup minced onion
3/4 cup chopped parsley
1/4 cup minced mint leaves

1/4 cup olive oil
1/4 cup lemon juice
1 tsp salt
1/4 tsp black pepper
Romaine lettuce
Greek olives, tomato wedges, mint sprigs

Place cracked wheat in medium bowl, add water to cover and let stand about 30 minutes, until wheat has doubled in size and most of the liquid is absorbed. Squeeze out excess water. Add tomatoes, onion, parsley and mint. Toss gently. Combine olive oil, lemon juice, salt and pepper. Add to wheat mixture. Toss to mix well. Refrigerate, covered, several hours or overnight. To serve, line salad bowl with romaine, mound wheat mixture in center. Garnish with Greek olives, tomato and mint.

Preparation time: 45 minutes
Serves: 6

COUSCOUS AND ORANGE SALAD [P]

1 large orange, peeled, pith and
   membrane removed
1 cup uncooked couscous
1-1/2 cups orange juice
1/4 cup vegetable oil (optional)
2 tsp fresh lemon juice

1 Tbsp grated fresh ginger
1 Tbsp grated orange peel
3 Tbsp raisins or currants
1/2 cup chopped walnuts, toasted
1/4 cup finely chopped parsley

Segment oranges and, leaving a few pieces whole, cut sections in half. Cook couscous according to package directions substituting orange juice for water. When cooked, transfer to a bowl and fluff, removing lumps as you go. Drizzle oil and lemon juice over while continuing to fluff. Add ginger, peel, orange pieces, raisins, walnuts, and parsley. Mix well and refrigerate several hours ahead. Decorate with remaining whole orange segments just before serving.

Preparation time: 20 minutes
Cooking time: 20 minutes
Serves: 4

SMOKED SALMON POTATO SALAD [P]

1-1/4 lbs new potatoes
6 Tbsp vinaigrette dressing*
1/2 lb smoked or barbecued salmon, diced
1/4 cup chopped dill pickle
2 green onions, chopped, white part only
2 Tbsp chopped parsley

1 tsp dried dill or 1 Tbsp chopped fresh dill
1/4 tsp freshly ground pepper
6 Tbsp mayonnaise
shredded lettuce
Parsley or dill sprigs

Cook potatoes, peel and slice. While still warm, toss in bowl with vinaigrette. Chill. Add salmon, dill pickle, green onions, parsley, dill and pepper. Add mayonnaise to moisten. Serve on a bed of shredded lettuce. Garnish with parsley.

Preparation time: 20 minutes
Cooking time: 30 to 45 minutes
Serves: 6

* May use commercially prepared dressing

OLD FASHIONED NEW POTATO SALAD [D/P]

4 to 5 lbs washed, unpeeled, cooked new potatoes
1 Tbsp rice vinegar
1 tsp sugar
6 green onions, chopped or 1 small red onion, chopped
1 cup dill pickle relish

1/2 cup Dijon mustard
3/4 cup light mayonnaise
1/4 cup light sour cream (optional)
6 hard boiled eggs, chopped (optional)
3 stalks celery, chopped
Salt and pepper to taste

Cube hot potatoes into large bowl. Sprinkle with vinegar and sugar. Mix the mustard, mayonnaise and sour cream together. Add all other ingredients. Toss to Blend.

Preparation time: 20 minutes
Serves: 10

PASTA GARDEN SALAD [D]

6 oz jar marinated artichoke hearts
yogurt vinaigrette dressing*
1 cup broccoli florets
1 small zucchini, cut matchstick
1 small carrot, julienne
1/4 lb green beans, cut 1 inch
4 medium mushrooms, sliced
2 Tbsp thinly sliced green onion
1 red pepper, thinly sliced
1/2 lb rotelle or other pasta
salt, pepper
chopped parsley

Drain artichoke hearts, reserving marinade. Cut artichokes if large. (Prepare yogurt vinaigrette dressing using marinade as part of olive oil, combining all ingredients except yogurt.) Steam broccoli until crisp-tender, about 3 minutes. Place in large bowl and add a little of the dressing. Steam zucchini, carrot and green beans separately, then transfer to bowl. Add mushrooms, green onion and red pepper. Add dressing to marinate vegetables. Vegetables may be cooked in a microwave until crisp-tender.

Cook rotelle in large kettle of boiling water until just tender. Drain and rinse under cold running water. Toss with a little of the dressing. When completely cold, combine with vegetables. Add yogurt to remaining dressing and toss some with salad to moisten just before serving. Add salt and pepper to taste and chopped parsley.

Yogurt Vinaigrette Dressing:
1/2 cup olive oil
2 Tbsp white wine vinegar
1 tsp Dijon mustard
1 large clove garlic, minced
1 Tbsp minced parsley
1/2 tsp basil, dried
1/2 tsp thyme, dried
1 tsp salt
1/4 tsp freshly ground pepper
1/4 cup yogurt*

Combine oil, vinegar, mustard, garlic, parsley, basil, thyme, salt and pepper. Blend well. Stir in yogurt.

Preparation time: 20 minutes
Cooking time: 10 minutes
Serves: 6
Makes: about 3/4 cup.

*Omit for a meat meal.

SMOKED PASTA SALAD [D]

Salad:
1 zucchini or crook-neck squash,
    washed unpeeled, sliced 1/4 inch pieces
4 to 5 firm white mushrooms, sliced
1/2 large red bell pepper,
    sliced into 1/4 inch slices
1 cup snow or sugar peas
8 cherry tomatoes, halved
1 avocado, peeled, pitted and
    cut into thin wedges
1 lb spiral pasta

Dressing:
1 cup dry sherry
1/2 cup oil
1 clove garlic, chopped
1/2 cup chopped onion
1/2 tsp hot pepper sauce or to taste
1 tsp salt
1 cup mayonnaise
2 to 3 Tbsp vinegar
freshly ground pepper
1/2 cup whole almonds,
    skin on slightly toasted
1/2 cup shredded smoked Gouda cheese

Prepare squash, mushrooms, bell pepper, snow peas and tomatoes. Prepare avocado last to avoid its turning brown. All ingredients should be slightly cooler than room temperature.

Cook pasta according to package directions. Don't overcook. Rinse in cold water and shake dry.

In small saucepan, over high heat, combine sherry, oil, garlic, onion, hot pepper sauce and salt. Bring to rapid boil. Boil 2 to 3 minutes then simmer about 10 minutes over low heat. Strain, discard garlic and onion and with whisk beat slowly into mayonnaise. Add vinegar and beat again. Toss first with pasta until it is coated, then add vegetables and toss lightly. Just before serving, sprinkle with toasted almonds and grated gouda. Offer a pepper mill with fresh black pepper. The dish should be served cool but not cold.

Preparation time: 30 minutes
Cooking time: 20 minutes
Serves: 8 as appetizer or 4 as main course

ALSATIAN CHEESE SALAD [D]

Salad:
14 oz Gruyere cheese

Dressing:
5 Tbsp fine olive oil
3 Tbsp red wine vinegar
1 Tbsp Dijon mustard
1/4 tsp salt

4 shallots, sliced into thin rounds
1/4 cup finely minced parsley

1/2 Tbsp freshly ground black pepper, or to taste
1 head butter lettuce, washed thoroughly and break into pieces

In a small bowl, coarsely grate cheese and toss with shallots and parsley. In a separate bowl, whisk oil, vinegar, mustard, salt and pepper. Add to cheese mixture. Cover at room temperature for 1 hour. Toss with lettuce and serve.

Preparation time: 10 minutes plus 1 hour to marinate
Serves: 4

TURKEY RICE SALAD [M]

Dressing:
1/4 cup seasoned rice vinegar
3 Tbsp oil

2 cups brown rice, cooked
1/2 cup wild rice, cooked
1 lb cooked turkey, diced
10 oz pkg frozen peas, thawed

2 Tbsp Dijon mustard
1-1/2 Tbsp fresh ginger, grated
1 tsp white pepper

1/2 cup chopped green onions
1/2 cup chopped red bell pepper
lettuce Cups
2/3 cup almonds, toasted

Whisk together dressing ingredients. Add rice, turkey and vegetables. Mix thoroughly. Spoon into lettuce cups and sprinkle with almonds.

Preparation time: 10 minutes
Serves: 6

OREGANO AND BASIL DRESSING [P]

3/4 cup oil
1/4 cup vinegar
1 tsp salt
1/2 tsp sugar

1 tsp oregano
2 tsp pepper
1-1/2 Tbsp fresh basil or 1-1/2 tsp dried
2 cloves garlic, minced

Combine all ingredients and shake vigorously. Refrigerate.

Preparation time: 5 minutes
Makes: 1 cup

BALSAMIC VINEGAR DIJON DRESSING WITH A SIMPLE SALAD [P]

2 Tbsp water
4 tsp balsamic vinegar
4 tsp olive oil
2 tsp Dijon style mustard

1 clove garlic, finely chopped
4 cups lettuce
4 large plum tomatoes, sliced

In bowl, combine water, vinegar, oil, mustard and garlic. Whisk together until blended. Pour over lettuce and tomatoes and serve.

Preparation time: 5 minutes
Serves: 4

OIL-FREE VINAIGRETTE DRESSING [P]

1 large shallot
4 sprigs parsley
1 tsp capers

1 cup tarragon vinegar
1 Tbsp honey
1 hard cooked egg white

Blend shallot, parsley, capers, vinegar, honey and egg white until smooth. Store in refrigerator.

Preparation time: 5 minutes
Makes: 1-1/4 cups

PICKLES AND SAUCES

***WAILING WALL*, BRONZE, SALVADOR DALI**

TISHA B'AV— Kosher Dill Pickles Add Interest to Meals Throughout the Year, and at Break the Fast after Tisha B'av.

92 PICKLES AND SAUCES

PICKLES AND SAUCES

Janet Salter

"I'm really in a pickle!" said Gideon, as he stood knee-deep in the vinegar barrel. He had been out in the garden, picking dozens of cucumbers for the family dinner, when he tripped and fell into the barrel. He had meant to store the ripe cucumbers in the dark shed, but the accident prevented the completion of his task. When he fell he also dropped the precious dill herbs which he kept between each cucumber for storage.

Acting quickly, Gideon leaped out of the barrel. Looking about for a means of covering his mistake, he spied a very large stone in the corner of the shed. He placed the large stone on top of the mixture and swiftly left the scene of his "crime."

In biblical times, like today, people rushed about preparing meals, with family members usually arriving late for dinner...and that is what happened that same evening. Fortunately, Gideon's mother neglected to ask for the cucumbers. In fact, she didn't even question him about them for several weeks. When she finally did, Gideon hung his head low and led her to the vinegar barrel, pointing inside. His mother reached in and drew out a large, dark green vegetable and said, "What in the world happened to our wonderful cucumbers?" as she raised it to her eyes. It was then that her nose captured the interesting aroma of the new creation, and she bit into it. "Why, this is delicious!" she shouted. "You mean I'm not in a pickle?" Gideon cried. "No, dear boy, you *CREATED* a pickle!"

MARINATED RED ONIONS   [P]

1/4 cup red wine vinegar
1/4 cup green onions, sliced
2 garlic cloves, minced
1 Tbsp sugar
1 tsp Hungarian sweet paprika
1 tsp dry mustard
1/2 tsp dried tarragon, crumbled

1/2 tsp dried thyme, crumbled
1/2 tsp dried oregano, crumbled
1/4 tsp salt
1/4 tsp freshly ground pepper
1 cup vegetable oil
1 lb red or sweet onions, cut into thin rings

Mix first 11 ingredients in a large nonaluminum bowl. Whisk in oil in thin stream. Add onions and toss well. Cover and refrigerate 2 to 7 days before serving.

Preparation time: 15 minutes
Processing time: 2 to 7 days
Serves: 4 to 6

RED ONION RELISH   [P]

2 cups thinly sliced red onions
2 cups boiling water
2 cups ice water
1/3 cup red wine vinegar

1 Tbsp sugar
10 black peppercorns
2 bay leaves, crumbled

Place onions in a bowl. Pour boiling water over and let steep for 30 seconds. Immediately drain in colander and immerse in ice water. Drain again. Pour vinegar over and add sugar, peppercorns and bay leaves. Cover and refrigerate at least 1 hour. This will keep for a week.

Preparation time: 5-8 minutes
Serves: 6

This is a good relish to serve with cold meat or cheese sandwiches. Try buttering pumpernickle bread, placing slices of cheese on top and top again with the drained onions. Cut small for appetizers or leave in halves for hearty lunch with a bowl of soup or salad.

ONION MARMALADE [P/D]

1/4 cup butter or pareve margarine
2-1/2 to 3 cups onions, chopped
1/2 cup red wine vinegar
1 cup red wine
5-1/2 Tbsp sugar
2 tsp salt
1 tsp white pepper
1/4 cup grenadine syrup

Melt butter in saucepan. Add onions and saute until tender but not brown. Add all other ingredients except grenadine. Simmer 5 minutes. Add grenadine. Cook until reduced to thick marmalade consistency about 45 minutes. If necessary add a little more wine or water to keep from scorching.

Preparation time: 5 minutes
Cooking time: 45 minutes
Makes: 1 cup

ROASTED YELLOW TOMATOES [D]

2 lbs yellow tomatoes
4 threads saffron
1 Tbsp grated orange zest
1 Tbsp grated lemon zest
1/4 cup orange juice
1/2 tsp cider vinegar
6 cloves roasted garlic, peeled
2 tsp tabasco sauce
1/2 tsp salt (optional)
1 tsp freshly ground pepper
1/4 cup chopped parsley
2 Tbsp minced mint, or 3/4 Tbsp dried
2 Tbsp minced basil, or 3/4 Tbsp dried
1 cup low fat cottage cheese

Preheat oven to 375 degrees.

Place whole tomatoes on baking sheet. Roast until skins blister about 15 minutes. Cool, then peel off skins.

Put tomatoes in a large, non-stick skillet. Add all ingredients, except cheese. Cook slowly over medium heat until mixture thickens into paste, approximately 20 minutes. Add cottage cheese. Store in refrigerator up to 3 days.

Preparation time:
Cooking time: 35 minutes
Serves: 8

MOROCCAN TOMATOES SALSA   [P]
Chuchukah

8 oz can stewed tomatoes, diced
4 oz can green chili peppers, drained and diced
2 cloves garlic, minced
1/2 tsp salt
1/2 tsp paprika
1 Tbsp olive oil

In a medium frying pan, simmer vegetables and spices about 30 minutes. Add olive oil. Cook 5 minutes. Let cool.

Preparation time: 10 minutes
Cooking time: 35 minutes
Serves: 4 to 6

A family favorite from Fez. Serve with fish, meat or poultry or as a dip with vegetables. Very versatile.

PEPPER MOSAIC RELISH   [P]

2 medium green peppers, seeded, sliced
2 medium red peppers, seeded, sliced
2 medium orange peppers, seeded, sliced
2 medium yellow peppers, seeded, sliced
2 large brown onions, sliced
1 whole head garlic, peeled, mashed
1 cup olive oil
1 tsp dried tarragon
1 tsp dried basil
1 tsp dried thyme
1 tsp dried rosemary
1 tsp dried parsley flakes
1 Tbsp sugar
2 Tbsp balsamic vinegar
1 tsp salt
1/2 tsp pepper

In a large skillet, saute vegetables for 15 minutes. Add seasonings, sugar and vinegar. Simmer 45 minutes, uncovered, stirring occasionally. Should cook to a marmalade-like consistency.

Serve hot or cold. Keep covered in refrigerator.

Preparation time: 15 minutes
Cooking time: 1 hour
Serves: 12 as a side dish.

PAPAYA-APPLE CHUTNEY [P]

1 clove garlic
1/2 cup golden raisins
1-1/2 papayas, peeled, seeded
2 medium tart apples, peeled, cored
1 medium yellow or red pepper, seeded
1 cup chopped red onion

1-1/2 Tbsp crystallized ginger
1/3 cup white vinegar
1/2 cup water
juice of 1 fresh lime
3/4 cup brown sugar

In food processor, coarsely chop fruit and vegetables. Put all ingredients in heavy pot. Cook, covered, over medium low heat for 30 minutes. Uncover and simmer for 30 minutes longer. Stir frequently. Store in refrigerator when cooled. May also be frozen.

Preparation time: 15 minutes
Cooking time: 60 minutes
Makes: 3 pints.

APPLE-PEAR CHUTNEY [P]

1 large apple, diced
1 firm, fresh pear, diced
1 small jalapeno pepper, seeded, diced very small (use rubber gloves when handling pepper)

1/2 bunch fresh mint leaves, chopped
1/2 cup raisins
1 Tbsp honey
2 Tbsp fresh lemon juice

Cover raisins with warm water to plump. Drain and combine all ingredients. Cover and refrigerate.

Preparation time: 15 minutes
Serves: 6

PEACH CHUTNEY [P]

1-1/2 lbs brown sugar
1/2 cup cider vinegar
1-1/2 lbs peaches, peeled, pitted and coarsely chopped
1 mango, coarsely chopped
1/2 large onion, chopped

1/2 cup golden raisins
2 Tbsp chopped candied ginger
1/4 tsp cayenne pepper
1/4 tsp cinnamon
1/4 tsp ground cloves
1 tsp mustard seeds

In a pot, mix brown sugar with vinegar and bring to a boil. Add all other ingredients. Simmer 3/4 hour. Put in sterile jars and keep refrigerated. Keeps indefinitely.

Preparation time: 30 minutes
Cooking time: 50 minutes
Makes: 2 pints

CURRIED FRUIT [P]

1 lb can pineapple slices in light syrup, drained
1 lb can apricot halves in light syrup, drained
1 lb can peach halves in light syrup, drained
1 lb can pear halves in light syrup, drained

2 bananas
any other fruit desired
3/4 cup brown sugar
1/2 tsp cinnamon
1 to 2 Tbsp curry powder
1/2 tsp chopped fresh ginger
2 Tbsp pareve margarine

Arrange fruit in casserole dish, sprinkle with sugar mixed with spices, dot with margarine. Cover with wax paper and microwave on high until hot, approximately 4 minutes. Time varies according to how much fruit is used. May be baked in a 350 degree oven for 45 minutes.

Preparation time: 10 minutes
Cooking time: 4 minutes in microwave or 45 minutes in oven.
Serves: 1 person per 1/4 lb of fruit.

CRANBERRY RELISH [P]

1 cup water
1 cup sugar
12 oz pkg cranberries, washed
1 pear, peeled, pitted and diced
1 orange, peeled, pitted and diced
1 tsp powdered ginger
3 tsp Amaretto

Boil water with sugar. Add berries and cook till berries pop, about 10 to 15 minutes. Add pears and orange and cook 10 minutes longer. Add powdered ginger and cool. Add Amaretto.

Preparation time: 10 minutes
Cooking time: 20 to 25 minutes
Serves: 6

CRANAPPLE SAUCE [P]

2 12 oz pkg cranberries, rinsed
2 cups water
1-1/2 cups sugar
4 to 5 golden delicious apples, peeled, cored and sliced

Place cranberries and water in a pan. Cover and bring to a boil. As cranberries begin to pop turn off burner and let berries finish popping. Puree berries with juices in a Foley food mill or use food processor with metal blade. Strain to remove skins. Add sugar to taste. Return pureed berries to pan and add apples. Bring to a boil, lower heat and simmer approximately 12 minutes or until apples are tender. Cool sauce and refrigerate.

Preparation time: 15 minutes
Cooking time: 15 minutes
Serves: 12

SUMMER PLUM SALSA   [P]

6 ripe red plums, diced
2 Tbsp red onion, diced
2 Tbsp sesame seeds

1 Tbsp sesame oil
1 Tbsp rice vinegar
1 tsp reduced salt soy sauce

Combine all ingredients, mixing thoroughly. Refrigerate 8 hours or overnight.

Preparation time: 7 to 8 minutes
Makes: 2 cups

FIG-ORANGE JAM   [P]

2 lbs black figs
1 large orange
1/4 cup water

2 cups sugar
3 Tbsp lemon juice

Wash figs, discard stems and slice. Measure 3-1/2 cups. Remove orange zest with vegetable peeler, finely chop and simmer in water until tender, about five minutes. Meanwhile, in a four-quart saucepan, combine figs and sugar. Peel white pith from orange and slice fruit. Add orange and drained orange zest. Bring mixture to a boil over medium heat. Reduce heat and cook, uncovered, stirring frequently, about one hour or until thickened. Remove from heat and stir in lemon juice. Meanwhile, prepare canning jars.* Carefully ladle hot jam into hot jars, filling to within 1/4 inch of rim. Seal. Process in boiling water bath 10 minutes.

Preparation time: 10 minutes
Cooking time: 1 hour
Makes: three to four 8 oz jars

* Wash all parts in hot, soapy water. Rinse. Boil 15 minutes in water to cover.

HERB VINEGAR [P]

3-1/2 cups rice vinegar or white wine vinegar
1 small fresh red Jalapeno pepper
1 stick cinnamon
1 sprig rosemary
1 sprig fresh thyme
1 clove garlic, peeled
1 strip lemon rind
4 whole cloves
4 whole allspice

Place all ingredients in decorative 1 quart bottle. Cover rim with plastic wrap and place in sunny spot 10 days before using. Store in refrigerator. Use on salads with a few drops of olive oil. If vinegar becomes cloudy, strain through paper coffee filter.

Preparation time: 5 minutes
Fills: 1 quart bottle

SWEET PICKLE CHIPS [P]

10 cucumbers, any variety
1 large red pepper, seeded, sliced
1 medium onion, sliced thin
1 tsp salt
2 Tbsp dill seed
3/4 cup sugar
1/2 cup white vinegar

Wash cucumbers. Do not peel. Slice into 1/8 inch thickness.

Combine with onion, salt and dill seed. Let stand 1 to 2 hours. Combine sugar and vinegar. Pour over cucumbers. Stir gently. Let marinate for 24 hours. Can stand for 3 weeks in glass jars in refrigerator.

Preparation time: 10 minutes
Processing time: 24 hours
Makes: 8 cups

SWEET & SOUR CUCUMBERS   [P]

1/2 cup sugar
1 tsp cornstarch
1/4 tsp salt

2 Tbsp water
1/2 cup white vinegar
3 cups cucumbers, finely sliced

In a saucepan, combine all ingredients except cucumbers. Bring to a boil, stirring contantly over medium heat. Continue cooking until thickened. Cool. Add to cucumbers and chill thoroughly before serving.

Preparation time: 5 minutes
Cooking time: 3 to 4 minutes
Serves: 12

CHINESE CUCUMBERS   [P]

1 medium cucumber, thinly sliced
2 Tbsp rice vinegar
1 Tbsp soy sauce

2 tsp sugar
1 Tbsp sesame seeds, toasted

Place cucumbers in a bowl. Add vinegar, soy sauce and sugar. Toss lightly. Chill. Sprinkle with sesame seeds.

Preparation time: 5 minutes
Serves: 3

AUTHENTIC DILL PICKLES   [P]

small pickling cucumbers or
    green tomatoes, scrubbed
fresh dill stalks, 3 per jar
garlic, 2 cloves per jar
celery, 1-1/2 stalks per jar
green bell pepper, 3 slices per jar
salt
water
celery leaves, a few per jar

Scald as many quart sized glass jars as you wish to fill. A quart jar should hold 5-6 cucumbers. Wash all other vegetables thoroughly.

Place cucumbers into jars.

For each jar, add 3 stalks dill, 2 cloves garlic, 1 1/2 stalks celery, 3 slices bell pepper, a few celery leaves.

To 1 quart tap water, add 1 Tbsp salt. Mix until dissolved. Fill jars to brim. Seal. Keep in a dark place at room temperature. Every other day, for two weeks, turn jars upside down and back. Pickles should be ready in two weeks. In very hot weather, they may be ready sooner.

Preparation time: 15 minutes
Processing time: 2 weeks.

PICKLED BEETS   [P]

1/2 lbs raw baby beets or
    1 lb can baby beets
1/2 cup white vinegar
6 to 8 Tbsp sugar
12 whole allspice
4 whole cloves
4 whole black peppercorns
1 small cinnamon stick
1 bay leaf, broken
1/2 medium onion, thinly sliced

Wash beets and trim their greens, leaving one-inch of tops and roots. Do not peel. Bring a large saucepan of water to a boil, add beets and simmer, covered, until tender when pierced with a fork, about 20 minutes. Drain through a cheese cloth, reserving 1/2 cup of the cooking liquid. Plunge beets into cold water. When cool enough to handle, slip off their skins and trim off tops and roots. Slice and place in a bowl.

In small saucepan, combine beet liquid (homemade or canned) with vinegar, sugar, allspice, cloves, cinnamon stick and bay leaf. Bring to a boil, reduce heat and simmer, uncovered, 15 minutes. Add onion, broken into rings, to bowl of sliced beets. Pour boiling liquid over them. Cool, then refrigerate overnight.

Preparation time: 5 minutes
Cooking time: 35 minutes
Serves: 4 to 6

PESTO [D]

2 cloves garlic
2 cups fresh basil, lightly packed
1/2 cup parsley
2 Tbsp pine nuts

1/2 cup Romano cheese, grated
1/2 tsp salt
1/8 tsp pepper
1/2 cup olive oil

Place garlic, basil, parsley and pine nuts in food processor or blender. Process until finely chopped. Add cheese, salt and pepper, blend. Gradually blend in oil until a smooth paste. Taste and correct seasoning.

May use at once, or transfer to a jar, film top with olive oil. Cover and refrigerate up to a week. If freezing, do not add cheese until defrosted.

To serve, toss about 1/2 cup pesto with four cups hot cooked noodles. Serve with additional cheese.

Preparation time: 10 minutes
Makes: 1-1/2 cups

VERY VERY TOMATO SAUCE [P]

3 Tbsp extra virgin olive oil
6 cloves garlic, minced
28 oz can Italian plum tomatoes or
    tomato puree

1 cup sundried tomatoes in oil,
    drained (reserve oil), coarsely chopped
1/2 tsp salt
1/2 tsp pepper, freshly ground

In skillet heat oil and gently cook garlic 3 minutes. Do not brown. Add tomatoes, simmer uncovered about 1 hour. Stir occasionally. Add sundried tomatoes. Remove from heat. Let stand for 5 minutes. Place in food processor and process until smooth. Slowly add 1/4 cup of oil (from tomatoes). Taste for seasoning. Refrigerate covered or freeze.

Preparation time: 5 minutes
Cooking time: approximately 1 hour
Makes: 3 cups

QUICK CLASSIC BROWN SAUCE   [M/P]

2 Tbsp olive oil
1/2 cup chopped onions
1/4 cup chopped carrots
1/2 cup flour
2 quarts beef or vegetable broth
8 peppercorns, ground

1 clove garlic
1 bay leaf
1 Tbsp chopped parsley
1/4 cup chopped celery
1/2 cup tomato paste

Heat oil in large pot and add vegetables. Cook and stir until limp. Add flour. Cook two minutes stirring constantly. Add stock, tomato paste and seasonings. Bring to a boil. Reduce heat and simmer 1 hour. Strain the sauce. Discard vegetables. Will keep in refrigerator for 2 weeks, or may be frozen.

Preparation time: 10 minutes
Cooking time: 1 hour and 10 minutes
Makes: 2 quarts

GLAZE FOR LAMB ROAST   [P]

2 Tbsp oil
2 shallots, minced
1 cup currant jelly
1/3 cup port wine
1 small orange, chopped

1 Tbsp grated orange zest
1/2 tsp cinnamon
1/8 tsp ground cloves
1/8 tsp dry ginger

In a saucepan, saute shallots in oil. Stir in rest of ingredients and cook 3 minutes. Baste meat while cooking with some of the glaze. Simmer remaining sauce and serve with the meat.

Preparation time: 8 minutes
Cooking time: 8 minutes
Makes: 1-1/2 cups

GINGER MUSTARD MARINADE AND GLAZE [P]

1 tsp dry ground ginger
1 Tbsp fresh ginger, grated
1 tsp dry mustard
1/2 cup dijon mustard
1 Tbsp sesame oil

1 Tbsp soy sauce
1/2 cup honey
1/3 cup rice vinegar
1/3 cup dark brown sugar, packed firmly

Mix all ingredients in non-stick saucepan. Simmer over medium heat 5 minutes, stirring constantly.

Preparation time: 5 minutes
Cooking time: 5 miinutes
Makes: about 1-1/2 cups of marinade.

MARINADE FOR MEAT OR CHICKEN [P]

14-oz bottle ketchup
1 onion, chopped
2 cloves garlic, chopped
1 Tbsp Worcestershire sauce

1/2 cup oil
1/4 cup wine vinegar
1/2 tsp pepper
1/4 cup chopped parsley

Mix all ingredients.

Marinate meat or chicken several hours or overnight in refrigerator. Discard remaining sauce.

Preparation time: 10 minutes

VIN CHAUD   [P]

1 bottle good red wine, Bordeaux type
4 oz lump sugar
2 lemons, sliced

2 cloves
1 cinnamon stick
2 drops orange flower water

Pour wine over sugar in a flameproof casserole. Place on stove and add spices. When very hot, stir once. When a white film appears on top, remove from stove. Serve in individual mugs with a slice of lemon.

Preparation time: 5 minutes
Cooking time: 10 to 15 minutes
Serves: 8

The better the wine the better the punch. For a cold winter night.

HOT CRANBERRY WINE CUP   [P]

2 pint bottles cranberry juice cocktail
2 cups water
1-1/2 cups sugar
1 4 inch stick cinnamon
12 whole cloves

zest of 1/2 lemon
2 large bottles California Burgundy or
    other red dinner wine
1/4 cup lemon juice
nutmeg

Combine juice, water, sugar, cinnamon, cloves and lemon zest in saucepan. Bring to a boil, stirring until sugar dissolves. Add wine and lemon juice. Heat gently, do not boil. Remove cloves and cinnamon. Serve in mugs and sprinkle nutmeg on top when ready to drink.

Preparation time: 5 to 10 minutes
Cooking time: 20 minutes
Serves: 24

CURRY SAUCE   [D]

3 tsp shallots or green onions, minced
1 tsp sesame oil
1 tsp curry powder

1 cup nonfat plain yogurt
1/2 ripe banana, mashed

In a non-stick pan, saute shallots in sesame oil for 2 minutes. Add curry powder and stir for 1 minute. Add yogurt and banana.

Preparation time: 5 minutes
Cooking time: 3 minutes
Serves: 8

DILL SAUCE FOR FISH   [D]

1 cup nonfat cottage cheese
1/3 cup nonfat yogurt
1/4 cup fresh dill
1 scallion, cut up

1 Tbsp lemon juice
1/2 tsp Dijon mustard
2 tsp grated Parmesan cheese

In blender or food processor add all ingredients. Process to blend well. Serve cold.

Preparation time: 5 minutes
Serves: 4

VEGETABLES

***HANUKKIA*, AMERICAN CONTEMPORARY, TREASURES OF JUDAICA**

HANUKKAH—FEAST OF LIGHTS—Candles are Lit in a Hanukkiah on Each of the Eight Nights of Hanukkah. Pancakes Are Fried to Commemorate the Miracle of the Oil.

HANUKKAH POTATO PANCAKES
Janet Salter

During the rebellion against the Greek-Syrian Governor, Antiochus IV, in 165 B.C.E., the five sons of the priest, Mattathias, hid in a cave near Modin. They lacked the necessary weapons to combat enemy troops, who used horse brigades and mounted elephants like modern tanks. One day, during a lull in the fighting, one of the wives ventured outside to cook pancakes made from potatoes. She left them on hot, flat rocks in the scorching sun. They doubled in size and became hard as rocks. The brothers cheered and shouted joyfully, "We can use them for chariot wheels!" They went into the forest, cut saplings for axles and built a brigade of mobile military weapons. This move turned the tide of the fighting and led to victory. The original recipe has been kept secret in the Dead Sea Scrolls, but our recipe will produce pancakes that are crisp and delicious on the outside and soft and nutritious in the inside. (Don't bake in the hot sun!)

JERUSALEM ARTICHOKES [P]

1 bowl water with juice of 1/2 lemon
1 lb Jerusalem artichokes
1-1/2 oz olive oil
1 medium onion, sliced thin

1/4 cup water or vegetable broth
1/2 tsp salt
1/2 tsp white pepper
2 Tbsp parsley, chopped

Peel artichokes, cut into pieces and immediately drop into lemon water. Heat oil, saute onion. When soft, add drained artichokes, 1/4 cup liquid and seasoning. Simmer gently 30 minutes. Drain and decorate with parsley.

Preparation time: 10 minutes
Cooking time: 30 minutes
Serves: 4

ARTICHOKES OF THE ITALIAN JEWS [M/P]

1 large bowl water with juice of 1 lemon
1 lb baby artichokes, sliced (choke and tough outer leaves removed) or
 2 10 oz pkg frozen
6 Tbsp olive oil
6 oz baby onions

4 garlic cloves, crushed
2 Tbsp capers, drained
1-1/2 cup water or chicken broth
1/4 cup chopped parsley
1 tsp salt (optional)
1/2 tsp pepper

Prepare artichokes as indicated above, dropping them immediately into lemon water.

Heat oil in heavy skillet. Saute onions for 5 minutes over medium heat. Add garlic, artichokes, capers, broth and seasoning. Cook gently for 20 minutes until artichokes are tender. Serve hot or cold. Sprinkle with parsley for garnish.

Preparation time: 15 minutes
Cooking time: 25 minutes
Serves: 4 to 6

This recipe is almost 2000 years old.

BRUSSELS SPROUTS WITH VERVE [P]

4 cups brussels sprouts
4 Tbsp pareve margarine
4 Tbsp chopped shallots
1/4 tsp ground black pepper

1/2 cup caraway seeds
2 Tbsp white wine
1/4 tsp salt

Wash and trim sprouts. In container, big enough to contain brussels sprouts, microwave margarine with shallots, pepper and seeds, 1 to 2 minutes, until limp. Add brussels sprouts and wine. Microwave on high 2 to 4 minutes. Add salt to taste.

Or, simmer brussels sprouts in water on top of stove for 5 to 7 minutes. Make sauce in small skillet. Place vegetables in serving dish and pour sauce over all. Toss gently.

Preparation time: 10 minutes
Cooking time: 10 minutes in microwave, 15 minutes on stovetop
Serves: 8 to 10

ASPARAGUS TARRAGON [P]

1-1/2 lbs asparagus
1/3 cup slivered almonds
6 Tbsp oil
1/4 cup vinegar

1 tsp tarragon
1 tsp sugar
1 tsp salt
1/2 tsp pepper

Break ends from asparagus and clean. Boil in 2 to 3 inches of water 3 to 5 minutes until just crisp. Drain and chill.

Saute almonds in 2 tablespoons of oil, stirring until golden brown. Add remaining ingredients. Heat for 1 minute. Pour over chilled asparagus. Turn to coat thoroughly.

Serve garnished with almonds and spoon small amount of dressing across spears.

Preparation time: 15 minutes
Cooking time: 5 minutes
Serves: 4 to 6

LIQUEUR GLAZED BABY CARROTS [D/P]

1 lb baby carrots, peeled and
   cut in 3 inch pieces
1 Tbsp butter or pareve margarine

2 Tbsp brown sugar
2 Tbsp honey
1 Tbsp orange liqueur

In a small saucepan, cook carrots in a little water until tender. Drain. Add rest of ingredients and continue cooking, turning often until carrots are lightly browned and well glazed.

Preparation time: 10 minutes
Cooking time: 15 minutes
Serves: 8

MUSTARD GLAZED CARROTS [D/P]

1-1/2 lbs carrots
1 tsp salt
2 Tbsp butter or pareve margarine
1/4 cup brown sugar, packed

1 Tbsp lemon juice
3 Tbsp Dijon mustard
1/2 tsp lemon pepper
1/4 cup chopped parsley

Scrape carrots* and cut into fourths lengthwise, then into 2 inch sections. In a saucepan, cook in salted boiling water until just tender, about 20 minutes. Drain well. In a small saucepan, blend butter, brown sugar, lemon juice, mustard and lemon pepper. Cook until syrupy, about 5 minutes. Pour over carrots and simmer 5 to 10 minutes longer. Sprinkle with parsley just before serving.

Preparation time: 5 minutes
Cooking time: 30 minutes
Serves: 8

*If carrots are very young and tender they are healthier to eat if left unscraped and washed well.

MOROCCAN CARROTS [P]

1/2 cup currants
1-1/2 lbs carrots, thinly sliced
1/3 cup unsalted pareve margarine
1/4 cup brown sugar, packed
1 tsp cinnamon
1/2 tsp ground cumin

1/4 tsp cayenne pepper, or to taste
1 cup fresh orange juice
1 Tbsp lemon juice
salt and freshly ground pepper
2 to 3 Tbsp chopped fresh mint or
   parsley for garnish

Soak currants in hot water, to cover, 15 minutes. Drain and reserve 1/4 cup liquid. In a large saucepan, heat margarine over low heat. Add sugar, spices and carrots. Cook, stirring constantly, 2 to 3 minutes. Stir in orange juice, lemon juice and currants with reserved liquid. Bring to a boil, reduce heat and simmer covered until tender about 20 to 25 minutes. Season to taste with salt and pepper. Sprinkle with mint or parsley and serve hot.

Preparation time: 25 minutes
Cooking time: 20 to 25 minutes
Serves: 6

CURRIED EGGPLANT [P]

3 lbs eggplant, washed
2 Tbsp oil
4 cups chopped onion
3 Tbsp minced fresh ginger
1 Tbsp minced garlic
2 Tbsp ground coriander
2 Tbsp ground cumin
2 tsp tumeric
1 minced jalapeno, seeded or
    1/2 tsp ground red pepper
1/4 cup fresh cilantro

4 chopped tomatoes
1/4 tsp ground cloves
1/2 tsp ground cinnamon
1/2 tsp ground black pepper
1 Tbsp ground cardamom
juice of 1/2 lemon
1 tsp sugar
salt to taste, or
    seasoned salt to taste
parsley, minced for garnish

Preheat oven to 450 degrees.

Slash about 12 one-inch cuts evenly around eggplants. Bake approximately 1 hour. Cool, peel and cut into chunks. Put into a large bowl. In a large pot, heat 2 tablespoons oil and saute onions. When the onions are translucent, add all ingredients except salt and eggplant. Cook until you can smell the spices. Add the eggplant, cook about 15 minutes over medium heat, stirring frequently. Taste and add salt and/or seasoned salt to taste. Put onto a serving plate or bowl and sprinkle with minced parsley for garnish.

Serve either hot, room temperature or cold. Use as a vegetable, salad, or appetizer.

Preparation time: 10 minutes
Cooking time: 1 hour 15 minutes
Serves: 6 as vegetable, 10 as salad, and 20 as appetizer

WARM VINAIGRETTE OF GREEN BEANS [P]

1 lb fresh green beans, washed and trimmed
1 Tbsp finely chopped shallots
1 Tbsp Dijon mustard
ground pepper to taste

1 Tbsp red wine vinegar
6 Tbsp oil
1/4 cup finely chopped fresh dill

Leave beans whole if very tender, or cut into 2 inch pieces. Drop into boiling salted water for 3 to 5 minutes. Do not overcook. Plunge into ice water, drain and dry. In a small saucepan, combine remaining ingredients, except dill. Warm over very low heat, stirring with a whisk until sauce is lukewarm. Do not cook too far in advance. When at room temperature, arrange beans on serving platter and add sauce. Sprinkle with dill. Serve warm.

Preparation time: 10 minutes
Cooking time: 5 minutes
Serves: 8

LIMA BEANS, CREOLE STYLE [P]

1 lb dried large lima beans, washed well
6 cups water
1 large onion, chopped
1 green pepper, diced
2 Tbsp oil
1 Tbsp all-purpose flour
2 tsp seasoned herbs

1/2 tsp salt
1/4 tsp pepper
2 tsp prepared mustard
1 tsp Worcestershire sauce
2 Tbsp brown sugar
15 oz can tomatoes

Cover washed beans with water, bring to boil, and simmer 2 minutes. Cover and let stand for 1 hour. Then cook until tender about 2 hours. Add more water if needed, to cover. In a medium skillet, saute onions and green pepper in oil 5 minutes. Blend in flour, seasonings and sugar. Add tomatoes and simmer uncovered 10 minutes. Add beans and heat, blending flavors.

Preparation time: 30 minutes
Cooking time: 2 hours 15 minutes
Serves: 12

LEEKS VICTOIRE [P]

4 leeks, white part only
1 cup vegetable broth
1 Tbsp olive oil
2 Tbsp tarragon vinegar
6 to 8 rolled anchovies with capers
    or flat anchovies

1 Tbsp chopped parsley
1 Tbsp capers if using flat achovies
1 cooked egg white, chopped
fresh ground pepper, to taste
pimiento for garnish

Cut leeks in half, lengthwise. Thoroughly clean white part, removing all sand, but keeping pieces intact as much as possible. Rinse under running water. Place leeks in container, pour broth over. Microwave 4 minutes or cook on top of stove, medium heat, until tender, 8 to 10 minutes. Drain. Place leeks in serving dish. Spoon oil and vinegar over them and add pepper. Decorate with anchovies, parsley, capers, chopped egg white and pimiento.

Preparation time: 10 minutes
Cooking time: 10 minutes
Serves: 4

This recipe may be made using celery in place of the leeks.

MUSHROOM MOUSSAKA [D/M]

1 Tbsp butter
1/2 cup chopped onion
1 clove garlic, minced
1 lb mushrooms, washed, dried and chopped
2 Tbsp minced parsley
1 Tbsp minced fresh mint
1/2 tsp salt
1/8 tsp pepper
1/2 tsp oregano
1/4 tsp cinnamon
2 Tbsp tomato paste
1/4 cup red wine
1-1/2 lb eggplant

oil
3 Tbsp butter
3 Tbsp flour
2 cups hot milk
2 large eggs, beaten
1 tsp salt
1/4 tsp white pepper
1/8 tsp nutmeg
1 cup cottage cheese
1/3 cup dry bread crumbs
1/3 cup shredded Romano or Parmesan cheese

In medium skillet, heat butter, add onion and garlic, and saute briefly. Add mushrooms and saute until all liquid evaporates, about 20 minutes. Add parsley, mint, salt, pepper, oregano, cinnamon, tomato paste and wine. Mix well and simmer until liquid evaporates again. Set aside to cool. Meanwhile, slice eggplant 1/2 inch thick. Place on oiled jelly roll pan and brush with oil. Broil just until tender and lightly browned. Turn and broil other side. Melt butter in saucepan, stir in flour and cook 1 minute. Gradually stir in hot milk. Cook and stir until smooth and thickened. Remove from heat and gradually beat into eggs, then return egg mixture to saucepan. Stir in salt, pepper, nutmeg and cottage cheese. Place a layer of eggplant in buttered 8 X 12 inch baking pan dusted with some of the bread crumbs. Combine remaining bread crumbs with Romano cheese. Sprinkle eggplant with half the cheese-crumb mixture. Top with mushrooms and sprinkle with remaining cheese crumb mixture. Arrange another layer of eggplant and top with custard sauce. Bake at 350 degrees for 1 hour or until top is golden and knife inserted comes out clean. Cool 10 minutes before cutting into squares to serve.

Lamb Moussaka: Omit butter, mushrooms, tomato paste and cheese. Brown 1 lb lean ground lamb in large skillet, breaking up meat. Add 1 cup chopped onion in place of 1/2 cup, increase salt to 1 tsp. Use 1/2 cup tomato sauce in place of tomato paste. Simmer meat mixture, uncovered, 30 minutes, until sauce is thickened.

Preparation time: 25 minutes
Cooking time: 25 minutes
Baking time: 1 hour
Serves: 8

VEGETARIAN MOUSSAKA   [D]

1 lb thin skinned potatoes, thinly sliced
1 medium eggplant, thinly sliced
3 medium zucchini, (1 lb),
   ends trimmed and thinly sliced
1/2 cup minced fresh basil or 1 Tbsp dried
2 jars marinated artichoke hearts
1/2 lb shredded Muenster cheese

Plunge potatoes into cold water until ready to cook. Drain. In an oiled 9 X 13 inch baking pan, layer potatoes, eggplant, zucchini and basil. Drizzle with artichoke marinade. Cover tightly with foil. Bake in a 400 degree oven until vegetables are very tender when pierced, about 1 hour. Uncover and tuck artichokes among the vegetables. Return to oven and bake uncovered until the liquid evaporates, about 30 minutes. Sprinkle cheese over vegetables and bake just until top is golden brown, about 10 minutes longer. Let stand 10 minutes before serving.

Preparation time: 20 minutes
Baking time: 1 hour 40 minutes
Serves: 8

VEGETABLE TEMPURA   [P]

Vegetables:
1 small sweet potato,
   peeled and thinly sliced, diagonally
1 carrot, peeled and thinly sliced, diagonally
1 small Japanese eggplant,
   thinly sliced, diagonally
12 snow peas
12 green beans
6 fresh mushrooms, halved, if large
1 red pepper, cut into rings
broccoli florets
oil for frying

Tempura Batter:
1 large egg
1-2/3 cup ice water
1/2 tsp baking soda
1 cup all-purpose flour
1 cup cornstarch

Tempura Dipping Sauce:
2 cups vegetable broth
1 Tbsp sake
1 tsp sugar
1 cup light soy sauce

Arrange vegetables on large platter. Heat at least 2 inches of vegetable oil in deep, heavy pan, skillet or wok to 375 degrees. Prepare batter just before frying. In a medium bowl, combine egg with ice water and baking soda. Lightly stir in combined flour and cornstarch with fork. Batter should be lumpy. Place bowl of batter inside a larger bowl with ice and water. Drop a few vegetables in batter, lift out, allowing excess to drain slightly. Slide gently into hot oil. Fry on one side. Turn and fry on other until golden and done, about 2 to 3 minutes. Drain on wire rack or paper towels. Occasionally skim oil with wire strainer to remove pieces of cooked batter. Combine vegetable broth, sake, sugar and soy sauce. Serve vegetables with dipping sauce.

Preparation time: 10 minutes
Cooking time: 30 minutes
Serves: 4

Can be reheated in 400 degree oven for five minutes.

STUFFED ONIONS [P/M]

8 large onions, white or brown
2 cups cooked rice, warm
1/2 cup chopped walnuts
1/2 cup currants
2 large tart apples, peeled and grated
3 Tbsp grated fresh ginger
3 Tbsp grated orange zest
1 tsp salt
1/4 tsp pepper
1/4 tsp allspice
1 cup water
3/4 cup apple juice

Peel onions. Cover with salted water and boil until almost tender, 7 to 8 minutes. Remove from water. Cool and remove inside of onion leaving 1/2 inch shell for stuffing. Invert and drain. Chop center part of onions and combine with other ingredients. Stuff onions. Place in baking dish. Surround with water and juice. Bake at 300 degrees for 25 minutes.

Preparation time: 15 minutes
Cooking time: 35 minutes
Serves: 8

May add 1 cup ground turkey, beef or lamb browned in its own pan juices.

SWEET AND SOUR BABY ONIONS [P]

2 lbs boiling onions
3 Tbsp raw sugar, or 2 Tbsp brown sugar
2 oz pareve margarine
1 Tbsp all-purpose flour
1/4 cup warm water
1 Tbsp white wine vinegar,
(use red wine vinegar if
you like rosy color)

Fill a saucepan with water and place onions in it for 10 minutes until skins can be rubbed off. Heat sugar in heavy skillet. Stir constantly until syrupy and light brown. Immediately add margarine and flour. Keep stirring until creamy. Add water. Boil mixture, then place onions in pan. Add water to cover onions, if necessary. Simmer 30 minutes. Add vinegar. Simmer 30 minutes more.

Preparation time: 15 minutes
Cooking time: 1 hour 10 minutes
Serves: 6

B'TAMPT POTATOES   [P]

8 unpeeled baking potatoes, sliced 1/2 inch thick
2 bunches scallions, cut into 1/4 inch pieces
1 cup melted pareve margarine
2 garlic cloves, chopped
coarse salt and pepper to taste

Preheat oven to 450 degrees. Stand sliced potatoes on end in a casserole and sprinkle with salt and pepper. Sprinkle scallions on top. Combine margarine with garlic and pour over potaoes. Bake uncovered 30 minutes. Reduce heat to 400 degrees and bake 30 minutes longer or until tender. Baste a few times during baking.

Preparation time: 10 minutes
Baking time: 1 hour
Serves: 8

CHEESE-POTATO BAKE   [D]

2 lbs potatoes, peeled, cut in chunks
3 large eggs
salt and pepper to taste
4 Tbsp butter
2 leeks, white part only, cleaned, chopped
3/4 lb farmer cheese
1 tsp salt
1/4 tsp pepper
1-1/2 cups shredded Muenster or Swiss cheese

Preheat oven to 375 degrees.

In boiling water, simmer potatoes until tender, about 10 minutes. Drain well, place in large bowl and mash. Add 1 beaten egg, salt, pepper and two tablespoons butter. Spread half of the potato mixture into a greased 8 X 12 inch baking dish. Saute leeks in 2 Tbsp butter for 5 minutes until tender. Remove from heat and let cool slightly. In mixing bowl, beat 2 eggs. Stir in farmer cheese, sauteed leeks, salt and pepper. Spread over potato mixture and sprinkle with 1/2 of the shredded cheese. Add another layer of potatoes, and top with remaining shredded cheese. Bake 30 minutes, until cheese is melted and filling is firm.

Preparation time: 10 minutes
Cooking time: 35 minutes
Serves: 12

FLAUMEN-POTATO TZIMMES [P]

1 cup thinly sliced onions
1/3 cup cooking oil
2 lbs white potatoes, cubed
1 lb pitted prunes, rinsed and drained
1 tsp salt (optional)
1 cup water
1/4 cup honey
1/8 tsp lemon juice

In a Dutch oven, saute onions in oil. Add potatoes, prunes, salt and water. Cover and cook 1 hour over low simmering heat. Add honey and lemon juice. Stir to mix. Cover and continue to simmer 1 hour. Stir occasionally.

Preparation time: 15 minutes
Cooking time: 2 1/4 hours
Serves: 6

This recipe freezes well in small containers. Braised lamb riblets and carrots may be added for a "meat" dish.

LACY POTATO PANCAKES [P]

1-1/4 lbs russet potatoes,
    peeled, finely shredded
1 Tbsp lemon juice
1/4 cup finely minced onion
2 large eggs, lightly beaten
3 Tbsp all-purpose flour
1 tsp baking powder
1 tsp salt
1/4 tsp white pepper
pinch sugar
oil for frying
cinnamon apple sauce, prepared

Squeeze shredded potatoes dry with hands. (A food processor simplifies shredding preparation, using a very fine blade.) Transfer to a mixing bowl and immediately toss with lemon juice. Add onion, eggs, flour, baking powder, salt, pepper and sugar. Heat about 1/8 inch oil in large, heavy skillet. For each pancake, drop potato mixtue by a heaping tablespoon into skillet, flattening with back of spoon to form a 2-1/2 inch pancake. Fry several at a time, without crowding pan. Fry until golden brown and crisp on each side, about 4 to 5 minutes. Drain on paper towels. Stir remaining potato mixture before frying a new batch, adding oil to pan as needed. Serve with cinnamon applesauce.

Preparation time: 15 minutes
Cooking time: 30 minutes
Serves: 4 to 6

Pancakes can be fried ahead, placed on rack over baking pan and kept warm at 250 degrees. If frozen, thaw slightly before reheating on a cookie sheet at 425 degrees for several minutes, until warmed through.

For onion potato latkes: add 1 minced shallot, 1 minced clove garlic and 2 Tbsp chopped chives.

MUSHROOM LATKES [D]

1 lb dried shitake mushrooms
1 medium onion, shredded
1/2 cup flour
4 large eggs
1/2 tsp salt

1/2 tsp pepper
vegetable oil for frying
sour cream
caviar

Place mushrooms in a large bowl and cover with warm water. When mushrooms are tender, drain and press out water with hands. Slice and remove stems. Meanwhile shred onions and mix in other ingredients. Add mushrooms. Heat 6 Tbsp oil in a large skillet. Drop mixture by tablespoon into oil and cook until brown on each side. Drain thoroughly on paper towel. Place on baking sheet. Keep warm in oven. May be frozen. Reheat at 400 degrees for 20 minutes. Serve with sour cream and caviar.

Preparation time: 15 minutes
Cooking time: 20 minutes
Serves: 6

ZUCCHINI PANCAKES [P]

1 lb zucchini, shredded
2 large eggs, lightly beaten
1 green onion, minced
1 tsp sugar
1/2 tsp salt

freshly ground pepper to taste
1/4 tsp oregano (optional)
1/4 tsp baking powder
2 to 4 Tbsp matzo meal
oil for frying

Squeeze zucchini dry in paper towels. In large mixing bowl, combine eggs, zucchini, green onion, sugar, salt, pepper, oregano and baking powder. Add enough matzo meal to make a batter. Heat oil in large skillet over medium-high heat. Skillet should be sizzling hot. Spoon about 2 tablespoons of zucchini mixture into skillet, flattening into a pancake. Repeat until skillet is filled, but not crowded. Fry until golden brown on one side, turn and brown other, pressing lightly with spatula. Transfer to paper-towel-lined baking sheet and keep warm in low oven. Repeat with remaining batter, adding oil as needed.

Preparation time: 5 minutes
Cooking time: 20 minutes
Serves: 4

Pancakes can be made in advance and reheated at 350 degrees about 10 minutes.

ZUCCHINI AND POTATO LATKES [P]

2 zucchini
2 russet potatoes, peeled
1 large egg

3 Tbsp flour
salt and pepper to taste
1/4 cup peanut oil

(Continued on Next page)

Grate zucchini and potatoes. Add egg, flour and seasoning to taste. Heat oil in skillet over high heat. Use large tablespoon and drop batter in skillet. Cook until golden brown on each side.

Preparation time: 10 minutes
Cooking time: 20 minutes
Serves: 4

TOMATO, ONION, POTATO MELANGE [P]

5 large tomatoes
5 large baking potatoes, thinly sliced
salt and pepper to taste
3 large onions, peeled, sliced
6 large garlic cloves, diced
1 Tbsp chopped fresh parsley
1 Tbsp chopped fresh oregano
1 cup dry white wine
1/4 cup virgin olive oil
2 Tbsp unsalted butter
1-1/2 cup seasoned bread crumbs

Blanch tomatoes in boiling water for 15 seconds in order to peel easily. Core and slice. If done ahead, cover and chill. Preheat oven to 400 degrees. In greased large baking dish that can be used for serving, arrange 1/2 of potatoes. Season with salt and pepper. Add 1/2 of onions and 1/2 of tomatoes, 1/2 of garlic and herbs. Season again with salt and pepper. Repeat. Pour wine and olive oil over. Bake 1-1/2 hours until almost all liquid is absorbed. Test for tenderness. Melt butter in large skillet over medium-high heat. Add crumbs and stir until golden brown about 5 minutes. Sprinkle on top. Cool 5 to 10 minutes before serving.

Preparation time: 20 minutes
Cooking time: 1 1/2 hours
Serves: 10 to 12

Substitute an equal amount of whole baby red potatoes and baby tomatoes and save time.

SWEET POTATO PUDDING [P]

4 cups sweet potatoes
3 large eggs, beaten
1/2 cup water
2 Tbsp lemon juice
2 Tbsp lemon zest, grated
1 tsp salt
1/2 cup oil
1/2 cup honey
1/4 cup sweet wine

Preheat oven to 350 degrees.

Cook potatoes in boiling water until done, about 30 minutes. Drain, peel and mash. Combine with other ingredients and place in well-greased mufffin pans, 2/3 full. Bake for 30 minutes.

Preparation time: 10 minutes
Cooking time: 1 hours
Serves: 12

Orange juice and zest may be substituted for lemon.

VEGETABLES

ORANGE AND YAM CASSEROLE [P]

6 medium yams, unpeeled
3 Tbsp cornstarch
1/2 cup brown sugar
1/2 cup sugar
1-1/2 cup orange juice
2 Tbsp butter or pareve margarine
8 oz can pineapple chunks or mandarine oranges (optional)

Preheat oven to 350 degrees.

Cook yams until tender, approximately 35 minutes. Cool. Peel and slice or cut into serving sized pieces. Make sauce of remaining ingredients. Place yams in baking dish and top with sauce. Bake 30 minutes. Casserole may be made 2 days ahead. If adding fruit, add just before reheating.

Preparation time: 15 minutes
Cooking time: 30 minutes
Serves: 6

CRANBERRY-GLAZED SWEET POTATOES [P]

1 cup canned whole cranberry sauce
1/2 cup water
1/4 cup sugar
1/2 tsp salt
1 tsp grated orange zest
1/2 tsp cinnamon
2 Tbsp pareve margarine
6 medium sweet potatoes, parboiled and peeled

Combine everything above except sweet potatoes and margarine. Simmer 5 minutes, then add margarine. Pour over sweet potatoes that are arranged in a baking dish. Bake 350 degrees for 40 minutes.

Preparation time: 15 minutes
Baking time: 40 minutes
Serves: 6

CREAMED SPINACH [M]

2 Tbsp oil
1 small onion, chopped fine
2 Tbsp flour
1 cup chicken broth
1/2 tsp salt
1/4 tsp nutmeg
1/4 tsp white pepper
1/2 cup non-dairy creamer
1 lb frozen spinach, thawed and squeezed dry

Heat oil. Cook onion in oil until limp. Add flour and cook, stirring constantly for 2 minutes. Add broth. Cook until boiling. Add seasonings and creamer. Add spinach. Put through food processor. Reheat about 5 minutes.

Preparation time: 10 minutes
Cooking time: 15 minutes
Serves: 4

NORTH AFRICAN STUFFED TOMATOES [P]

8 small tomatoes
3/4 cup chopped onion
2 Tbsp oil
2 cups cooked rice
1 cup mixed dark and light raisins
reserved tomato pulp
2 Tbsp orange marmalade
2 Tbsp lemon juice
1 Tbsp chopped fresh mint or 1 tsp dried

1 Tbsp honey
1/2 tsp allspice
1/2 tsp cinnamon

Topping:
1/4 cup marmalade
2 Tbsp honey
1 tsp cinnamon

Preheat oven to 350 degrees.

Cut 1/2 inch off tops of tomatoes. Remove pulp, drain, and reserve. In large skillet, saute onion in oil. Add remaining ingredients and stuff tomatoes. Drizzle topping made with marmalade, honey and cinnamon over tomatoes. Bake for 15 minutes. Chill. Serve cold as a first course.

Preparation time: 15 minutes
Baking time: 15 minutes
Serves: 8

SUN-DRIED TOMATOES [P]

3 pounds firm, ripe Italian plum tomatoes
whole peeled garlic clove (optional)
1 Tbsp dried basil, rosemary or oregano

olive oil
salt

Slice tomatoes lengthwise in halves. Pat dry. Place cut side up on wire racks in two shallow 10 X 15 inch baking pans. Sprinkle lightly with salt. Bake at 200 degrees 7 to 9 hours until shriveled and dry, but still flexible, not brittle. Pack loosely with basil, in 1 pint jar. Pour in olive oil to cover. May add whole peeled garlic. Cover and refrigerate.

Preparation time: 5 minutes
Cooking time: 7 to 9 hours.

MEDITERRANEAN ZUCCHINI BAKE [D]

2-1/2 lbs zucchini, sliced
28 oz can whole peeled tomatoes,
    drained and cut up
8 oz can tomato sauce
1 tsp salt

1/2 tsp pepper
1/4 tsp thyme
1/4 tsp basil
1/4 tsp oregano
1 cup grated sharp cheddar cheese

Combine vegetables in 9 X 13 inch casserole and top with seasonings and cheese. Bake in 350 degree oven for 30 minutes until vegetables are tender and cheese is melted.

Preparation time: 10 minutes
Baking time: 30 minutes
Serves: 8

VEGETABLES

CITRUS SQUASH [D]

3 small acorn squash or 2 butternut squash
1 Tbsp butter or pareve margarine
1/2 cup orange marmalade
1 Tbsp candied ginger, finely diced
1 Tbsp lemon juice
pinch of nutmeg

Preheat oven to 350 degrees. Grease baking pan.

Cut squash in half lengthwise. Remove seeds. Brush with melted butter or margarine. Place cut side down on pan. Bake 30 to 40 minutes. Remove from oven.

Fill cavities with mixture of marmalade, ginger, lemon juice and nutmeg. Return to oven and bake 15 minutes more or until tender.

Preparation time: 5 minutes
Cooking time: 55 minutes
Serves: 6

SUMMER SQUASH CHEESIES [D]

10 to 12 large summer squash (patti pan)
1/4 lb cheddar cheese, sliced
1/4 lb Swiss or Mozzarella cheese, sliced
1 tsp garlic salt
1 tsp paprika
1/4 tsp oregano, thyme, basil and parsley
1/4 tsp seasoned pepper
1-1/2 Tbsp butter
1/4 cup Parmesan cheese

Cut squash horizontally, but not completely in half. Cook 2 minutes in salted water. Drain and cool. Arrange squash in buttered baking dish. Lift up top of squash and insert cheeses...like a sandwich. Sprinkle liberally with seasonings. Dot with butter. Bake at 350 degrees for 20 to 30 minutes until squash is tender. Sprinkle with Parmesan cheese before serving.

Preparation time: 10 minutes
Cooking time: 20 to 30 minutes
Serves: 6

GINGER BEANS [P]

1 lb fresh green beans
2 Tbsp fresh ginger, peeled and chopped
1/4 tsp coriander seeds
1 Tbsp pareve margarine
2 Tbsp chopped chives

Wash beans, trim ends, leave whole or cut into slices. Bring to a boil enough water to cover beans. Add beans, ginger and coriander. Cover and simmer 5 minutes. Melt margarine. Drain beans and toss with chives and margarine and cook another 5 minutes, shaking pan constantly.

Preparation time: 10 minutes
Cooking time: 10 minutes
Serves: 4

Can be made in the microwave. 4 minutes for the beans, spices and margarine. 1 minute for the chives.

CASSEROLES

***"THE COMMANDMENTS,"* BRONZE,
GIFT OF SID LEVINE**

SHAVUOT—Noodle Kugel is a Holiday Tradition at Shavuot, When Dairy Products are Featured.

128 CASSEROLES

CASSEROLES
Janet Salter

The real reason King David invited Bathsheba to his palace....

One lovely day King David was standing on his roof, when he noticed a tantalizing smell in the air. He traced it to a nearby dwelling and spied Bathsheba relaxing in her bath after putting a noodle pudding in the oven to bake. The sweet smell of that "kugel" was so overpowering that he sent for Bathsheba to come immediately to the palace to prepare one for him, saying "One could kill for such a kugel!!!"

And that is exactly what David did! As Bathsheba was married, at the time, to a soldier named Uriah. King David sent him off to battle. He instructed his generals to position Uriah in the very front line of battle where, of course, he would be killed.

A high price to pay for a slice of kugel. But perhaps not, if one could also have the "kugel-maker!"

CARMELIZED KUGEL [P]

1/4 cup pareve margarine
1/2 cup dark brown sugar, packed
1 cup whole pecan halves
1 lb medium noodles, cooked and drained

4 eggs, beaten
1/4 cup pareve margarine, melted
1/3 cup sugar
1 tsp salt

Preheat oven to 350 degrees.

Melt 1/4 cup margarine in 10 inch bundt pan. Sprinkle brown sugar at bottom and around side of pan. Press pecan halves firmly into bottom of pan.
Mix other ingredients into noodles. Pour into pan and bake 1 hour. Cool and unmold.

Preparation time: 20 minutes
Baking time: 1 hour
Serves: 6

BUTTERMILK NOODLE PUDDING [D]

4 large eggs
1 qt buttermilk
1/2 cup butter, melted
1/2 cup sugar
1 lb wide noodles, cooked al dente
grated zest from 1 lemon (optional)

Topping:
2 cups crushed corn flakes
1/2 cup brown sugar, packed
3 Tbsp butter

Preheat oven to 350 degrees. Butter 9 X 13 inch pan.

In a bowl, beat eggs, add buttermilk, butter and sugar. Stir in noodles. Pour into pan. Bake 45 minutes.

In medium bowl, combine corn flakes, brown sugar and butter. Crumble topping over casserole. Bake an additional 15 minutes.

Preparation time: 20 minutes
Baking time: 1 hour
Serves: 6 to 8

CLASSIC NOODLE PUDDING   [D]

1 Tbsp butter to grease baking dish
12 oz pkg wide noodles
3 large eggs
3/4 to 1 cup sugar
1 tsp vanilla

2 cups cottage cheese
2 cups sour cream
1/2 cup golden raisins
1 tsp cinnamon
1 Tbsp butter

Preheat oven to 300 degrees. Butter 2 Qt baking dish.

Boil noodles according to package directions. Drain.

Beat eggs, add sugar, vanilla, cottage cheese, sour cream and raisins. Thoroughly mix into noodles. Pour into baking dish. Sprinkle with cinnamon and dot with butter. Bake 1-1/4 to 1-1/2 hours until brown.

Variations:
Low fat cottage cheese and yogurt may be substituted for regular (4%) cottage cheese and sour cream. Sliced almonds may be scattered over top. A cup of canned pineapple or chopped apple may be added for variety.

Preparation time: 15 minutes
Baking time: 1-1/2 hours
Serves: 10 to 12

GREEN CHILI QUICHE   [D]

10 large eggs
2 cups small curd cottage cheese
1 tsp baking powder
10 drops hot pepper sauce

1/2 cup all-purpose flour
1 lb Jack cheese, shredded
7 oz can diced green chiles, drained
1/2 cup melted butter

Preheat oven to 400 degrees. Coat 13 X 9 inch baking dish with non-stick spray or butter.

In mixer, blend first 6 ingredients. By hand, stir in the chiles and butter. Pour into baking dish and bake 15 minutes. Reduce to 350 degrees and bake 25 to 30 minutes. Cut into large squares or bite-size squares for hors d'oeuvres.

Preparation time: 15 minutes
Cooking time: 45 minutes
Serves: 8 large or 24 bite-size pieces

VEGETARIAN QUICHE [D]

8 inch pie shell, baked
1/2 cup grated Mozzarella cheese
1/2 cup cooked spinach, chopped
1/2 cup cooked broccoli, chopped
2 large eggs, slightly beaten

milk to make 1 cup
1/4 tsp garlic powder
1/4 tsp black pepper
1/4 cup grated Parmesan cheese

Preheat oven to 350 degrees.

Take one baked pie crust, layer with grated Mozzarella cheese, spinach and broccoli. In a one cup measuring container, place 2 eggs, fill cup with milk to measure one cup. Stir. Pour over vegetables. Sprinkle with garlic powder and black pepper, then Parmesan cheese. Bake 35 minutes or until knife inserted in center comes out clean.

Preparation time: 15 minutes
Baking time: 35 minutes
Serves: 8

QUICHE PROVENCALE [D]

1 medium onion, sliced
1/2 cup chopped green pepper
1 Tbsp oil
2 medium tomatoes, cut in wedges
1 cup sliced zucchini
1 Tbsp chopped parsley
1 tsp garlic salt

1/2 tsp dried basil
1/4 tsp pepper
1 unbaked 9 inch pastry shell
6 large eggs, beaten
1-1/4 cups half & half, may use non-dairy liquid creamer

Preheat oven to 450 degrees.

In a large skillet, saute onion and green pepper in oil over medium heat until onion is transparent, about 5 minutes. Add tomatoes, zucchini, parsley, garlic, salt, basil and pepper. Cook, uncovered, 10 minutes, stirring frequently. Drain well. Brush inside of pastry shell with small amount of beaten egg. Bake shell 5 minutes, or until light golden brown. Set aside. Reduce oven temperature to 350 degrees. Combine eggs and half and half. Pour into pie shell. Spoon in drained vegetable mixture. Bake 30 to 35 minutes or until knife inserted in center comes out clean. Let stand 5 minutes.

Preparation time: 30 minutes
Baking time: 35 minutes
Serves: 6

MAMALIGA BAKED WITH CHEESE AND TOMATO SAUCE [D]

3 cups yellow or white cornmeal
2 cups cold water
4 cups water
2 Tbsp salt
2-1/2 cups grated cheddar cheese
2 Tbsp butter
8 oz can tomato sauce or
 1 cup prepared spaghetti sauce

Preheat oven to 375 degrees.

In medium bowl, stir cornmeal with cold water, using wooden spoon to remove lumps. In large saucepan, boil 4 cups water with salt, gradually add cornmeal mush. Stir constantly. Simmer 10 minutes until very thick. Remove from heat. Use wooden spoon, dipped in cold water to push cornmeal to center of pot without stirring. Cook over low heat for 1 to 2 minutes to release steam and loosen from bottom of pan. Turn out onto baking sheet. With wet metal spatula spread smoothly to cover pan. Top with 2 cups of cheese and dot with butter. Roll up as jelly roll.* Sprinkle top with 1/2 cup cheese. Cover with tomato sauce. Bake 30 minutes. Slice and serve.

Preparation time: 20 minutes
Baking time: 30 minutes
Serves: 12

* A sheet of foil or waxed paper underneath will make rolling simple.

CORNMEAL PUDDING [D]

1 cup cornmeal
1 cup cold water
2 cups boiling water
1 tsp salt, or to taste
1 small onion, diced
1/2 green pepper, diced
1 Tbsp oil or butter
1 tsp cumin
1/4 cup sour cream
sour cream topping (optional)
paprika

Preheat oven to 350 degrees.

Combine cornmeal and cold water. Add cornmeal slowly to boiling salted water, stirring constantly. Bring cornmeal mixture back to a boil and continue stirring until mixture thickens, about 4 to 5 minutes. In a small skillet, saute onion and green pepper in oil until onion is translucent. Add to cooked cornmeal. Season with cumin and sour cream. Spoon into buttered 2 quart casserole. Top with a layer of sour cream (optional). Sprinkle with paprika and bake until pudding is hot and golden, about 40 to 60 minutes.

Preparation time: 10 minutes
Baking time: 40 to 60 minutes
Serves: 6

This can be prepared a day ahead, refrigerated, and baked just before serving. If the pudding is cold, allow for extra time.

GARDEN LASAGNA [D]

1/4 cup butter
1-1/2 cups chopped onion
2 cups cubed zucchini
2 cups cubed eggplant
1 cup sliced mushrooms
6 garlic cloves, minced
1-1/2 tsp Italian seasoning

3 cups vegetarian spaghetti sauce
12 pieces lasagna noodles,
   cooked and drained
12 oz pkg grated mozzarella cheese
1/2 cup grated Parmesan cheese
2 cups cottage cheese

Preheat oven to 350 degrees. Grease a 10 X 15 inch baking dish.

In a large skillet, saute butter and onions. Add vegetables, garlic and seasonings and cook until vegetables are crisp tender. Stir in spaghetti sauce. A little water may be added, if needed.

Layer a third of the lasagna on bottom of baking dish. Add half of sauce mixture, Mozzarella and Parmesan cheeses. Layer a third of noodles and top with cottage cheese. Layer remaining noodles, sauce, Mozzarella and Parmesan cheeses. Bake 45 to 50 minutes or until cheese is lightly browned. Allow to stand 10 minutes before serving.

Preparation time: 45 minutes to 1 hour
Cooking time: 45 to 50 minutes
Serves: 10 to 12

GREEK STUFFED TOMATOES [M]

6 large tomatoes or 12 small, unpeeled
2 Tbsp oil
2 cloves garlic, crushed
1 small onion, diced
1/2 cup ground lamb
2 cups cooked rice
1/4 cup pine nuts
1/2 tsp salt (optional)

1/2 tsp black pepper
1 tsp dried oregano
1 tsp dried rosemary
1 tsp dried basil
1 Tbsp lemon juice
1/4 cup olive oil
1 tsp red wine vinegar (optional)

Preheat oven to 350 degrees.

Cut a slice from the top of each tomato. Hollow with a grapefruit knife. Reserve tomato pulp. Turn tomatoes upside down on paper towel and drain.

In a skillet, heat 2 tablespoons of oil, add garlic and onions and saute until limp. Add meat and saute lightly. Add rice, nuts and seasonings. Simmer 1 minute. Cool slightly. Stuff tomatoes. Place in 2 qt baking dish. Mix tomato pulp with lemon juice and olive oil.

Bake 30 minutes. Serve hot or cold. If serving cold, add 1 tsp red wine vinegar to the tomato topping. Pour over tomatoes.

Preparation time: 20 minutes
Cooking time: 30 minutes
Serves: 6

BARLEY CASSEROLE [M]

2 cups pearl barley
1/2 cup pareve margarine
1 cup sliced mushrooms
1/2 pkg onion soup mix

2 cups chicken broth
1/2 cup sliced almonds, toasted
2 Tbsp sherry

Preheat oven to 350 degrees.

In a large saucepan, brown barley in margarine. Combine mushrooms, soup mix, chicken broth and sherry. Combine the two mixtures in a greased casserole. Bake covered, 1-1/2 hours. Stir once or twice during baking. Before serving, sprinkle with almonds.

Preparation time: 15 minutes
Baking time: 1-1/2 hours
Serves: 8

WILD RICE WITH PEAS [M]

1 cup uncooked wild rice
3 cups chicken broth
1 cup pecans, toasted
1 cup currants, plumped*

grated zest of orange
1/3 cup orange juice
10 oz pkg frozen tiny peas
pepper to taste

Rinse rice under cold water. In a 2 quart saucepan, combine rice, water and broth. Cover and bring to a boil. Reduce heat and simmer uncovered for 35 to 45 minutes or until rice is tender. Combine rice with remaining ingredients except peas. Mix well. Add peas last. Serve at room temperature.

Preparation time: 10 minutes
Cooking time: 45 minutes
Serves: 6

* Cover currants with boiling water and let stand about 15 minutes. Drain. Repeat process, soaking another 15 minutes. Currants will then be plump and ready to use in recipe.

RISI BISI WITH PINE NUTS [M]

2 Tbsp olive oil
1 onion, finely chopped
1-1/2 cups long-grain white rice
1 tsp ground turmeric
1/2 tsp crumbled thyme

4 cups chicken broth
1 cup frozen or fresh peas
salt and pepper to taste
1/2 cup toasted pine nuts

In medium saucepan, heat oil. Add onion and saute until tender, about 3 minutes. Add rice, turmeric, thyme and broth. Stir. Bring to boil. Cover, reduce heat to low and cook 15 to 20 minutes or until rice is tender and liquid is absorbed. Add peas and heat 2 minutes longer. Taste for seasoning. Add salt and pepper if desired. Spoon into serving dish and top with pine nuts.

Preparation time: 10 minutes
Cooking time: 30 minutes
Serves: 6

An Italian speciality. For a dairy variation, use vegetable broth, sprinkle with 1/4 cup Parmesan cheese.

SPICED RICE [P]

1 cup currants
1 cup water
2 Tbsp pareve margarine or oil
2 cloves garlic
1-1/2 cups dry white wine
2 cups water
1 tsp salt

2 cups rice
1/4 tsp pepper
1/4 tsp nutmeg
1/4 tsp allspice
2 Tbsp sugar
2/3 cup chopped or
    slivered Brazil nuts, toasted

In a saucepan, cover currants with water. Bring to a boil. Remove from heat. Drain after 5 minutes and reserve liquid. In same saucepan, melt margarine, add garlic and saute 5 minutes. Discard garlic. Add wine, water, reserved currant liquid and salt to pan. Bring to a boil and stir in rice, spices and sugar. Bring to a boil. Reduce heat, cover and simmer 25 minutes or until liquid is absorbed. Stir in currants and nuts.

Preparation time: 10 minutes
Cooking time: 35 minutes
Serves: 8

CONFETTI RICE, MICROWAVABLE [M]

1 cup finely chopped onion
1/3 cup chopped celery
1 cup uncooked long grain rice
2 cups chicken broth
1/2 tsp salt
1/4 tsp pepper
1/2 cup chopped ripe olives
1 cup fresh sliced mushrooms
4 oz jar pimientos, undrained
1-1/2 Tbsp diced green chiles

In 2 qt casserole, combine onion, celery, rice, broth, salt and pepper. Cover. Microwave on high 20 minutes, stirring after 10 minutes.

Add remaining ingredients. Mix well. Microwave on high 2 to 4 minutes longer. Stir before serving.

Preparation time: 10 minutes
Microwave time: 20 minutes
Serves: 6 to 8

BROWN RICE WITH BLACK BEANS [P]

1 medium onion, chopped
1 Tbsp oil
14-1/2-oz can stewed tomatoes
1/4 cup tomato salsa
16 oz can black beans, undrained
1 tsp dried oregano
1/2 tsp garlic powder
1-3/4 cups instant brown rice

Cook and stir onions in hot oil until soft. Add all ingredients except rice. Bring to boil. Stir in rice. Cover. Reduce heat. Simmer 20 minutes. Remove from heat. Let stand covered for 5 minutes.

Preparation time: 10 minutes
Cooking time: 30 minutes
Serves: 6 to 8

BUKHARIAN PILAF [P]

1 Tbsp oil
3/4 cup grated carrot
1 small onion, chopped
1 clove garlic, chopped
1 cup white rice

2 cups boiling water
1 tsp turmeric
1/2 tsp salt (optional)
1/4 tsp pepper
1 Tbsp chopped parsley

In a saucepan, heat oil and add vegetables and saute lightly. Add rice and water to vegetables and return to a boil. Reduce heat, stir, cover and cook without stirring for 30 minutes until liquid is absorbed.

Preparation time: 10 minutes
Cooking time: 30 minutes
Serves: 4 to 6

FRIED RICE [M]

1 large egg
2 Tbsp oil
1 cup diced mushrooms
3 to 4 water chestnuts, diced
3 to 4 Tbsp canned, diced bamboo shoots

1/2 cup diced cooked chicken (optional)
1 green onion, diced fine
2 cups cold, cooked rice
1 Tbsp soy sauce, or to taste
dash pepper

In skillet, scramble egg in oil, breaking into very small pieces. Add mushrooms, water chestnuts, bamboo shoots, chicken, green onion and rice. Cook five minutes. Toss. Add soy sauce and pepper. Continue cooking until heated through.

Preparation time: 20 minutes
Cooking time: 10 minutes
Serves: 8

FARFEL [M]

2 Tbsp oil
1 large onion, minced
1 cup sliced mushrooms
2 cup farfel, toasted according to pkg directions
1/2 tsp sweet basil
4 cups chicken broth
1/4 tsp salt
1/4 tsp white pepper

In a large heavy pot, heat oil. Saute onion and mushrooms until limp. Add farfel and basil. Stir until grains are coated. Add broth and bring to boil. Add salt and pepper. Cook over low heat 25 to 30 minutes or until all liquid is absorbed.

Preparation time: 5 minutes
Cooking time: 40 minutes
Serves: 8

VEGETABLE CHOLENT [M]

1/2 cup kidney, pinto or red beans
1 Tbsp oil
1 large onion, sliced
2 large cloves garlic, minced
1/2 cup barley
2 small white potatoes, peeled and cut in thirds
2 medium carrots, sliced diagonally
4 tsp instant chicken or beef-flavored soup mix
1-1/2 cups boiling water
1-1/2 tsp salt
1/2 tsp freshly ground pepper
1-1/2 tsp sweet paprika
1 bay leaf

Wash beans and soak overnight in water to cover. In a 2 qt flameproof casserole, heat oil, add onion and garlic and saute until soft. Drain beans and add along with barley, potatoes and carrots. Dissolve chicken soup mix in boiling water, add salt, pepper and paprika. Pour over bean mixture. Add bay leaf. Bring to a boil. Cover and bake at 350 degrees 2-1/2 hours, stirring occasionally, until beans are tender and most of the liquid is absorbed. Add more liquid if needed.

Preparation time: 15 minutes
Cooking time: 2 hours 30 minutes
Serves: 4

ISRAELI CHAMIN OR CHOLENT [M]

1 cup dried small white beans
1/4 cup oil
6 small white potatoes, whole
2 large onions, sliced
3/4 cup barley
2 lbs boneless short ribs
1 beef marrow bone, cut in quarters, or soup bones
1 head garlic, cloves separated, but unpeeled

3 large eggs, in shells
12 pitted prunes
14-1/2 oz can chicken broth
14-1/2 oz can beef broth
water (hot)
2-1/2 tsp salt
1 tsp coarsely ground black pepper
2 tsp sweet paprika
2 tsp honey

In medium bowl, soak beans in cold water to cover for 6 hours or overnight. In large Dutch oven, heat oil, add potatoes and brown on all sides. Add onions and saute lightly. Remove and set aside. In bottom of Dutch oven, place drained beans, barley, short ribs,* bones, reserved potatoes and onions, garlic and prunes. Gently add eggs. In small saucepan, heat broth and add to Dutch oven. Add enough hot water to barely cover mixture in Dutch oven. Add salt, pepper, paprika and honey. Cover and bake at 250 degrees 8 hours or until meat is tender, most of liquid is absorbed, checking occasionally to add more water, if needed. Skim off fat.

Preparation time: 30 minutes plus soaking time
Cooking time: 8 hours
Serves: 6 to 8

*Pre-roast ribs and bones at 450 degrees 30 minutes before adding to recipe.

ZUCCHINI FRITTATA [P]

2 cups tightly packed, shredded zucchini
1/2 cup tightly packed, grated carrots
1/2 cup pareve margarine, melted
1/3 cup flour or matzoh cake meal
2 large eggs, beaten
1/2 tsp salt (optional)

Preheat oven to 375 degrees. Grease 9 inch pie pan.

In a bowl, mix vegetables together. Add margarine and flour. Stir in eggs. Press into prepared pan. Brush with a little margarine. Bake 30 to 40 minutes or until knife inserted in center comes out clean. To serve cut into wedges.

Preparation time: 10 minutes
Baking time: 30 to 40 minutes
Serves: 4

BEAN CASSEROLE [P]

2 15 oz cans butter beans, drained
2 15 oz cans kidney beans, drained
2 15 oz cans baked beans
1 large onion, chopped
1 clove garlic, chopped
1 Tbsp oil
2 Tbsp brown sugar
3 Tbsp cider vinegar
1 tsp pepper
1 tsp salt
1/2 tsp dry mustard
3/4 cup catsup

Preheat oven to 350 degrees.

Place beans in a large casserole. In a skillet, saute onions and garlic in oil. Add sugar, vinegar, spices and catsup. Cook 2 minutes. Add to beans. Bake uncovered 1 hour.

Preparation time: 10 minutes
Baking time: 1 hour
Serves: 12

BLACK BEAN CHILI   [D]

2 cups black beans, rinsed and soaked 6 hours or overnight
1/4 cup olive oil
1 large onion, finely chopped
1 medium green pepper, chopped
1 clove garlic, minced
1 tsp ground cumin
1 tsp paprika
1/2 tsp cayenne pepper
1 Tbsp basil
1/2 tsp salt
1-1/2 cups canned crushed tomatoes
1/2 cup finely chopped jalapeno chili pepper
1 cup jack or cheddar cheese, grated
1/4 cup green onion, finely chopped
1/3 cup sour cream
cilantro (optional)

Place beans in a large pot and cover with water to several inches above top of beans. Cover and bring to a boil. Reduce heat and cook for 1-3/4 hours or until tender. Add more hot water if necessary. When beans are cooked, drain. Reserve 1 cup cooking water and add back to the beans. Add oil to saucepan and saute onion, pepper, garlic and cumin. Add seasonings. Cook 10 minutes or until onions are tender. Add tomatoes and chili pepper. Add all to beans and stir. To serve, place in bowl and top with cheese, onion, or sour cream. Garnish with cilantro.

Preparation time: 20 minutes
Cooking time: 2 hours 20 minutes
Makes: 3 qts

INDIAN FRUIT AND VEGETABLE CURRY   [P]

4 Tbsp pareve margarine or oil
1 medium onion, chopped
1 Tbsp flour
2 tsp curry powder, or to taste
1 cup vegetable broth
2 Tbsp orange juice
2 bananas cut in 1 inch chunks placed in bowl with 1 tsp lemon juice and water to cover
2 Tbsp lemon juice
1 Tbsp apple juice
1/2 firm-fleshed melon, cut in chunks
2 tomatoes, cut in 1/8's
1 carrot, sliced thin
1 green pepper, diced
1/2 cup peapods
1/4 cup slivered almonds
1/4 tsp hot pepper sauce (optional)

In a large heavy skillet, heat margarine and saute onions. Add flour and curry powder. Cook 2 minutes, stirring constantly. Add broth and fruit juices. Simmer 3 minutes. Drain bananas and add with remaining ingredients, except peapods. Cook over low heat until carrots are almost tender. Add peapods. Garnish with almonds. Season to taste with hot pepper sauce.

Preparation time: 20 minutes
Cooking time: 10 minutes
Serves: 6

BLINTZES [D]

Batter for crepes:
3 large eggs
3/4 cup all-purpose flour
1/2 cup water
1/2 cup milk
1/4 tsp salt
(This can be made with all water or all milk)

Filling:
3/4 lb hoop cheese
3/4 lb farmer cheese
1 large egg
1 egg yolk
grated zest of 1 lemon
2 Tbsp sugar
1/4 cup crushed corn flakes
pinch of salt
1/2 tsp cinnamon (optional)
Unsalted butter or margarine for frying

To make the crepes:
Beat eggs, add other ingredients and beat till smooth. Drop batter, 2 tablespoons at a time into a 6 to 7 inch buttered frying pan. Tip pan to spread batter over entire pan. Fry only on one side until top is dry and starts to blister. Turn out on a towel. Mix all ingredients for filling. On each blintz place filling and fold sides inward, then roll to make envelope. Fry or bake blintzes in a well buttered pan or baking dish at 400 degrees until golden brown.

Preparation time: 30 minutes
Cooking time: 15 to 30 minutes
Serves: 4 to 6

You may substitute cottage cheese for one of the cheeses, or both, but you may have to use a little more corn flakes to thicken the mix.
Serve with sour cream, jam and fresh fruit or cinnamon sugar (1/2 cup sugar to 2 tsp cinnamon).

HERBED FRENCH CREPES   [D]

1/2 cup cold water
1/2 cup cold milk
2 large eggs
1 cup sifted all-purpose flour

2 Tbsp oil or butter
1/3 cup mixed finely chopped dill,
    chives and parsley
oil for frying

In blender or food processor, place all ingredients. Blend just until smooth. Refrigerate, covered, 3 hours. Using a crepe pan or small skillet, lightly brush with oil and place over high heat. When hot, remove from heat and quickly place about 1/4 cup batter into pan, tilting it. Return to heat. Cook until just set, about 1 minute. Turn and cook on other side for 30 seconds. Stack between waxed paper layers. Wrap in foil for freezing. These crepes may be frozen for up to two weeks or refrigerated for 2 days. Reheat in oven 5 to 10 minutes in the foil. Use filling of your choice: Roll up, drizzle with a little butter and heat in 325 degree oven about 15 minutes or until warmed through.

Suggested filling: smoked salmon with creme fraiche. Decorate with dill.

Preparation time: 25 minutes
Cooking time: 20 to 25 minutes
Serves: 6

ONION SOUFFLE   [D]

2 medium onions, peeled and diced
2 Tbsp butter or margarine
3 Tbsp butter
3 Tbsp flour
1 cup milk, warmed

3 large egg yolks
4 large egg whites, room temperature
1/4 tsp salt
1/4 tsp cream of tartar

All ingredients must be at room temperature when putting souffle together before baking. In a small saucepan, over medium heat, saute onions in 2 tablespoons of butter until soft and light brown. In a food processor with metal blade, pulse onion until pureed and measures 1 cup. In same pan, melt 3 tablespoons butter, blend in flour until a paste forms. Cook 1 minute. Beginning slowly, blend in warmed milk. Cook and stir until thickened. Add onions. Cool. Beat egg yolks. Gradually add a little at a time to cooked mixture. About 1 hour and ten minutes before planned serving time, beat whites until foamy. Add salt and cream of tarter. Continue beating until stiff peaks are formed. Stir a little of whites into cooked mixture, then fold, lightly, until just blended. Place in an ungreased 6 cup souffle dish. Bake at 350 degrees for 1 hour. Souffle may be left in oven about 10 minutes after cooking but do not delay serving any longer or it will fall.

Preparation time: 20 minutes
Baking time: 1 hour
Serves: 4

FISH

WALL HANGING, PHILIP RATNER

YOM KIPPUR—Many Families Break the Fast After Yom Kippur with Gefilte Fish.

YOM KIPPUR

Janet Salter

You may trick your friends by asking, "What do we eat on Yom Kippur?" After they have described the crown-shaped challah and the fish steamed in its own juices, the golden soup, boiled chicken, fruit compote and tea, you tell them, "We don't eat anything on Yom Kippur, silly." However, what comes before our most sacred day and what follows it are important meals.

Erev Yom Kippur we serve food that is a bit bland, sparing with salts and spices to avoid the torments of a terrible thirst while fasting. After Yom Kippur we break the fast judiciously, restoring salt to our bodies with the salt fishes, but avoiding the pitfall of trying to make up for lost calories with too much rich food.

One of our confessions on Yom Kippur is for the sin of gluttony. We must be careful not to commit it again the minute the Shofar is blown.

Break the Fast

Almost as earthshaking a discovery as finding the Dead Sea Scrolls was the unearthing of the fossilized skeleton of a little round fish, which once swam in the Sea of Galilee, and was called "Gefilte". Its memory never disappeared from the Jewish psyche, and so to make up for its absence, resourceful Jewish "balabustas" took carp, whitefish and pike, ground them until they were unrecognizable, formed the mix into a ball with their bare hands. Then they slightly flattened the fish balls to simulate the "Gefiltes" of old.

Scientists in Israel, subsidized by the Horseradish Cartel, are working diligently on gene-altering to bring back the original Gefilte. Housewives worldwide are breathlessly awaiting the results. Until that day, purist cooks will keep grinding, while others will visit the supermarket and pass off their purchases as their own original recipes.

BAKED STUFFED GEFILTE FISH   [P]

Sauce:
2 tsps margarine or oil
2 large onions, diced
6 carrots, diced
6 celery ribs, diced
1 green pepper, diced
1/2 lb mushrooms, sliced

1/4 lb fresh green beans, cut
28 oz can tomatoes, mashed
15 oz can tomato sauce
2 or 3 cloves garlic, crushed
2 bay leaves
salt and pepper to taste

Fish Mixture:
1 large whitefish, boned (2-1/2 to 3 lbs)*
1 Sucker, boned (3 lbs)*
1 to 1-1/2 lbs black cod, boned*
2 medium onions

3 large eggs
1/2 cup matzo meal
1/4 cup water
2-1/2 to 3 tsps salt
2 tsp white pepper

Preheat oven to 350 degrees.

Prepare sauce: melt margarine in an oversized oblong casserole (12 X 18 inch). Add remaining ingredients for the sauce and bake about 30 minutes or until very hot.

Rinse fish. Remove skin from fish and keep intact. Grind fish, add onions, eggs, matzo meal, water and seasonings. Makes enough fish to fill 2 complete fish skins.

To stuff fish skins: Be sure the skins are free of scales. Place 2 of the skins on a flat surface and rub with a little salt. Place fish mixture on the skin in the shape of a fish then place 2 skins on top of the fish. Using 2 spatulas, carefully lift stuffed fish and place them side by side in the hot vegetables, covering fish with some of the sauce.

Cover with foil and bake 1-1/4 hours, basting several times.

To Serve: Cool slightly and remove entire fish to a serving platter, surround with the vegetables. Cut the fish into slices and serve with horseradish.

Preparation time: 45 minutes.
Cooking time: 1 1/4 hours
Serves: 10

* Fish can be skinned and ground at your fish market.

ITALIAN FISH STEW [P]

6 anchovy fillets
2 Tbsp pine nuts
1 Tbsp anise seeds
1 small onion, chopped
1 large clove garlic, mashed
1 Tbsp chopped parsley
2 Tbsp oil

28 oz can tomatoes, chopped
1/4 cup dry red wine
1 oz dried mushrooms, reconstituted
3 lbs mixed fish (use firm varieties)
salt (optional)
1/2 tsp pepper

Sauce: Grind together in a processor with a metal blade, anchovies, nuts and anise seeds. In a large skillet, saute onion, garlic and parsley in oil until limp. Add to the skillet, tomatoes, wine, mushrooms and anchovy mixture.

Rinse fish and pat dry. Place fish in skillet, cover with sauce and cook over low heat 15 minutes or until fish is just tender. Season with salt and pepper.

Preparation time: 20 to 25 minutes
Serves: 8 to 10

FRENCH FISH STEW [P]

zest only of 2 oranges
3 medium potatoes, thinly sliced
3 medium onions, thinly sliced
16 small mushrooms
2 cloves garlic, thinly sliced
8 artichoke hearts, quartered
2 medium tomatoes, peeled,
   cored and chopped
1 large sprig fresh thyme or 1/2 tsp dried
2 bay leaves
3 Tbsp olive oil

2 qts water
1 tsp salt
1/2 tsp white pepper
1/2 cup minced parsley
2 lbs firm fish such as halibut,
   cod or whitefish cut into 1/2 inch slices

4 slices French bread
   cut 1/2 inch thick (or more if desired)
1 clove garlic
1 Tbsp olive oil

In a large pot, combine first 14 ingredients. Bring to a rapid boil for 15 minutes. Add fish and lower heat to simmer. Cook 5 minutes.

Preheat broiler: Spread bread on both sides with oil and garlic. Toast until light brown. Place a slice of bread into each bowl. Place a slice of fish on top of bread. Remove zest and bay leaves. Ladle the remaining ingredients over fish. Serve with extra garlic bread.

Preparation time: 15 minutes
Cooking time: 20 minutes
Serves: 4

STUFFED FISH IN LETTUCE PACKETS [P]

4 Tbsp pareve margarine
5 Tbsp minced shallot
1 lb fresh mushrooms, minced
1 tsp tarragon, (dried)
4 4 oz pieces of thick-cut, filleted fish, (cod, or halibut)
1/2 bunch watercress leaves, cleaned and stemmed
1/2 tsp salt (optional)
1/2 Tbsp pepper
1 tomato, chopped (optional)
1 large head iceberg lettuce

In a small skillet, melt margarine. Add shallots, mushrooms and seasonings. Cook over low heat until liquid evaporates. Place lettuce leaves in a collander placed over a pot. Pour boiling water over lettuce. Keep submerged until limp. Rinse fish and pat dry. Season fish with salt and pepper. Split fish in half horizontally, but do not cut through. Divide mushroom mixture between fish steaks. Drain and dry lettuce. Roll each piece of fish in double lettuce leaves to make a packet (rolling up like a blintz). Place fish in a steamer rack and steam for 10 minutes. Remove packets carefully. Place on individual plates and garnish with watercress and chopped tomato.

Preparation time: 15 minutes
Cooking time: 10 minutes
Serves: 4

SICILIAN FRESH TUNA [P]

6 slices tuna, 1/4 inch thick
4 oz white wine
1/2 lemon, juiced
1/4 tsp salt
1/4 tsp white pepper
1/8 tsp nutmeg
1 Tbsp fresh rosemary or 1 tsp dried
2 small cloves garlic, peeled and crushed
6 anchovies, drained and rinsed (optional)
1 Tbsp capers (optional)

Place fish in glass container. Pour wine, lemon juice, salt, pepper and nutmeg over fish. Refrigerate for 2 hours. Drain fish, sprinkle with rosemary and garlic. Grill, basting with dressing, for 3 to 4 minutes on each side. Decorate with pieces of anchovies and capers, if desired.

Preparation time: 10 minutes
Plus refrigeration time: 2 hours
Cooking time: 6 to 8 minutes
Serves: 6

WALNUT STUFFED TROUT [P]

2 cups finely chopped walnuts
2 cups finely chopped onions
1 cup finely chopped parsley
1 tsp salt (optional)
1/2 tsp white pepper

6 boned trout
1 cup yellow cornmeal
3 Tbsp oil
12 slices lemon
parsley for garnish

In food processor with metal blade, mix walnuts, onions, parsley, salt and pepper. Wash fish, split open and pat dry. Evenly divide filling between the split fish and spread evenly. Close fish.

Alternate cooking methods:

1. Dip fish in cornmeal and brown on each side in hot oil in a skillet.
Cook 5 minutes on each side

2. Wrap each fish in foil. Grill on each side for 5 minutes over hot coals. Decorate with lemon slices and parsley.

Preparation time: 10 minutes
Cooking time: 10 minutes
Serves: 6

POACHED SALMON WITH CAPER SAUCE [P]

- 1 whole salmon, salmon steaks or fillets, at least 5 pounds total or enough to serve 10. If you use fillets, there will be less waste and more meat.
- 10 cups water
- 2 carrots
- 2 celery stalks
- 1 large onion, sliced
- 2 sprigs parsley, 1 bay leaf, 1 tsp thyme, wrapped together in cheesecloth bag
- 6 peppercorns
- 2 Tbsp wine or lemon juice
- 1 tsp salt
- lemon slices

Rinse fish and dry. In a deep roasting pan, combine all ingredients except salmon. Cover and bring to boil. Lower heat and simmer 15 to 20 minutes.

Wrap fish in parchment paper and place in broth. Liquid should just cover fish. Return broth to boil, reduce heat and simmer 20 to 30 minutes. Drain well, remove skin, if desired. Place on platter and chill. Surround with sliced lemons and serve with caper sauce.

CAPER SAUCE

- 1 Tbsp red wine vinegar
- 1 Tbsp white wine vinegar
- 1 tsp dry mustard
- 2 tsp anchovy paste or mashed whole anchovy
- 2 Tbsp finely chopped parsley
- 1 Tbsp onion, minced
- 1/3 cup capers, drained
- 1/4 tsp garlic powder
- 1 cup mayonnaise

In blender, combine all ingredients. Refrigerate overnight. (Must be prepared in advance.)

An alternative cooking method: On a large sheet of foil, place fish. Cover with caper sauce. Wrap securely and grill or barbeque 10 to 15 minutes for small serving or 30 minutes for whole fish. Turn fish once while cooking.

Preparation time: 15 to 20 minutes for fish, 10 minutes for sauce
Cooking time: 20 to 30 minutes
Serves: 10

PICKLED SALMON   [P]

2-1/2 cups water
1 cup white wine (optional)
1 cup white wine vinegar
1-1/2 onions, sliced
2 tsp salt

3 Tbsp sugar
1 Tbsp pickling spices
1 Tbsp fresh dill or 1 tsp dried dill
2 lbs salmon, cut in chunks

Rinse fish and pat dry.

In a large pot, combine water, white wine, white vinegar and onions. Bring to boil and simmer for 15 minutes. Add salt, sugar, spices, dill and salmon. Cover and simmer 10 minutes or until salmon is tender.

Remove salmon to glass baking dish. Strain sauce to remove herbs and spices and pour sauce and onions over salmon. Cover and cool. Refrigerate

Preparation time: 15 minutes
Cooking time: 10 minutes
Serves: 6 to 8

MICROWAVE POACHED SALMON   [P]

1/2 cup diced carrots
1/2 cup diced onion

1/2 cup diced celery
2 Tbsp water

1 lb salmon
fresh dill weed,
lemon slices

juice of 1/2 lemon
1 to 2 Tbsp white wine
salt and pepper to taste

Scatter diced vegetables and water on bottom of microwave proof utensil and cook on high for 1 minute. Rinse fish and pat dry. Place salmon steaks or fillets over cooked vegetables. Sprinkle with salt and pepper. Place dill and lemon slices on each piece of fish. Drizzle white wine and lemon juice over fish. Lightly moisten paper towel, wetting it and wringing out. Stretch towel on top of salmon. Microwave on high about 5 minutes. Test for doneness. It should flake easily but still be moist.

Preparation time: 15 minutes
Cooking time: 5 to 10 minutes
Serves: 4

SMOKED PEPPERED SALMON [P/D]

Salmon Preparation:
1 salmon fillet with skin, 3 to 3-1/2 pounds, 1-1/2 inch thick
1 Tbsp honey

1/2 cup mixed whole peppercorns (pink, green, white, & black: for mildest flavor use mainly pink and green peppercorns), lightly crushed

Marinade:
1 cup brown sugar, packed
6 Tbsp salt
1 Tbsp minced fresh ginger or 1 tsp dry ginger

2 or 3 bay leaves
1 tsp crushed whole allspice
1-1/2 cups water

Condiments:
1/2 cup capers, drained
1 cup red onions, minced
1 Tbsp lime or lemon juice

1 cup sour cream (optional)
lemon slices or dill for garnish
thin toast

Barbeque:
1/2 cup apple or hickory wood chips briquets

Rinse salmon, pat dry, and place flat, skin down. Prepare marinade by mixing all marinade ingredients in saucepan. Bring to a boil. Remove from heat. Let cool slightly.

Pour marinade over salmon. Cover pan tightly and chill fish at least 4 or up to 24 hours. Occasionally spoon marinade over the fish.

Pour enough hot water over peppercorns to float them. Soak 15 minutes.

Prepare fire: Mound hot briquets so that there is an opening in the middle for fish. Soak wood chips for 15 minutes.

Prepare to barbeque fish: Pour off marinade, rinse fish with cool water and pat dry. Set skin-side down on a large piece of heavy foil. Cut or shape foil along outline of fish.

Rub honey over top of fish. Drain peppercorns and scatter evenly over fish, patting lightly in place. Drain wood chips and scatter on coals. Place salmon on coals in middle of grill. No coals should be directly beneath fish. Close barbeque and vents, leaving 1/4 inch opening in vents. After 30 minutes, check coals to be sure temperature stays at 160 degrees. Add wood chips as needed to produce a faint, steady stream of smoke. Cook salmon until thermometer registers 140 degrees in center of thickest part (about 1 to 1-1/2 hours). Remove fish carefully to a large flat dish. Serve warm, cool or chilled. Garnish with onion and dill. Lift off skin. Cut fish across grain into 3/4 inch slices. Serve with condiments.

Preparation time: 30 minutes
Cooking time: 1 to 1-1/2 hours
Serves: 12 to 14

SALMON WITH RED CURRANTS [P]

1 leek, white part only, washed well
1/2 cucumber
3 small carrots
4 sprigs parsley
1 tsp salt

5 ounces fresh red currants or 2 Tbsp dried
4 filets of salmon or salmon trout
1 to 2 cups dry white wine
fresh mint sprigs

Preheat oven to 400 degrees. Rinse fish and pat dry.

Chop vegetables and herbs and place in bottom of 8 X 12 inch baking dish. Sprinkle with currants, then top with salmon. Arrange mint over salmon. Add wine to barely cover fish. Cover with foil and bake 20 minutes.

Preparation time: 10 minutes
Cooking time: 20 minutes
Serves: 4

SHERRIED SALMON [D]

5 green onions diced
2 Tbsp butter
salt and pepper

4 salmon steaks, 1/2 inch thick
3/4 cup cream sherry

Rinse fish and pat dry.

Using a large heavy skillet, saute the onions in butter. Season the salmon with salt and pepper. Using high heat saute salmon on each side until the fish changes color to pink. Remove fish, cover and keep warm. Add sherry to pan and boil down, uncovered, until the sauce is reduced by half. Return fish to sauce and heat to serving temperature. Serve immediately.

Preparation time: 15 minutes
Cooking time: 10 to 15 minutes (test for doneness)
Serves: 4

ORANGE ROUGHY EN RAMEKIN   [D]

6 5 oz fillets orange roughy
   (or other filleted fish)
1 large onion, chopped
2 Tbsp butter or oil
1/2 tsp salt, or to taste

1/2 lb mushrooms, sliced
1/2 cup sour cream
10-1/2-oz can tomato soup
dash pepper

Preheat oven to 350 degrees. Rinse fish and pat dry.

Roll each fillet and place in individual ramekin. (This recipe is not successful in large casserole). In skillet, melt butter and saute onion until tender. Add salt if desired. Add mushrooms and continue sauteing until tender. Spoon over each fillet. In bowl, combine soup and sour cream, mixing well. Pour over fish to 1/4 inch or less to top of ramekin. Add pepper. Dot with butter if desired. Place ramekins on baking sheet. Bake 45 to 50 minutes.

Prepartion time: 15 minutes
Cooking time: 45 to 50 minutes
Serves: 6

MOROCCAN FISH   [P]

1 lemon, peeled and sliced
1 large tomato, sliced thin
1/2 tsp cilantro (dried) or 1 Tbsp
   fresh or Italian parsley
4 fish fillets (cod or orange roughy),
   one inch thick

1/2 tsp dried red pepper flakes
1 tsp cumin
1-1/2 tsp garlic powder
1 tsp paprika
1 tsp salt (optional)

Rinse fish and pat dry.

In a large pan, combine lemon, tomato, cilantro and pepper flakes. Place fish on top. Cook over low heat for 10 to 15 minutes or until fish is almost done. Mix cumin, garlic powder, paprika and salt. Sprinkle over fish and simmer on low heat for 10 minutes or until fish flakes easily.

Preparation time: 5 minutes
Cooking time: 25 minutes
Serves: 4

FISH ESPANOL [D]

olive oil
3 cups sliced onions
1/2 tsp paprika
1 tsp sugar
1-1/2 lbs fish fillets or steaks
 (firm white fish)
1 lemon
1 tsp salt

1/4 tsp pepper
1/8 tsp cayenne
2 large tomatoes, peeled and sliced
1/2 lb mushrooms, sliced
5 green onions, chopped
1/4 cup dry sherry
1/2 cup buttered bread crumbs

Preheat oven to 400 degrees.

Brush shallow baking dish with 1/2 teaspoon olive oil. Set aside. Heat 1 Tablespoon olive oil and saute onions until transparent. Season with paprika and sugar and cook 1 minute longer. Cover bottom of 8 X 12 inch baking dish with cooked onions. Rinse fish and pat dry. Rub fish with cut lemon and arrange fish fillets or steaks over onions. Sprinkle with salt, pepper and cayenne. Top with tomatoes. In a small skillet, heat 2 tablespoons olive oil and saute mushrooms 2 to 3 minutes. Add sherry to pan and cook 1 minute longer. Stir in green onions. Spoon mushroom mixture over fish. Cover loosely with oiled parchment or waxed paper and bake 10 minutes. Uncover and top with buttered crumbs. Bake 10 minutes longer or until fish flakes easily with a fork. Let rest 5 to 7 minutes before serving.

Preparation Time: 20 to 30 minute
Cooking time: 20 Minutes
Serves: 4

HALIBUT IN DIJON VINAIGRETTE [P]

1 lb halibut fillet or steak or cod, flounder, or perch
pepper to taste
1 Tbsp Dijon mustard
1/4 cup vinegar or white wine
1 tsp Worcestershire sauce
salt and pepper to taste
1/2 cup olive oil
1/4 tsp onion powder
1/4 tsp basil
1/2 tsp paprika

Rinse fish and pat dry.

Place fish in microwave-proof dish. Cover with a paper towel. Microwave on high for one minute. Remove paper towel. Combine mustard, vinegar, Worcestershire sauce, oil and seasonings. Pour over fish. Cover fish with waxed paper and secure. Microwave on high, turning pan once. Cook for 6 to 8 minutes depending on power of your microwave. Check for doneness and rotate dish in microwave after 4 minutes. Cook until fish is flaky. Sprinkle with paprika for color.

Preparation time: 5 minutes
Cooking time: 6 to 8 minutes for microwave
Serves: 3 to 4

HALIBUT CREOLE [P]

1 Tbsp oil
1 Tbsp all-purpose flour
2 onions, chopped
2 cloves garlic, crushed
1 large green pepper, chopped
2 tsp chopped parsley
28 oz can tomatoes, undrained
1/8 tsp cayenne pepper
1/2 tsp salt
2 bay leaves
1/3 tsp celery seeds
1/4 tsp powdered thyme
2 lbs halibut steak cut into 1" pieces
2 tsp Worcestershire sauce

Rinse fish and pat dry.

In a heavy iron pot, make a roux with the oil and the flour, cooking and stirring until golden brown. Add the onions, garlic, pepper and parsley. Stir until the onions are slightly brown. Mash the tomatoes and add. Season with cayenne pepper, salt, bay leaves, celery seeds, and thyme. Add the halibut. Cover and cook over low heat 15 minutes. Add the Worcestershire sauce. Cook 5 minutes longer or until fish flakes. Serve over cooked rice.

Preparation time: 15 minutes
Cooking time: 15 minutes
Serves: 4

PECAN LEMON HALIBUT [D]

1 cup fine bread crumbs
1/2 cup coarsely chopped pecans
salt and pepper to taste
grated zest of 1 lemon
2 to 3 Tbsp chopped parsley
juice of 1 lemon

2 lbs halibut fillets
1/2 cup flour
1 large egg
2 Tbsp milk
4 to 6 Tbsp butter or oil
parsley and lemon slices for garnish

Mix together bread crumbs, pecans, salt, pepper, lemon zest and chopped parsley. Rinse fish and pat dry. Squeeze lemon juice over halibut. Dredge fish in seasoned flour. Beat egg and milk together and dip fish in egg mixture. Then dip in pecan mixture. In large skillet, heat butter and fry halibut on each side for 3 to 4 minutes, until light brown and crisp. Garnish with lemon slices and parsley.

Preparation time: 15 minutes
Cooking time: 6 to 8 minutes
Serves: 4 to 6

GEFILTE FISH LOAF [P]

5 lbs mixed chopped fish, whitefish,
    black cod and pike
5 egg whites
1-1/2 onions, peeled and cut into chunks
1 carrot

4 Tbsp matzo meal
3 to 4 oz water
1/2 tsp salt
1/2 tsp white pepper

Place all ingredients in food processor. Process until thoroughly chopped and blended together. Rinse two 9 X 5 X 3 inch pans with water. Add fish mixture to pan and level top. Bake at 350 degrees for 50 minutes. Check with cake tester for doneness. Immediately turn out onto a platter. The juices will jell when refrigerated. Serve hot or cold with horseradish.

Preparation time: 10 to 15 minutes
Baking time: 50 minutes
Serves: 10 to 12

BASS POACHED WITH FENNEL AND ORANGES [P]

Marinade:
1/4 cup fresh lemon juice
3 cloves garlic, peeled and minced
1/4 cup dry sherry
4 bass fillets

Poaching liquid:
1 cup white wine
1 clove garlic, peeled and minced
1/2 to 1 tsp fennel seeds
1/2 small onion peeled and thinly sliced
1/4 tsp saffron threads (optional)
2 oranges, peeled and cut into sections
1 lemon, peeled and cut up
1/4 tsp salt
freshly ground pepper to taste
8 fresh basil leaves, cut into strips
8 sliced stuffed green olives for garnish

For the marinade, combine the lemon juice, garlic and sherry in a shallow dish. Add bass and marinade 20 minutes, turning once. For poaching liquid, place wine, garlic, fennel seeds and onion in saucepan large enough to cook fish. Bring to boil, reduce heat and simmer, covered, 10 minutes. Add saffron and simmer 1 minute. Remove bass from marinade and place in poaching liquid. Cover and simmer 4 minutes. Add orange and lemon sections, cover and simmer 2 minutes more. Season with salt and pepper to taste. Add basil leaves and/or olives.

Preparation time: 10 minutes, plus marinating time: 20 minutes
Cooking time: 17 minutes
Serves: 4

ONION MARMALADE AND TOMATO BUTTER FOR FISH   [D]

Marmalade:
4 medium red onions, minced
1/2 cup sherry wine vinegar (if not available, mix 1/4 cup sherry with 1/4 cup white wine and let stand for a few days)
1-1/4 cup dry red wine
1/4 cup water
1 tsp honey
1 tsp unsalted butter or margarine
1/2 tsp fresh ground pepper
1/2 tsp salt (optional)

To prepare marmalade: Combine onions, wine, vinegar, water, honey, salt and pepper in a large saucepan. Cook, uncovered, over low heat until all liquid is absorbed (at least 45 minutes).

Stir occasionally. (This may be done in advance and refrigerated.)

Tomato Butter:
1 Tbsp unsalted butter or margarine
10 tomatoes, cored and chopped or 2 cups canned tomato puree

To prepare tomato butter: In food processor, with metal blade, puree tomatoes. Press through sieve to remove seeds. Pour remainder into a small saucepan. Cook over medium heat until reduced 2/3. Add butter until completely blended. Add salt and pepper to taste.

Warm onion marmalade over low heat. Place a portion on each plate and surround with tomato butter. Place broiled fish on top and drizzle with a little tomato butter.

Preparation time: 20 to 25 minutes
Cooking time: 45 minutes to 1 hour
Makes: 2 cups of each

PAPAYA RELISH FOR FISH   [P]

1 papaya, peeled, seeded and chopped
1 red bell pepper, chopped
1 red onion, chopped
2 Tbsp lime juice
2 Tbsp mint leaves, chopped
1/2 tsp salt
1/4 tsp pepper

In a bowl, combine papaya, red pepper, onion, lime juice and seasonings. Cover and chill. Serve with salmon or red snapper.

Preparation time: 5 minutes
Makes: about 2 cups

BASS STEAKS WITH TOMATOES AND BLACK OLIVES [P]

1 large ripe tomato, cored and quartered
1/2 cup dry white wine
1 tsp grated lemon zest
1/2 tsp salt to taste
8 1 inch thick bass steaks

1/4 cup chopped tomatoes
1 Tbsp pitted and chopped black olives
1 tsp chopped fresh rosemary
freshly ground pepper to taste
1 tsp fresh chopped chives

In food processor, with steel blade, process tomato until finely chopped. Press through sieve lined with cheesecloth to remove pulp and seeds. 1/2 cup tomato liquid should be reserved. Add wine, lemon zest and salt. Bring to boil over medium heat in saucepan large enough to cook bass. Reduce heat and simmer, adding bass. Cover and poach until just cooked through, about 5 to 7 minutes. Remove from heat and add chopped tomatoes, olives and rosemary. Add salt and pepper to taste. Garnish with chives.

Preparation time: 5 minutes
Cooking time: 5 to 7 minutes
Serves: 4

MEAT

ETHROG BOX, PORTUGAL, SILVER, TREASURES OF JUDAICA

SUKKOT—At Sukkot Families Enjoy Stuffed Foods Such as Sweet and Sour Cabbage Rolls.

SUKKOT
Janet Salter

In ancient times, the contracting firm of Aram & Beryl did all of the sukkot-building work, including the Sunrise Senior Sukkot Housing Project. They were leaders in their field until the Holiday Help-Yourself chain forced them into Chapter 11 (This Chapter does not appear in the bible). King Solomon, master builder, conceived the plan of do-it-yourself stores, and the chain flourished. Franchises were sold all over Israel and included a grove of palm trees. The store's free offers of palm fronds made them successful.

Since that time, it has become a tradition to build one's own sukkah. There, savory meals can be enjoyed for a week, along with the knowledge that the dwelling was built with loving care.

SWEET AND SOUR STUFFED CABBAGE [M]

1 large cabbage, washed and frozen for 2 days. Defrost night before cooking. Alternative: Cabbage may be cored and blanched in boiling water until outer leaves are soft and pliable.
28 oz can tomatoes
15 oz can tomato sauce
1/4 cup lemon juice
1/2 cup brown sugar, packed
1 cup water
2 cloves garlic, minced
1/2 cup golden raisins
8 gingersnaps, crushed (optional)
2 large onions, sliced
1 lb ground beef
1/4 cup uncooked rice
1 large egg
1/4 tsp salt
1/4 tsp pepper
1 medium onion, grated
1 large carrot, grated

For sauce:
In a saucepan, bring tomatoes, tomato sauce, lemon juice, brown sugar and water to boil. Simmer 10 minutes. Add garlic, golden raisins, gingersnaps and onions.

Meat Mixture:
In a mixing bowl combine ground meat, rice, egg, salt, pepper, grated onion and carrot.

Assembly:
Remove core from head of cabbage. Separate leaves. Place a ball of the meat mixture in center of each leaf and roll up, tucking ends in securely. Place cabbage rolls into large pot on top of onions and remaining cabbage leaves. Pour sauce over rolls and cook over moderate heat 45 minutes to an hour. Then bake 350 degrees 2 to 3 hours, covered. Longer cooking improves flavor.

Preparation time: 45 minutes
Cooking time: 45 minutes
Baking time: 2 to 3 hours.
Serves: 6

STUFFED CABBAGE HUNGARIAN STYLE [M]

Large head of cabbage, cored
2 lbs ground beef
1/4 cup instant rice
1/2 cup finely minced onion
2 large eggs
1 Tbsp lemon juice
2 tsp salt
1/4 tsp pepper
1/2 large onion, sliced

28 oz can tomatoes
8 oz can tomato sauce
2 lb jar sauerkraut
3/4 to 1 cup dark brown sugar, packed
1/3 cup golden raisins
1/2 tsp ginger
1/2 tsp coarsely ground pepper
1 bay leaf
24 inch square of cheesecloth

Steam cabbage over boiling water 10 to 12 minutes to soften leaves. Drain. Separate leaves and if leaves are not flexible, steam longer. Trim veins off leaves with peeler to flatten. In a bowl, combine beef, rice, onion, eggs, lemon juice, salt and pepper. On a 24 inch square of cheesecloth, overlap six outer cabbage leaves in circle with stem ends facing. Put a cabbage leaf in center. Spread about 1/3 meat mixture over leaves, leaving two-inch border of cabbage. Make a second circle of cabbage leaves. Spread 1/3 of meat mixture over this layer. Continue layering meat and cabbage, so there are five cabbage layers and four meat layers in all. Bring corners of cheesecloth together, transfer to a medium bowl to form cabbage shape, tie cheesecloth with string and cut off excess cheesecloth.

In eight-quart Dutch oven, layer remaining cabbage and onion, then place packet, tied side down, on top. Add tomatoes, tomato sauce, sauerkraut with juice, brown sugar, raisins, ginger, pepper and bay leaf. Bring to a boil. Cover and remove from stove. Bake at 350 degree oven 2 hours, basting occasionally. Remove cheesecloth from cabbage. Return to oven and bake uncovered one hour more, basting occasionally, until sauce is reduced.

Preparation time: 30 minutes
Baking time: 3 hours
Serves: 6 to 8

STUFFED CABBAGE WITH APRICOTS   [M]

12 or more dried apricots
1 large head cabbage
2 lbs ground beef, veal or turkey
1 large egg
1/2 cup water from apricots
3 Tbsp uncooked rice

1/2 tsp salt
1/8 tsp pepper
1/4 tsp garlic powder
2 large onions, diced
2 Tbsp oil

Sauce:
2 15 oz cans tomato sauce
1 tsp salt

1/8 to 1/4 tsp pepper
1/2 cup brown sugar, packed
juice of small lemon

In a small bowl, soak apricots in warm water. Core cabbage and blanch in boiling water until outer leaves are soft and pliable. Remove from water and drain. In a bowl, combine meat, egg, apricot water, rice and seasoning.

Stuff each leaf by tucking sides in as you roll. In a Dutch oven saute onions in oil. Layer apricots and cabbage rolls over the onions. Combine sauce ingredients. Pour over all. Cover and simmer 3 hours or until sauce thickens.

Preparation time: 30 minutes
Cooking time: 3 hours
Serves: 6 to 8

BRISKET WITH COFFEE AND WINE   [M]

4 medium onions, sliced
2 large cloves garlic, minced fine
2 Tbsp oil
4 to 5 lbs brisket
salt and pepper to taste

1/4 tsp cumin
1 tsp paprika
1 cup strong coffee
1 cup red wine

Preheat oven to 350 degrees.

In skillet, saute onions and garlic in oil. Season meat with salt and pepper. Place 2/3 of onions in bottom of roasting pan with meat. Sprinkle with cumin, paprika and remaining onions. Add coffee and wine. Cover tightly and roast for 2-1/2 to 3 hours. Cool and slice. Strain and reheat remaining liquid and use as gravy over meat before reheating brisket.

Preparation time: 10 minutes
Cooking time: 2-1/2 to 3 hours
Serves: 8

ISRAELI STEAK SANDWICH   [M]

- 4 minute steaks
- 1/2 tsp salt
- 1/2 tsp fresh ground pepper
- 1/2 tsp paprika
- 1/4 tsp coriander
- 1/2 tsp ground cumin
- 1/8 tsp hot pepper (optional)
- 4 pita breads (very fresh)
- 2 dill pickles, sliced thin
- 2 cups mixed chopped tomatoes, onions, parsley and cucumber
- 1 cup tahini dressing

Place steaks between waxed paper. Flatten by hitting with side of cleaver. Slit steaks in three places. Mix 6 spices and rub into steaks with hands. Grill over high heat or broil on high for 4 to 5 minutes on each side. Warm and split pita, and place steak and salad items in pocket. Top with tahini dressing.

Preparation time: 20 minutes
Cooking time: 8 to 10 minutes
Serves: 4

TAHINI DRESSING   [P]

- 1-1/2 cups sesame seed paste
- 1 cup water
- 1/2 cup fresh lemon juice
- 1 tsp salt
- 2 cloves garlic, mashed
- 1/2 tsp paprika
- 1/4 tsp white pepper

In food processor with metal blade, blend all ingredients until smooth.

Preparation time: 5 minutes
Makes: 3 cups

Will keep well in refrigerator

GLAZED BEEF BRISKET [M]

4-1/2 to 5 lb fresh beef brisket
3 cups beef broth, heated
1 medium onion, quartered
8 whole cloves
4 cloves garlic
5 peppercorns
1 bay leaf
1 cup currant jelly
1/4 cup Dijon mustard
2 green onions, minced
1 tsp curry powder
1/2 tsp coarsely ground black pepper

Preheat oven to 350 degrees.

Trim fat from meat. In large Dutch oven or deep skillet, brown brisket on both sides, starting with fatty side. Pour off excess fat. Add hot broth, onion studded with cloves, garlic, peppercorns and bay leaf. Bring to a boil and then place in oven. Bake 2-1/2 hours or until tender. Drain brisket, reserving cooking liquid and place in shallow, non-stick baking pan. In small saucepan, combine jelly, mustard, green onions, curry powder and pepper. Heat until jelly melts, stirring from time to time. Brush meat with glaze and roast 30 minutes longer, basting frequently with glaze. Heat remaining glaze with 1/4 cup reserved cooking liquid for gravy. Carve brisket into thin slices and serve with gravy.

Preparation time: 15 minutes
Cooking time: 3 hours
Serves: 8

BAR-B-Q BRISKET [M]

Meat:
4 lb brisket
1 tsp garlic powder
1 tsp onion powder
1 tsp seasoned salt

Sauce:
1/3 cup red wine
2 Tbsp Worcestershire sauce
2 Tbsp teriyaki sauce
2 cups water with 1 bouillon cube
 or 1 cup beef broth

Season brisket with garlic powder, onion powder and seasoned salt. Cover and refrigerate overnight. Grill on both sides over charcoal about 45 minutes or until browned. May be done in two steps. Grill one day, refrigerate and roast the next day.

In a roasting pan, pour sauce over brisket and roast, covered, at 350 degrees until tender, 2 to 2-1/2 hours. Remove from roaster, cool, slice and replace in roaster to reheat.

Preparation time: 15 minutes
Cooking time: 2-3/4 to 3-1/4 hours
Serves: 8

ESSIG FLEISCH (SWEET AND SOUR) [M]

3 to 3-1/2 lb boneless chuck roast
1 Tbsp oil
salt, pepper to taste
2 onions, chopped
1/2 cup chopped celery
2 to 3 cloves garlic, pressed

1 cup water
3 Tbsp brown sugar
3 Tbsp wine vinegar
1/2 cup raisins
1 Tbsp grated fresh ginger
2 tsp candied ginger, cut into slivers

Wipe roast with paper towel, sprinkle with salt and pepper and rub with 1 clove garlic pressed through garlic press.

Heat pan, add oil, onions and celery. Stir until onions are browned.

Push vegetables to side of pan and sear meat on both sides. Add water and 2 cloves garlic and stir vegetables and water so that meat is surrounded. Add brown sugar and vinegar. Combine with gravy. Bring mixture to boil, then turn down heat to simmer until meat is almost tender, about 1-1/2 hours.

Add raisins, fresh ginger and candied ginger. Continue to cook until meat is tender, about 1 hour.

Preparation time: 20 minutes
Cooking time: 2-1/2 to 3 hours
Serves: 4

AUSTRO-HUNGARIAN BEEF [M]

4 to 6 lbs beef roast, fat removed
1/2 tsp oregano
1/4 tsp basil
1/2 tsp white pepper
1 tsp paprika
2 cloves garlic, mashed
1/2 cup dry sherry or red wine

2 carrots, chopped
1 onion, chopped
2 stalks celery, chopped
2 Tbsp parsley, chopped
1/2 cup chicken or beef broth
1/2 lb mushrooms, sliced

In the morning: take a large sheet of heavy foil and double it, making sure not to tear it. Place meat on foil and rub with spices and garlic. Pour wine over meat. Seal package tightly and refrigerate, turning occasionally. May marinate all day. Preheat oven to 450 degrees. Remove from refrigerator one hour before cooking. Just before roasting, unfold foil and place all vegetables, except mushrooms, around meat. Reseal and roast 15 to 18 minutes per pound. Remove meat from package and set aside. Place cooked vegetables in food processor and blend until smooth. In saucepan, add vegetable mixture, broth and mushrooms. Cook 5 minutes. Slice meat and serve with sauce.

Preparation time: 15 minutes
Cooking time: 1 to 2 hours
Serves: 6 to 8

ITALIAN-STYLE POT ROAST [M]

2 Tbsp oil
3 to 4 lbs chuck roast
2 large onions, sliced
2 cloves garlic, minced
2 medium carrots, sliced
salt and pepper to taste
3 plum tomatoes, sliced
1/4 tsp dry rosemary

1/4 tsp dry basil
1/4 tsp dry thyme leaves
1/4 tsp dry mustard
2 bay leaves
1/2 cup dry sherry
1/2 cup water
8 oz mushrooms (optional)

Preheat oven to 350 degrees.

In Dutch oven, using 1 tablespoon of oil, brown meat on all sides. Remove meat and set aside. Saute onions in remaining oil until tender. Add garlic and carrots. Season meat with salt and pepper and return to pot. Add tomatoes, seasonings, sherry, and water. Cover pot and place in oven. Bake 2 to 3 hours until meat is tender. Add mushrooms in last 1/2 hour, if desired. Remove bay leaves. When done, strain gravy and refrigerate a few hours till fat has solidified. Remove fat. Blend gravy with the cooked vegtables. This can be left as is or put into a blender. Slice meat and reheat in gravy.

Preparation time: 15 minutes
Cooking time: 2 to 3 hours
Serves: 4 to 6

FRENCH MUSTARD POT ROAST [M]

2 Tbsp oil
3 to 4 lb chuck roast
2 large onions, chopped
2 Tbsp Dijon mustard
2 Tbsp brown sugar
2 Tbsp lemon juice

2 Tbsp Worcestershire sauce
1 tsp garlic powder
1/2 tsp salt
1/2 tsp pepper
1/2 cup water

Preheat oven to 325 degrees.

In a heavy pot, using 1 tablespoon of oil, brown meat on all sides. In separate skillet, saute onions in remaining oil until tender. Spread mustard over meat and add onions. Mix brown sugar, lemon juice, Worcestershire sauce, garlic powder, salt, pepper and water. Pour over roast. Cover and bake 2 to 3 hours. Strain gravy, reserve onions and refrigerate until fat has solidified. Remove fat and place onions and gravy in food processor with metal blade. Process until smooth. Slice meat and heat in gravy.

Preparation time: 15 minutes
Cooking: 2 to 3 hours
Serves: 4 to 6

SHORT RIBS TZIMMES [M]

14 prunes, pitted
water to cover
3 lbs beef short ribs
1-1/2 tsp salt
1/4 tsp pepper
1 Tbsp oil

1 large onion, coarsely chopped
1/4 cup honey
juice of 1 medium lemon
2 to 3 medium sweet potatoes,
  peeled, cut into chunks

Soak prunes in water. Sprinkle ribs with salt and pepper. In large Dutch oven, heat oil, add and brown ribs, drain off excess fat. Add onion and cook over low heat until tender. Skim off fat as it accumulates. Add water in which prunes were soaked, honey and lemon juice. Cover and cook over low heat 1-1/2 hours. Add prunes and sweet potatoes. Taste and add more honey or lemon juice as needed. Cook 30 minutes longer, or until sweet potatoes and meat are tender.

Preparation time: 30 minutes
Cooking time: 2 hours
Serves: 4 to 6

INDONESIAN BAR-B-Q BEEF RIBS [M]

4 lbs short ribs, well trimmed
2 Tbsp sesame oil
1/4 cup soy sauce
2 large cloves garlic, minced
1-1/2 tsp vinegar

1/4 tsp pepper
1 Tbsp toasted sesame seeds, crushed
dash hot pepper sauce
1 green onion, sliced

Cut short ribs, 1/2 inch deep at 1/2 inch intervals, then score in other direction. Combine sesame oil, soy sauce, garlic, vinegar, pepper, sesame seed, hot sauce and green onion in shallow dish, mixing well. Place scored meat in marinade, turning to coat well. Cover and refrigerate four hours, turning once.

Place meat, bone side down, on barbecue grill over high heat or broil, then turn bone side up. When brown, turn and cook meaty side. Turn meat several times during cooking to brown all sides, about 15 minutes. Meat should be well-browned but medium done.

To toast sesame seeds: Bake sesame seeds at 350 degrees about 10 minutes, until golden brown. Watch carefully they burn easily. Crush in a mortar with a pestle or in an electric blender.

Preparation time: 20 minutes, marinate 4 hours
Cooking time: 15 minutes
Serves: 4

BEEF WITH CHINESE PEAS [M]

1 scant tsp sugar
1 scant tsp cornstarch
4 Tbsp soy sauce
1-1/2 lbs minute, flank or
    skirt steak cut into strips
1/2 cup dry sherry
1/2 lb Chinese peas, string removed
5 oz can water chestnuts, drained
5 to 6 fresh mushrooms, sliced
3 Tbsp peanut oil

In a bowl, combine sugar and cornstarch. Add soy to make a paste. Then add wine. Add meat strips and marinate 30 minutes in the refrigerator.

In a heavy skillet, heat 1 tablespoons of oil. Add peas, mushrooms and water chestnuts. Stir-fry for a few minutes. When mushrooms soften and peas are crisp-tender, remove from pan.

Add remaining oil to pan. Heat. Add meat and marinade. Cook quickly for a few minutes, till meat is barely cooked through and sauce thickens. Return vegetables to pan. Heat and serve immediately with steamed or fried rice.

Preparation time: 20 minutes
Cooking time: approximately 15 minutes
Serves: 5 to 6

CREOLE CHILI [M]

1/2 cup chopped onions
2 Tbsp oil
1 lb ground chuck
1 lb can kidney beans, drained
2 1 lb cans tomatoes
6 oz can tomato paste
1 clove garlic, minced
2 to 3 tsp chili powder
1-1/2 tsp oregano
1/4 tsp pepper
1 bay leaf
dash hot pepper sauce
1 cup water
1 cup chopped celery
1 cup chopped green pepper
onion chopped for garnish

In large skillet, saute onions in hot oil until tender but not brown. Add meat, brown lightly. Add beans, tomatoes, tomato paste, seasonings, water and 1/2 cup each of celery and green pepper.

Simmer, uncovered, 1 hour. Add remaining celery and green pepper. Simmer 10 minutes longer. Garnish with onion, if desired.

Preparation time: 20 minutes
Cooking time: 1 hour 10 minutes
Serves: 6 to 8

Recipe may be increased to serve a crowd. Can substitute ground turkey for beef, adding more chili powder to taste.

STUFFED LAMB SHOULDER   [M]

5 lbs lamb shoulder, boned to form pocket
6 cloves garlic
3/4 lbs ground lamb
1-1/2 cups cooked rice
6 to 8 green onions, chopped
1/2 cup chopped parsley
1/2 cup pine nuts
1/2 cup currants
1 Tbsp turmeric
seasoned salt
3 Tbsp tarragon leaves preserved in vinegar, or soak 2 tsp tarragon in 3 Tbsp vinegar, seasoned salt and freshly ground pepper overnight.

Have lamb at room temperature. Slash and insert 4 cloves of slivered garlic. Set aside. Combine ground lamb, rice, remaining garlic, chopped onion, parsley, pine nuts, currants, turmeric, salt and pepper. Place stuffing in the pocket of meat and sew with string or secure with skewers.

Season outside of meat with seasoned salt and pepper. Place half the tarragon on top of the meat. Roast at 450 degrees 10 minutes. Reduce heat to 375 degrees and continue roasting 1-1/2 hours or until meat is tender. Ten minutes before removing lamb from oven, place remaining tarragon over meat.

Let stand in a warm place 10 to 15 minutes before carving.

Preparation time: 15 minutes
Cooking time: 1 hour and 40 minutes
Serves: 6 to 8

LAMB WITH PLUM SAUCE   [M]

6 large lamb chops
1/2 tsp salt
1/4 tsp white pepper
1 tsp garlic powder
1 tsp rosemary
1 tsp curry powder
1/2 cup plum jam
1/4 cup sherry
3 Tbsp lemon juice
1 lemon, sliced for garnish

Season chops with salt, pepper, garlic powder and rosemary. Grill on both sides until done as desired.

Sauce: Heat together, curry powder, jam and sherry until melted. Add lemon juice. To serve, place lemon slice on each chop. Pour on sauce.

Preparation time: 10 minutes
Cooking time: 30 minutes
Serves: 6

LAMB STEW AND COUSCOUS [M]

3 lamb shanks or (2-1/2 lbs) boneless lamb shoulder cut into 1 inch cubes
salt and pepper
flour for dredging
1 Tbsp oil
1 onion, chopped
1 garlic clove, minced
1 lb can tomatoes with liquid
1 cup tomato juice
1 cup water
1-1/4 lbs zucchini, cut in 1 inch chunks
1-1/2 cups canned, drained garbanzo beans
1/2 tsp thyme
1/2 tsp oregano
2 bay leaves
1 yellow turnip (1 to 1-1/2 lbs)
1 large green pepper, cut in strips
1/3 cup raisins, soaked in water
1/3 cup walnuts, large pieces
1-1/2 cups couscous
2 Tbsp melted pareve margarine
fresh parsley, minced for garnish

Dust lamb with salt, pepper and flour and brown in oil in heavy pan. Lower heat. Add onions, garlic, tomatoes, tomato juice, water, 1/2 the zucchini, garbanzos, thyme, oregano, bay leaves, salt and pepper to taste. Cover tightly and simmer one hour.

Pare turnip and cut in large cubes. Add green pepper, turnip and rest of zucchini to pot. Cover and cook 1 hour.

Remove lamb shanks and strip meat from bones. Discard bones, return meat to pot. Add raisins and walnuts.

Cook couscous according to package directions using chicken stock in place of water. Let stand few minutes as directed. Add melted margarine and fluff with fork.

To Serve: Place couscous in warmed large serving dish, pour lamb stew on top and around it. Sprinkle with parsley.

Preparation time: 30 minutes
Cooking time: 3 hours
Serves: 6

This is a basic Moroccan recipe. One can add chicken pieces, cabbage, carrots, fresh tomatoes, halved onions as desired. May flavor couscous with saffron.

INDIAN LAMB CURRY [M]

- 3 Tbsp oil
- 1 large onion, chopped
- 1 clove garlic, minced
- 2 Tbsp curry powder
- 2 large ripe tomatoes, peeled and chopped
- 1 medium green tomato, peeled and chopped
- pinch ground ginger
- 1 cup green peas
- 2 medium carrots, chopped
- 1 medium apple, chopped
- 1 Tbsp raisins
- 2 lbs lamb stew, cubed
- 1 neck of lamb, chopped
- 1 cup boiling water
- dash pepper
- 1 tsp salt
- 1 Tbsp apricot jam

Use two skillets. In one pan, heat the oil. Saute onions and garlic until brown. Add curry powder and heat until well combined, stirring constantly. Add tomatoes, ginger, vegetables, chopped apple and raisins. Remove from heat. In the second pan, sear the cubed meat in its own fat. When the meat is brown, add it to the curry mixture. Add boiling water, salt and pepper. Simmer gently until tender, for about 2 hours. Add boiling water as needed. Add apricot jam at end of cooking. Serve with rice and accompaniments such as fruit-chutney, hard-cooked sieved eggs, chopped green onions, toasted coconut, chopped peanuts and tomatoes.

Preparation time: 20 to 25 minutes
Cooking time: 2-1/2 hours
Serves: 8

May also be made with cooked leftover lamb. Just add cooked meat to other ingredients. Cook 1 hour over medium heat.

OSSO BUCCO (VEAL SHANKS) [M]

6 veal knuckles (1-1/2 to 2-1/4 inch thick)
3 Tbsp olive oil
1 cup flour, seasoned with salt and pepper
1 clove garlic, chopped
1 carrot, chopped or thinly sliced

3 Tbsp chopped parsley
zest of 1/2 lemon
2 Tbsp lemon juice
1 cup dry vermouth
1 to 1-1/2 cups beef broth

Preheat oven to 325 degrees.

Heat oil in a Dutch oven. Roll veal in seasoned flour and brown on all sides. Add rest of ingredients. Bake covered 1-1/2 to 2 hours until tender. Add more broth if needed. Serve with a small fork for marrow.

Preparation time: 10 minutes
Cooking time: 2 hours
Serves: 4 to 6

SHERRIED VEAL [M]

2 Tbsp pareve margarine
2 Tbsp olive oil
salt (optional)
white pepper to taste
1 lb veal scallops
1/2 cup all-purpose flour
1 cup beef broth

1/2 cup chicken broth
2/3 cup dry sherry
2 Tbsp lemon juice
4 clove garlic, chopped
1/2 tsp Worcestershire sauce
fresh parsley, minced for garnish

In heavy skillet over medium heat, melt margarine and oil. Season veal with salt and white pepper. Dredge in flour, shaking off excess. Place meat in pan, careful not to overlap scallops. Saute 1 minute on each side. Remove meat to heated platter and keep warm. Add rest of ingredients. Bring to boil and lower heat, stirring occasionally, until reduced to 3/4 cup. Return meat to skillet and heat through. Sprinkle with parsley before serving.

Preparation time: 15 minutes
Cooking time: 5 minutes
Serves: 4

VEAL STEW WITH GREEN OLIVES [M]

5 Tbsp olive oil
3 large onions, chopped coarsely
4 cloves garlic, minced
15 oz can tomatoes
3-1/2 lbs veal stew
   (chicken can be substituted)
1/2 cup beef broth, salt free preferred
1/2 tsp marjoram
1/4 cup chopped parsley
1 bay leaf
pepper to taste
1 cup green olives, rinsed twice and pitted

Heat oil in large skillet. Add onions, garlic and simmer over low heat 3 to 4 minutes. Add tomatoes, stock, veal stew, marjoram, bay leaf and some of the chopped parsley. Cover and simmer 3 hours. Stir occasionally. About 30 minutes before stew is done, add olives. Continue cooking, adding pepper at the end, as olives will add salt automatically. Add remaining parsley and serve hot.

Preparation time: 20 minutes
Cooking time: 3 hours
Serves: 8

BRAISED VEAL ROAST [M]

2 Tbsp oil
3 to 4 lbs boned veal roast
1/2 cup Port, Madeira or Marsala wine
1 tsp green peppercorns, ground
salt and pepper to taste
1 clove garlic, pressed
1 shallot, minced

In a large heavy pot, heat 2 tablespoons oil and brown meat over high heat. Pour off excess fat. Add wine, crushed green peppercorns, salt, pepper, garlic and shallot. Turn veal over and around in the juices. Cover and cook over low heat 1 to 2 hours until the juices run clear. Baste from time to time during cooking.

Preparation time: 10 minutes
Cooking time: 1 to 2 hours
Serves: 4 to 6

RIB ROAST
WITH MUSHROOM SAUCE   [M]

3 to 4 lbs rib roast	1 can beef broth
1 lb button mushrooms, cleaned and sliced	1 small clove garlic, crushed (optional)
3 Tbsp pareve margarine	1/2 cup dry sherry
1 to 2 tsp flour	salt and pepper to taste

Allow roast to stand at room temperature for at least one hour before cooking. Roast on a rack uncovered according to chart below.

Timing for roasting:
    rare meat: 18 to 20 minutes per lb
    medium rare: 22 minutes per lb
    well done: 25 minutes per lb

When using a meat thermometer in an oven temperature of 375 degrees:
    rare meat: 130 degrees
    medium meat: 140 degrees
    well done: 160 degrees

Sauce:
Saute mushrooms in margarine. Sprinkle flour over sauted mushrooms and shake pan to absorb flour. Add broth, garlic and wine. Stir constantly, until sauce thickens. Add salt and pepper to taste. Serve hot in sauce boat with meat.

Preparation time: 30 minutes
Cooking time: 1 hour or until desired doneness
Serves: 4

POULTRY

"ACTION CAUSES MORE TROUBLES,"
FROM THE SERIES, ***"TRUISMS,"*** **MARBLE, JENNY HOLZER, 1988**

LAG B'OMER—At Lag B'omer Picnics and Outdoor Festivities, Poultry is a Good Choice.

LAG B'OMER

Janet Salter

If you think Lag B'Omer is a picnic...well, it is! It is really the granddaddy of the modern passion for getting out of the house in Springtime—going to the great outdoors and battling crawling and flying insects to build a roaring fire with which to char/burn chickens and call it a barbecue. (Not to be confused with a Bar Mitzvah.) During the picnic, the children play outdoor games in imitation of the students who armed themselves with bows and arrows and pretended to hunt game, when in reality they visited their rabbinical teachers who were in hiding from the Romans. In this manner they were able to continue their studies.

In Israel today, the army holds marksmanship competitions and builds campfires for its own cookouts. Everyone enjoys this playful holiday, except, of course, the chickens!

BASIC ROAST CHICKEN [M]

1 roasting chicken, 4 to 5 lbs
1 large clove garlic
1 small or 1/2 large onion
1/2 apple, sliced

seasoned salt (optional)
1/2 tsp white pepper
2 cloves garlic, crushed
1 tsp tarragon, dried or fresh

Preheat oven to 450 degrees.

Spray roasting pan with non stick substance. Season chicken inside and out with salt and pepper. Place garlic, onion and apple inside cavity of chicken. Rub chicken with garlic and tarragon and roast 60 minutes. Do not baste or turn. Test for doneness by inserting fork into thigh area. Juices should run clear. Discard garlic, onion and apple after cooking.

Preparation time: 5 minutes
Cooking time: 50 to 60 minutes
Serves: 6

Very moist chicken with very crisp skin.

BESTILLA (CHICKEN IN FILO) [M]

3-1/2 lb broiler-fryer, cut up
1 cup onion, minced
1 clove garlic, minced
3/4 cup parsley, minced
1/3 cup cilantro, minced
1 tsp salt (optional)
1 scant tsp pepper
1/8 tsp ground saffron
1/4 tsp turmeric
1/4 tsp coriander
1/4 tsp cumin
1/2 tsp ginger
1 tsp cinnamon

2 3 inch cinnamon sticks
2 cups water
3 Tbsp lemon juice
6 large eggs
salt to taste
2 Tbsp oil
12 oz blanched almonds
1/4 cup powdered sugar
2 tsp cinnamon
3/4 cup unsalted, pareve margarine, melted
1/2 lb filo
powdered sugar
cinnamon

Wash chicken thoroughly and pat dry.

Place chicken in Dutch oven. Add onion, garlic, parsley, cilantro, salt, pepper, saffron, turmeric, coriander, cumin, ginger, cinnamon and cinnamon sticks. Add water. Cover and bring to a boil. Reduce heat and simmer about one hour, turning occasionally, until chicken is tender. Remove chicken from broth and set aside to cool. Cut chicken from bones and into bite size pieces. Bring broth to a boil and reduce to about 1-1/4 cups. Skim off excess fat. Remove cinnamon sticks. Add lemon juice. Beat eggs lightly, pour into simmering broth. Add salt. Cook and stir until eggs are set. Cool and reserve. Heat oil in large skillet. Fry almonds, stirring constantly, until golden brown. Drain on paper towels. Cool and grind in food processor. Set aside about 1/2 cup. Mix remaining almonds with 1/4 cup powdered sugar and 2 tsp cinnamon.   **(Continued on Next Page)**

To Assemble:
Coat bottom and sides of paella pan or deep dish pie pan with melted margarine. Brush a sheet of filo with melted margarine, arrange in pan, allowing excess dough to hang over edge. Sprinkle lightly with almonds. Repeat layers using about half the filo. (Keep unused filo covered with a damp cloth to prevent drying). Turn chicken into pan. Top with egg mixture, then sweetened almonds. Top with remaining layers of filo. Fold ends of filo, one at a time over filling, to make a pie, brushing top and sides of each with margarine, sprinkling with almonds. Brush top with margarine. Bake at 425 degrees 20 to 25 minutes. Invert bestilla onto baking sheet and bake 10 to 15 minutes longer, until golden brown. Turn out onto serving dish. Sprinkle with powdered sugar. Crisscross with cinnamon, forming a diamond pattern. Serve at once.

Preparation time: 45 minutes
Cooking time: 50 minutes
Serves: 12 as appetizers or 8 as an entree.

ARTICHOKE CHICKEN [M]

- 1 chicken, cut up
- 1/2 lb fresh mushrooms, sliced
- 1/4 cup flour
- 1 lb can tomatoes
- 2 cloves garlic, minced
- 1 small jar marinated artichoke hearts, drain and save oil for sauteing chicken.
- 1-1/4 tsp salt (optional)
- 1/2 tsp pepper
- 1/2 tsp dried oregano
- 1/2 tsp dried basil
- 1/2 cup dry sherry
- 1 tsp chicken bouillon

Preheat oven to 375 degrees.

Wash chicken thoroughly and pat dry. Add enough oil from artichokes to cover bottom of large skillet. Saute chicken until lightly brown on both sides.
Remove chicken and place, skin side up, in a 10 X 13 pyrex dish.

Shake the mushrooms in the flour and saute lightly in the same skillet, scraping the bottom of the pan. Add the rest of the ingredients, except the artichokes, to the skillet and bring to a boil, then pour over chicken, cover with foil and bake 40 minutes. Add the artichokes and bake another 10 minutes or until the chicken is done. If doubling the recipe, do not double the wine or the bouillon.

Preparation time: 30 minutes
Cooking time: 50 minutes
Serves: 4 to 5

Can be prepared in advance. Freezes well.

MIDDLE EASTERN CHICKEN [M]

1 cup blanched almonds
1 clove garlic
1/2 inch slice fresh ginger
1/4 tsp ground cumin
1 tsp paprika

1/4 tsp pepper
1 tsp salt (optional)
2-1/2 to 3 lbs chicken, cut up
1/2 cup margarine, melted

Preheat oven 375 degrees.

Place almonds, garlic, and ginger in a food processor with a metal blade or blender and grind finely. Add cumin, paprika, pepper, and salt. Wash and dry chicken thoroughly. Dip chicken into margarine and then roll in almond mixture. Place chicken, skin side up, in 13 X 9 inch baking dish. Bake, uncovered, 55 to 60 minutes. If using boned chicken decrease baking time.

Preparation time: 10 minutes
Cooking time: 55 to 60 minutes
Serves: 6 to 8

JAMAICAN CHICKEN [M]

3-1/2 lb broiler-fryer chicken, quartered
4 large cloves garlic
1 to 2 jalapeno peppers
4 green onions, cut up
3 Tbsp red wine vinegar
3 Tbsp water
2 Tbsp olive oil

2 Tbsp honey
1 tsp salt (optional)
2 tsp ground allspice
2 tsp leaf thyme
1-1/2 tsp ground black pepper
1 bay leaf

Wash chicken thoroughly and pat dry.

In food processor with a metal blade, mince garlic and jalapeno pepper, add green onions and chop finely. Add remaining ingredients, except chicken. Process until smooth paste forms. Coat chicken, placing some of the mixture under the skin. Place chicken in baking dish, cover and let marinate in refrigerator for one hour or overnight. Remove chicken from refrigerator, remove from marinade, and place over medium hot grill. Grill 45 minutes to one hour until cooked through, but still moist, turning and basting at least once. Alternate method of cooking: Bake in oven at 375 degrees about one hour, turning once. Discard marinade.

Preparation time: 5 minutes
Cooking time: 45 to 60 minutes
Serves: 4

SESAME CHICKEN [M]

3 chickens (or chicken parts)
1/2 cup salad oil
2 medium lemons, juiced
1/2 cup soy sauce
6 cloves garlic, crushed

2 tsp ginger (or 3 to 4 tsp fresh ginger, grated)
1/2 cup white wine
1 cup sesame seeds
1/2 cup bread crumbs

Wash chicken thoroughly and pat dry.

Combine oil, lemon juice, soy sauce, garlic, ginger and white wine. Pour over chicken. Marinate chicken overnight or several hours. May place chicken in plastic bag with marinade. Turn pieces of chicken in marinade to coat evenly. Line a baking pan with extra-heavy aluminum foil. Combine sesame seeds with bread crumbs. Dip each piece of chicken, skin side only, in the mixture. Place on pan, skin side up. Bring marinade to boil, cook 5 minutes, then pour around chicken. Bake 30 to 40 minutes in 400 degree oven. Do not overcook chicken. Boned breasts only need 20 to 25 minutes. Serve hot or cold.

Preparation time: 15 minutes
Cooking time: 40 to 45 minutes
Serves: 12 or more

HONEY GLAZED CHICKEN WITH APPLES [M]

2 frying chickens, cut up
pepper to taste
salt (optional)
garlic powder to taste
3 Tbsp pareve margarine, melted
8 apples, peeled, cored, quartered

1/2 cup honey
1/2 cup apple juice
1 Tbsp brown sugar
2 tsp grated lemon zest
2 tsp grated orange zest
1/2 cup orange marmalade

Preheat oven to 375 degreees.

Wash and dry chicken thoroughly. Sprinkle chicken pieces with pepper and garlic powder. Melt margarine. Place apples around edges of two 9 X 13 inch casserole dishes. Place chicken in center. Drizzle margarine over all. Roast for 30 minutes. Drain liquid. In small pan heat apple juice, honey, brown sugar, lemon and orange rind. Baste chicken and apples with this mixture. Continue baking for 15 to 25 minutes, basting every 10 minutes to glaze.

Preparation time: 20 minutes
Cooking time: 45 to 55 minutes
Serves: 8

ISRAELI POMEGRANATE CHICKEN   [M]

1 frying chicken, cleaned and quartered
1 qt pomegranate juice (available in health food or Middle Eastern shops)
2 cloves of garlic, crushed
1/2 tsp pepper
1/2 tsp ground cumin
2 Tbsp olive oil
1 large onion, chopped
1 can black or green olives, drained
1/2 cup pine nuts

Wash and dry chicken thoroughly.

Marinate chicken overnight in pomegranate juice, garlic, pepper and cumin. Remove from marinade. Pat chicken dry. In saucepan, reduce marinade by boiling, about 10 to 15 minutes. Reserve. Heat oil in a large skillet, brown chicken over high heat. Add onions, olives, pine nuts, and reduced marinade. Reduce heat to low and cook chicken one hour or until chicken juices run clear.

Preparation time: 20 minutes
Cooking time: 1 hour
Serves: 4

CHICKEN FIDEO   [M]

1 large egg
1 Tbsp lemon juice
1/4 cup flour
1/4 tsp garlic powder
1/4 tsp paprika
4 chicken breasts, skinned and boned
1/4 cup pareve margarine
3/4 cup chicken broth
3 Tbsp lemon juice

Wash chicken thoroughly and pat dry.

Beat egg with 1 tablespoon lemon juice. Combine flour, garlic powder and paprika. Dip chicken in egg mixture and then in flour mixture. In a large skillet, melt margarine. Add chicken and brown on both sides.

Add broth and remaining lemon juice. Cover and simmer 20 to 25 minutes. Serve over fideo noodles. See following recipe.

Preparation time: 10 minutes
Cooking time: 20 to 25 minutes
Serves: 4

FIDEO (COIL VERMICELLI)   [P]

8 coils vermicelli
2 Tbsp oil
3-1/2 cups hot water
Salt and pepper to taste

In non-stick frying pan, with lid, saute noodles in oil to brown slightly. When brown, add water carefully. Cover and cook about 5 minutes. With a fork, break coils open. Recover. Cook 5 minutes until water is absorbed and fideo are al dente.

Cooking time: 10 minutes

CHICKEN PUERTO VALLARTA [M]

5 chicken breasts
1/2 cup bread crumbs or matzo meal
1/3 cup oil
1/2 medium onion, minced
1 medium green pepper, diced
2-1/2 cups canned tomatoes
1 cup raisins, steeped in 1/4 cup sherry
6 oz can black olives
1 tsp cumin
2 tsp oregano
salt and pepper to taste
2 large limes, sliced

Wash and dry chicken thoroughly.

Roll chicken in crumbs. Heat oil in skillet and brown chicken. Remove chicken. In same skillet, saute onions and green pepper until golden. Add tomatoes, raisins, olives and seasoning. Simmer, covered, for 25 minutes. Line bottom of casserole with slices of lime. Layer sauce, then chicken, and then more sauce. Bake, covered, for 30 minutes at 350 degrees.

Preparation time: 15 minutes
Cooking time: 55 minutes
Serves: 5

KABUKI CHICKEN [M]

1 small red pepper, seeded and chopped
1 Tbsp chopped green onion
1-1/2 Tbsp sesame seeds, ground in blender
2 Tbsp soy sauce
2 Tbsp sake (Japanese rice wine), or dry sherry
10 to 14 oz boneless chicken breast cut in thin strips
1 small tomato, diced
1 small cucumber, peeled and diced
2 Tbsp rice noodles, reconstituted
1 Tbsp sesame oil or peanut oil
2 Tbsp rice vinegar
1 tsp white pepper
1 Tbsp sugar

Mix red pepper, onions, sesame seeds, soy sauce and sake to make a marinade. Add chicken and marinate for 1 hour. Soak noodles in hot water for 5 minutes until soft. Drain. Heat oil in a large skillet or wok. Remove chicken from marinade and reduce marinade by boiling for 5 minutes. Saute chicken in skillet for about 5 minutes until opaque. Combine rice vinegar, white pepper, and sugar. Add to chicken and cook for 5 minutes. Add marinade and cook 1 minute more. Add tomato and cucumber to noodles. Toss with chicken.

Preparation Time: 15 minutes
Cooking time: 10 to 12 minutes
Serves: 2 to 3

ORANGE GINGER CHICKEN [M]

8 chicken breasts, skinned, bone in
1/2 cup soy sauce
1/3 cup honey
2 oranges juiced

2 Tbsp orange zest
3 cloves garlic, minced
2 Tbsp fresh ginger, grated

Preheat oven to 350 degrees.

In a large baking pan, place chicken, bone side up in a single layer. Combine soy sauce, honey, orange juice, grated orange zest, garlic and ginger. Pour 3/4 of mixture over chicken. Bake 30 minutes, basting occasionally. Turn chicken and pour remaining sauce over all. Baste and bake another 30 minutes or until juices run clear. If using boneless chicken, decrease cooking time.

Preparation time: 15 minutes
Cooking time: 1 hour
Serves: 8

CHICKEN WITH DRIED FRUIT [M]

6 lbs chicken (2 fryers, quartered)
1 inch piece fresh ginger, peeled and
   sliced (or 1 tsp dry ginger)
1-1/2 cups orange marmalade
Fresh ground pepper to taste
1 tsp salt (optional)

1/2 cup orange juice
1/2 cup apple juice
8 oz dried nectarines, peaches or
   apricots, chopped
1 cup currants or raisins
1/2 cup dark brown sugar

Preheat oven 375 degrees.

Wash and dry chicken, place in pan, skin side up. Season with ginger, salt and pepper. Dab marmalade on each piece of chicken. This will form a glaze. Add juices and bake 25 minutes. Add fruit and brown sugar. Bake another 45 minutes, basting occasionally.

Preparation time: 15 minutes
Cooking time: 70 minutes
Serves: 6 to 8

HONEY NUTTY CHICKEN [M]

1/4 cup honey
2 Tbsp Worcestershire sauce
2 Tbsp vegetable oil
1 Tbsp lemon juice
salt and pepper to taste

1-1/2 to 3 lbs chicken, cut up
3/4 cup crushed cornflakes or
   cornflake crumbs
1/3 cup finely chopped peanuts
   (salted may be used)

Wash chicken thoroughly and pat dry.

Combine honey, Worcestershire sauce, oil and lemon juice. Add salt and pepper to taste. Pour over chicken, coating completely. Cover and refrigerate overnight turning once.

(Continued on Next Page)

Combine cornflake crumbs and nuts. Lift chicken pieces from marinade. Coat with crumb mixture. Arrange on rack, skin side up in a shallow pan. Bake in a 350 degree oven until chicken is fork tender, about one hour.

Sauce:
2 Tbsp pareve margarine
2 Tbsp water
2 Tbsp honey
1/4 cup chopped nuts
1 tsp prepared mustard

In a heavy saucepan, melt margarine over medium heat. Add remaining sauce ingredients, stirring to blend. Continue cooking over medium heat until sauce comes to full boil (1 to 2 minutes). Serve honey sauce to spoon over chicken.

Preparation time: 20 minutes
Cooking time: 1 hour
Serves: 4

CHICKEN STIR-FRY [M]

3/4 lb boneless, skinless chicken breast, cut into bite sized pieces
2 Tbsp dry sherry
1 Tbsp soy sauce
1/2 tsp sugar
1/8 tsp pepper
1 Tbsp cornstarch
3 Tbsp oil
1 clove garlic, minced
1 inch piece fresh ginger, peeled and minced
1 medium onion, sliced
2 stalks celery, sliced diagonally
1/2 green pepper, sliced
2 green onions, cut into 1 inch pieces
2 to 3 stalks bok choy, sliced diagonally
3 slices jicama, sliced julienne or 1/2 can water chestnuts, sliced
4 medium mushrooms, sliced
2 oz Chinese pea pods
1/4 lb bean sprouts
3/4 cup chicken broth
1/2 tsp sugar
2 Tbsp soy sauce
1 Tbsp cornstarch
1 Tbsp cold water
hot cooked rice

Wash chicken thoroughly and pat dry.

In small bowl, combine sherry, soy sauce, sugar and pepper. Add chicken and marinate 10 minutes. Blend in cornstarch. In wok or large skillet, heat 1 tablespoon oil to very hot. Add garlic and ginger and saute briefly. Add chicken, cook and stir until opaque. Remove from pan and reserve. To juices remaining in pan, add onion, celery and green pepper. Stir-fry 1 minute. Add green onion and bok choy and saute 1 minute longer. Remove to plate. In same pan, heat 1 tablespoon oil, add jicama and mushrooms and stir-fry 30 seconds, add pea pods and bean sprouts and stir-fry 30 seconds longer. Return chicken and vegetables to pan. Add chicken broth mixed with sugar and soy sauce. Add cornstarch blended with water. Cook and stir until thickened, 5 minutes. Add additional soy sauce if desired. Serve with hot cooked rice.

Preparation time: 25 minutes.
Cooking time: 10 to 15 minutes
Serves: 4

May substitute boned turkey breast and/or any firm, sliced, fresh vegetables you have on hand.

APPLES STUFFED WITH CURRIED CHICKEN [M]

8 large cooking apples
1/2 cup raisins
1/2 cup brandy
2 Tbsp pareve margarine
2 Tbsp flour
1 cup chicken broth
1/2 lb cooked chicken, ground
4 cups cooked rice

1/2 cup chopped walnuts
2 Tbsp brown sugar
1/2 tsp cinnamon
1/2 tsp powdered cloves
1/2 tsp powdered ginger
1 tsp curry powder
2 cups green peas, parboiled

Preheat oven to 300 degrees. Grease baking dish and oven proof bowl.

Core apples. Scoop out leaving 1/2 inch of shell. Set apple shells aside. Save pulp for another use. Soak raisins in brandy.

In a large skillet, melt margarine. Sprinkle with flour. Cook about 2 minutes, stirring constantly, until it boils. Add remaining ingredients, except peas. Mix well. Stuff apples. Place extra stuffing in bowl and stuffed apples in baking dish. Cover both containers with foil and place in pans half filled with water. Bake 40 minutes or until apples are tender. On a large platter, unmold stuffing in center. Surround with apples.

Sprinkle peas over center mixture.

Preparation time: 30 minutes
Cooking time: 40 minutes
Serves: 8

APRICOT CORNISH HENS [M]

12 oz apricots, dried
1 cup brown sugar
1-1/2 cup water
1/2 cup apricot preserves
1/3 cup soy sauce

1/2 cup dry sherry
3 cloves garlic, pressed
1 Tbsp wine vinegar
1 Tbsp fresh ginger, grated
4 Cornish hens, cut in half

In a saucepan combine apricots, brown sugar and water. Cook 20 minutes over medium heat. Remove from heat and add preserves, soy sauce, sherry, garlic, vinegar and ginger. Wash hens, pat dry and remove excess fat. In bottom of a roasting pan, spoon a little sauce and place hens one layer deep, cut side down. Pour remaining sauce over hens. Marinate several hours in refrigerator. One hour before baking, remove from refrigerator.

Place in 350 degree oven for 1 hour or until juices run clear when pierced with a fork. Baste occasionally.

May be kept in a 275 degree oven for 10 to 15 minutes before serving.

Preparation time: 25 minutes
Cooking time: 1 hour
Serves: 8

GREEK STYLE CORNISH GAME HENS [M]

4 large game hens or 8 small, split
1 jar grape leaves, drained
8 slices kosher beef-fry (optional)
4 Tbsp white wine
giblets from hens
1 lb fresh mushrooms, sliced
1 Tbsp olive oil
1 Tbsp Madeira wine
1 Tbsp red wine
1 tsp salt (optional)
1 tsp white pepper
1 whole shallot, chopped fine

Preheat oven to 350 degrees. Wash hens thoroughly and pat dry. Remove excess fat from hens.

Rinse grape leaves several times to remove salt. Place game hens on rack and cover with grape leaves, beef-fry (optional) and secure with string. If not using beef-fry, salt and pepper before wrapping leaves around game hens. Roast for 1 hour, basting every half hour, using white wine to keep leaves moist and turning hens every time.

In a small saucepan place giblets, cover with water. Bring to a boil and simmer 30 minutes. Remove neck bone and place remainder in a food processor and grind.

Saute mushrooms and shallot in oil until brown. Add giblets, Madeira and red wine to this mixture. Simmer 5 to 10 minutes. Season with salt and pepper to taste. Remove hens from oven and remove string. Place on platter and spoon sauce over and around hens.

Preparation time: 25 minutes
Cooking time: 1 hour
Serves: 8

GROUND TURKEY OR CHICKEN LOAF [M]

1 lb ground turkey or chicken breast
3 green onions, chopped
1 cup soft bread crumbs
1 cup salt-free chicken broth
2 tsp curry powder
2 tsp rosemary, dried or 1-1/2 Tbsp fresh
1 large egg white

Glaze:
1 Tbsp soy sauce
1 tsp brown sugar
2 Tbsp water

Preheat oven to 350 degrees.

Using a food processor with a metal blade, chop onions then add other ingredients and mix. Turn mixture into a 5 X 8 inch loaf pan. Combine soy, brown sugar and water. Pour over loaf, cover with foil and bake 30 minutes. Uncover and bake 30 minutes longer.

Preparation time: 10 minutes
Baking time: 1 hour
Serves: 4 to 6

DO AHEAD TURKEY ROAST [M]

13 to 14 lb turkey
salt (optional)
pepper and paprika
4 large onions, sliced
5 large cloves garlic, minced

2 Kosher beef bouillon cubes
   dissolved in 2 cups hot water
1/2 cup dry white wine
a few sprigs of fresh rosemary
a few sprigs of fresh basil

Preheat oven to 425 degrees. Wash turkey thoroughly inside and out.

Season with spices. Rub all over with garlic. Fill cavity with 1 cup of chopped onions. Place sprigs of rosemary and basil inside of cavity and under wings. In large roasting pan, place remaining onions. Over onions, pour broth made by dissolving beef cubes in hot water and wine. Place turkey on top of onions, breast side down. Cook turkey for 40 minutes, covered loosely. Reduce oven to 350 degrees and continue to cook for another two hours. Turn turkey over and continue cooking for another 45 minutes. Remove turkey to a platter. Deglaze pan with water or wine. Strain pan juices and refrigerate. Remove any fat that has formed on top of pan juices. Reheat gravy and serve with turkey.

If made a day ahead, turkey is easily sliced and may be heated in gravy.

Preparation time: 12 to 15 minutes
Cooking time: 3-1/2 hours
Serves: 12 to 14

SMOKED TURKEY [M]

10 to 12 lb turkey
salt and pepper
4 cloves garlic, sliced
1/3 cup liquid smoke

1 bay leaf
6 peppercorns
1 Tbsp mustard seeds
1 cup boiling water

Wash turkey thoroughly and pat dry.

Rub turkey in and out with garlic, salt and pepper. Insert sliced garlic under skin with knife. Brush in and out with liquid smoke. Add spices. Refrigerate overnight.

Preheat oven to 500 degrees. Place turkey in roasting pan and bake 20 minutes. Pour 1 cup boiling water in pan. Reduce oven temperature to 375 degrees and continue to bake for 2-1/2 hours. Cool. Best served cold

Preparation time: 10 minutes
Cooking time: 3 to 3 1/2 hours
Serves: 12

TURKEY BREAST CHAMPAGNE [M]

1/2 tsp celery salt
1/4 tsp pepper
3 Tbsp pareve margarine, melted
1 whole turkey breast (5 to 6 lbs)
2 leeks, sliced and washed well
1-1/2 cups chicken broth
1 Tbsp parsley, minced
1 tsp orange zest
1/4 tsp thyme
1/4 tsp tarragon
2 cups champagne or dry white wine

Wash turkey thoroughly and pat dry.

Combine celery salt, pepper and margarine. Brush over turkey breast. Place in pan on low rack of oven and roast at 425 degree for 20 minutes. Combine remaining ingredients (except wine) and pour over turkey. Reduce heat to 350 degrees for 1/2 hour. Pour wine over turkey and continue cooking for 1-1/2 hours. Baste frequently.

Preparation time: 10 minutes
Cooking time: 2 hours and 20 minutes
Serves: 6

TURKEY CHILI [M]

2 medium onions, diced
2 cloves garlic, minced
1 medium green pepper, diced
2 lbs ground turkey
28 oz can peeled tomatoes, drained and liquid reserved
30 oz can vegetarian chili beans
27 oz can vegetarian kidney beans, rinsed and drained.
1 Tbsp chili powder
1 tsp cumin powder
1 bay leaf
salt, pepper and cayenne pepper to taste

In a saucepan, sprayed with non-stick spray, saute onions, garlic and green pepper. Reserve. Saute ground turkey until no longer pink. Add reserved vegetables, tomatoes, chili beans, with liquid, and kidney beans. Add chili powder, cumin, bay leaf and spices. Simmer until flavors are blended. Cook 30 minutes. Add juice from tomatoes as needed. Season to taste. May be frozen.

Preparation time: 20 to 25 minutes
Cooking time: 35 minutes
Serves: 8 to 10

TURKEY MOLE [M]

6 to 8 lb turkey, cut up
water to cover turkey plus 2 inches
2 tsp salt (optional)
3 medium green peppers
2 Tbsp sesame seeds
6 garlic cloves
1 slice dry white toast
1/2 cup almonds, ground

8 tomatoes
1/2 tsp cinnamon
1/4 tsp pepper
2 to 3 Tbsp chili powder (start with
    2 Tbsp and add more to taste)
2 oz unsweetened chocolate, grated
1/4 cup olive oil

Wash turkey thoroughly.

Cover turkey with water in a deep soup kettle. Cook until turkey is thoroughly done, about one hour. Drain turkey, reserving 2 cups of stock. Pat turkey dry with paper towels. While turkey is boiling, grind remaining ingredients, except oil, in blender. Heat oil in a large skillet and brown turkey. Remove from pan and cut into bite-size pieces. In same pan cook the spice mixture for 5 minutes on a low flame, stirring constantly. Add reserved turkey stock. Place turkey and all ingredients in a flame proof casserole and cover. Cook on top of stove, stirring occasionally, over a low flame, or 350 degree oven, for 2 hours.

Preparation time: 20 minutes
Cooking time: 3 to 4 hours.
Serves: 12

CRANBERRY CHESTNUT STUFFING [M]

12 oz fresh cranberries
2-1/2 cups chicken broth
8 cups stale challah, torn into
    bite-size pieces
11 oz can or jar whole chestnuts, with juice
2 Tbsp oil
4 stalks celery, chopped

2 large onions, chopped
1 Tbsp dried parsley or
    4 Tbsp fresh, chopped
1 cup pecans
2 large eggs, beaten
1 tsp white pepper

Preheat oven to 350 degrees.

In a large bowl place bread and broth. Mix to moisten. Add cranberries and chestnuts with juice. In a skillet, heat oil, saute vegetables until limp but not brown. Add to bread mixture. Add pecans, eggs and pepper. Mix well. Place mixture in a three quart baking dish. Cover with foil and bake 1 hour. May be frozen.

Preparation time: 25 minutes
Cooking time: 1 hour
Serves: 10 to 12

FRUIT STUFFING [P]

(for 20 lb turkey)

1 cup dried apricots
1 cup raisins
1 cup pitted prunes
1/2 cup currants
1/4 cup Grand Marnier or Curacao
1/4 cup pareve margarine
3 large tart apples, diced, unpeeled
3 large onions, diced
3 stalks celery, diced
1 cup unsalted cashew nuts
1 cup pecans
1 cup almonds
12 oz fresh cranberries
1 tsp ground ginger
1 tsp cinnamon
1 tsp tarragon
1 cup minced fresh parsley
2 tsp salt
2 large eggs, beaten

Mix dried fruit together with liqueur and marinate overnight in refrigerator. In large pan, melt margarine and saute apples, onions and celery for 10 minutes. Mix in remaining ingredients. May be used to stuff a 20 lb turkey or baked in a greased casserole for one hour, at 350 degrees.

Preparation time: 30 minutes
Cooking time: 1 hour

Never leave stuffing inside turkey before or after cooking.
This is a very rich and delicious alternative to a bread stuffing.

DIFFERENT WAYS WITH DUCKLING [M]

General instructions for cooking duck:

1 duck
1 tsp salt
1/2 tsp white pepper

Preheat oven to 375 degrees.

Clean and remove as much fat as possible from duck. Prick skin all over with fork. Mix together salt and pepper and spread lightly with fingers inside and outside of duck. Roast about 2 hours. Prick with fork into leg meat. When juice runs clear, duck is done. Duck should be brown all over and skin should be crisp.

Remove from oven. Let cool. Pour juices in jar. Refrigerate and when cold remove fat. Cut duck into quarters. To finish cooking, see page 198.

Serves: 4

Stock for sauce:

neck, gizzard and heart of duck
1/2 onion
1 carrot
1 stalk celery
1/2 cup parsley
1/2 tsp salt
1/4 tsp pepper
water to cover plus two inches

Cook all ingredients over high heat to boiling. Reduce heat and simmer until giblets are soft when pierced with a fork. Strain and reserve broth.

Makes: about 3 to 4 cups.

CHERRY STUFFING [P]

1 cup canned or dried cherries,
    drain and reserve liquid
2 cups rice, cooked
1/2 tsp salt
1 cup syrup from canned cherries or
    1 cup water if dried cherries are used

1/2 cup orange juice
1 Tbsp mixed Italian herbs
    (oregano, basil, thyme)
1/2 cup onion, chopped
2 Tbsp pareve margarine
2 Tbsp parsley, chopped

Mix together. Place in casserole and heat in oven while duck is reheating in sauce.

MANGO SAUCE [M]

2/3 cup orange juice
1 cup fresh, frozen or
    canned mango, mashed
1/2 Tbsp pareve margarine
2 Tbsp cornstarch

3 Tbsp duck stock
1 Tbsp cognac
2 tsp sugar
1 tsp orange rind, grated
pinch of salt

In a heavy skillet, melt margarine, add cornstarch and stir well. Add liquids a little at a time. Add rest of ingredients and bring to a boil. May be thinned with a little additional stock.

Reheating in sauce:

Preheat oven to 350 degrees.

Place duck in a roasting pan, cover with sauce. Reheat in oven for 3/4 to 1 hour until it is heated through.

GREEN PEPPER SAUCE [M]

12 Tbsp duck stock
pan juices from duck (skim of fat)

4 Tbsp olive oil
1/2-oz green peppercorns

Add pan juices to stock. Boil until consistency of cream. Pass through a sieve. Add oil and peppercorns. Reheat duck in this sauce.

Good if you want a variation that is not sweet.

Preparation time: for duck, 15 minutes
                for stock, 10 minutes
                for stuffing, 15 minutes
                for mango sauce, 15 to 20 minutes
                for green peppercorn sauce, 10 minutes

This recipe from Australia is a nice variation from the traditional orange flavored French style. However, any recipe for duck should follow the basic instructions. This method insures that all fat will be removed before the final cooking and serving.

Note: Most domestically raised ducks have a small amount of flesh. One duck should serve 4. It is always as easy to cook more than one at a time. Leftovers can be frozen. The cherry stuffing mix could serve 8 to 10.

COOKIES

"TREE OF LIFE," **WALL HANGING, PHILIP RATNER**

PURIM—Hamantaschen (Haman's Pockets) Say "Purim" With Their Distinctive Shape and Varied Fillings.

200 COOKIES

PURIM
Janet Salter

The two thousand year war ended among the growers and producers of apricots, prunes and poppyseeds in the 20th century. It was finally determined that as long as you add a cup of chopped walnuts (or pecans or almonds) to the filling of the hamantaschen you can't go wrong!

Now, whether cookie dough or yeast dough should form the three-cornered goodies…that comes from your own bubbie. Ours always said, "As long as you make it with love it will be a success!"

HAMANTASCHEN [D]

Yeast Dough
2 pkg active dry yeast
1/2 cup warm water
1/2 cup sweet butter
3 Tbsp sugar
3 large egg yolks
2-1/4 cups all-purpose flour
4 Tbsp non-fat dry milk powder
1/4 tsp salt

Dissolve yeast in warm water. Cream butter with sugar. Beat in egg yolks. Combine 2 cups flour, non-fat dry milk and salt. Add yeast mixture alternately with flour mixture. If dough is sticky, add remaining flour until smooth. Place dough in an oiled bowl, turning to grease top of dough. Cover and refrigerate several hours or overnight. Divide dough into quarters. Divide each into 12 sections. Roll each on floured board to 3-1/2 or 4 inch rounds. Brush edges of round with water. Place a spoonful of filling in center and pinch three sides together to form triangle. Place on greased baking sheets. Bake at 350 degrees for 15 minutes, until lightly browned. After 10 minutes of baking, if seams open, pinch together gently and continue baking. Remove to wire rack to cool.

Preparation time: 30 minutes, plus refrigeration
Baking time: 15 minutes
Makes: 20 to 24

[P] Cookie Dough:
3 large eggs
3/4 cup sugar
1/2 cup oil
juice and zest of 1/2 lemon
juice and zest of 1/2 orange
1 tsp vanilla
3-1/2 to 4-1/2 cups all-purpose flour
2 tsp baking powder

Beat eggs, add ingredients except flour and baking powder. Combine flour and baking powder and work into other ingredients until dough can be handled. Turn out on floured board and knead until dough does not stick to your hands. Cut dough into quarters. Roll out to 1/8 inch thickness. Using 4 inch round cutter, cut out circles of dough. Fill each with a tablespoon filling. Pull up two sides, then the third and pinch edges together to form 3 cornered pocket. Place on greased cookie sheet. Brush tops with slightly beaten egg yolk. Bake at 375 degrees 20 minutes until nicely browned.

Preparation time: 30 minutes plus refrigeration
Baking time: 20 to 25 minutes
Makes: 30 large

[D] Pastry Dough:
1-1/2 cups sifted all-purpose flour
1/4 cup sugar
1/2 tsp salt
1 cup sweet butter
3 large egg yolks
3 Tbsp white or cider vinegar
3 Tbsp cold water
1 cup sifted all-purpose flour

In mixing bowl, combine flour, sugar, salt and butter, rubbing butter into flour with fingers. Mix egg yolks with a fork, add vinegar and water. Add remaining flour, mixing together lightly. Combine both mixtures, blending well with a fork. Cover and refrigerate several hours or overnight. Pinch off walnut size balls and roll out on floured board to 3-1/2 inch

(Continued on Next Page)

rounds. Place a spoonful filling in center. Pinch sides together, forming a closed triangle. Seal well. Place on ungreased cookie sheet. Bake at 375 degrees 20 minutes, until golden brown. Remove to wire rack to cool.

Preparation time: 20 minutes plus refrigeration
Baking time: 20 minutes
Makes: 3 dozen

Dough may be mixed in food processor until it forms a ball, using on/off pulse speed.

Dried Fruit Filling:
10 oz pitted prunes
1/4 pound dried apricots
water or sweet wine to cover
3/4 cup chopped walnuts
2 Tbsp sugar or to taste
grated zest and juice of 1 lemon
1/2 tsp cinnamon
2 Tbsp prune liquid

In a saucepan, cook prunes and apricots in water until tender, about 30 minutes. Drain and reserve liquid. Chop in food processor. Add nuts and process until finely chopped. Add sugar, lemon peel and juice, cinnamon and prune liquid, mixing well.

Preparation time: 10 minutes
Cooking time: 30 minutes
Makes: filling for 2 dozen

Apricot filling:
1/2 pound dried apricots
1/4 cup apricot nectar or water
grated peel of 1 lemon
1 tsp lemon juice
1/4 cup finely chopped walnuts

In small saucepan, combine apricots, apricot nectar, lemon peel and juice. Cook 20 minutes until apricots are tender. Remove from heat and let cool. Process in food processor until pureed, add nuts and process until blended.

Preparation time: 5 minutes
Cooking time: 20 minutes
Makes: filling for 2 dozen

Poppy Seed Filling:
12 oz can poppy seed filling
1 cup raisins, plumped in
   hot water 15 minutes
rind of 1 lemon
rind of 1 orange

In mixing bowl, combine all ingredients.

Preparation time: 5 minutes
Makes: filling for 1 recipe of dough

ITALIAN HAMANTASCHEN [P]

1/2 cup plus 2 Tbsp sweet wine
2 cups flour
1 Tbsp sugar

1/2 cup olive oil
1 Tbsp grated orange rind
1/4 tsp ground cinnamon

Heat wine (do not boil). Mix all ingredients with hands and knead as you go until dough is smooth and elastic. Cover and refrigerate until ready to use (about 3-1/2 hours).

Filling:
3/4 cup dark raisins
2 Tbsp sweet wine
1/2 cup pecans, chopped

1 oz semisweet chocolate, chopped
1/2 tsp grated lemon rind
2 Tbsp honey
1/2 cup powdered sugar

Marinate raisins in wine for 3 hours. Drain. Combine all ingredients and add raisins. Preheat oven to 350 degrees.

Roll out dough to 1/8 inch on floured surface. Cut into 4 inch rounds. Place filling evenly on each round. Shape into triangles and moisten edges with water to seal, leaving a little open space at top. Place on cookie sheet. Bake for 20 minutes or until browned. Dust with powdered sugar when cool.

Preparation time: 30 minutes plus 3 hours of marinating
Baking time: 20 minutes
Makes: 24

CINNAMON MANDELBRODT [P]

3 large eggs
1 cup sugar
3/4 cup oil
1 tsp almond or vanilla extract
pinch of salt

3-1/4 cups flour
2 tsp baking powder
3/4 cups almonds, chopped
2 tsp cinnamon

Preheat oven to 375 degrees. Grease cookie sheet

In a bowl, cream eggs and sugar. Add oil, almond or vanilla extract and salt. Beat in flour, baking powder and nuts. Divide batter into 4 parts on a large cookie sheet. Shape into long rolls and sprinkle with cinnamon. Bake for 30 minutes or until brown. Remove each roll carefully, slice immediately into diagonal slices about 1/2 inch thick. Lay each flat on cookie sheet and return to a low oven (250 degrees) until nicely browned.

Preparation time: 30 minutes
Baking time: 50 to 60 minutes
Makes: 4 dozen

CHOCOLATE CHIP MANDELBRODT [P]

3 large eggs, beaten
1 cup sugar
1 cup oil
3 cups sifted all-purpose flour
1 tsp baking powder

1 tsp cinnamon
2 tsp almond or vanilla extract
1/2 to 1 cup ground almonds
8 oz chocolate chips
1/2 tsp salt

For topping:
2 Tbsp sugar and 1 tsp cinnamon

Preheat oven to 350 degrees. Oil cookie sheet.

Mix all ingredients together. May use processor. Pat into 3 rolls. Place rolls on cookie sheet. Sprinkle top with sugar and cinnamon. Bake for 30 minutes. Remove from oven and cut into 1/2 inch diagonal slices. Return to oven at 250 degrees for 20 minutes or until golden brown. Cool on racks. Store in air tight container. Variation: May add 1 cup chopped dried fruit.

Preparation time: 25 minutes
Baking time: 1 hour
Makes: 5 dozen

RUGELACH [D]

Filling:
1 cup ground pecans
1 cup currants
1/2 cup sugar
1 tsp cinnamon
12 oz apricot jam

Dough:
1/2 lb cream cheese, room temperature
2 sticks butter
2 cups all-purpose flour
2 Tbsp sugar
Powdered sugar

For filling: Combine pecans, currants, sugar and cinnamon

For dough: Combine cream cheese, butter, flour and sugar in a large bowl or mix in food processor for a few seconds until it forms a ball. Divide dough into four pieces. Dust each with flour, shaking off excess. Roll each piece between sheets of waxed paper into 10 inch circle. Refrigerate 1 hour.

Preheat oven to 375 degrees. Line baking sheet with foil, shiny side up. Spread each circle of dough with apricot jam. Divide filling among circles spreading evenly. Cut into 12 wedges. Roll up each wedge from bottom edge to point. Arrange on prepared sheet, point side down. Bake until golden, about 20 minutes. Transfer to wire rack to cool. Dust with powdered sugar. Store cookies in airtight container.

Preparation time: 25 minutes
Baking time: 20 minutes
Makes: 48

TRADITIONAL PFEFFERNUESSE [P]

2-1/2 cups all-purpose flour
1/4 tsp ground black pepper
1/2 tsp salt
1/2 tsp anise seed
1/2 tsp ground cinnamon
1/4 tsp baking soda
1/4 tsp ground allspice
1/8 tsp ground cloves
1/8 tsp ground nutmeg
1/2 cup pareve margarine
1/2 cup light, unsulphured molasses
1/2 cup sugar
1 large egg
1 tsp water
1 cup pecans, finely chopped
powdered sugar

In a medium bowl, combine flour and spices. In another bowl, using an electric mixer, combine margarine, molasses and sugar. Beat until fluffy. Beat in egg and water. At low speed add dry ingredients, gradually, until combined. Roll dough in pecans. Wrap tightly in plastic wrap and refrigerate until firm (at least 6 hours or overnight).

Preheat oven to 350 degrees. Grease cookie sheets. Roll dough into balls and place 1-1/2 inches apart. Bake until edges are brown and firm to touch about 16 minutes. Transfer to rack and cool. Dust with powdered sugar. Will keep 1 week at room temperature or may be frozen.

Preparation time: 15-20 minutes, plus six hours
Baking time: 16 minutes
Makes: 30

MOCK STRUDEL [D]

1 cup margarine
1 cup sour cream
1/2 tsp salt
2 tsp grated orange rind
1 cup ground nuts
4 oz grated coconut
2 cups all-purpose flour
3/4 to 1 lb apricot-pineapple preserves
1 egg yolk, lightly beaten

Preheat oven to 350 degrees. Grease cookie sheet.

Blend first five ingredients, wrap in waxed paper and refrigerate overnight. Divide dough into 4 parts. Set aside 3 and place the 4th on a floured board. Roll with a rolling pin into a rectangle about 10 X 14 inches. Spread surface, not quite to the edges, with 1/4 of the preserves. Sprinkle with 1/4 of the nuts and 1/4 of the coconut. Roll like a jelly roll from the widest end. Place on cookie sheet. Repeat the process with each of the other pieces of dough. Brush with egg yolk. Bake for 35 minutes or until slightly brown. Remove rolls to a board. When cool cut into 1 inch pieces. Dust with powdered sugar.

Preparation time: 20 minutes
Baking time: 35 minutes
Makes: 35 to 40 pieces

An equal amount of nuts may be substituted for coconut. Cut longer slices for a dessert; smaller slices for cookie platter.

LEBKUCHEN [P]

1 lb dark brown sugar, packed
4 large eggs
1-1/2 tsp cinnamon
1/8 tsp ground cloves
1/8 tsp ground allspice
1-1/2 cups flour
1-1/2 tsp baking powder
3/4 cup walnuts, chopped

Preheat oven to 350 degrees.

Grease 9 X 9 baking pan.

In a large bowl, mix sugar and eggs, add other ingredients. Put in pan. Bake 25 minutes. Cool 10 to 15 minutes. Cut while warm.

Preparation time: 10 minutes
Baking time: 25 to 40 minutes
Makes: 2 dozen

These should have a chewy consistency. This recipe is over 100 years old.

CHOCOLATE BISCOTTI [P]

1-1/4 cups whole almonds, blanched
3 large eggs
1/2 cup dark brown sugar, packed
1 tsp vanilla
1 tsp almond extract
2 cups sifted all-purpose flour
1-1/2 tsp baking powder
1/4 tsp salt
1 tsp ground white pepper
1/3 cup Dutch process cocoa, unsweetened
2 Tbsp instant espresso powder
1/2 cup sugar
4 oz bittersweet chocolate, ground fine
2 Tbsp flour
1 tsp cocoa
4 oz bittersweet chocolate (optional)

Toast almonds at 375 degrees for 10 to 12 minutes, stirring once during baking time. Cool.

Line 2 cookie sheets with parchment paper. Turn oven down to 300 degrees. Place oven racks 1/3 from top and bottom of oven. In a small bowl beat eggs, sugar, vanilla and almond extract. In a large bowl, sift flour, baking powder, salt, pepper, cocoa, espresso powder and sugar. In food processor with metal blade, add chocolate with 1/2 cup of flour mixture and process until fine powder. Combine eggs and nuts. Lightly flour a board with 1 tablespoon of flour mixed with 1 teaspoon cocoa. Place dough on board, then sift a little more flour and cocoa mixture on top. Cut dough in two. Shape into logs about 3/4 inches high 2-1/2 inches wide. Transfer to 2 cookie sheets, reshaping if necessary.

Bake for 50 minutes, shifting pans once during baking. Remove from oven. Remove parchment paper. Reduce oven temperature to 275 degrees. Cut loaves into 2/3 inch slices, cut on an angle. Replace on pans cut side down and bake an additional 30 to 40 minutes turning over once until dry. Do not overbake.

May be frosted on one side with 4 oz melted bittersweet chocolate spread on top side of slice. Refrigerate on waxed paper until firm.

Preparation time: 25 minutes
Baking time: 65 to 70 minutes
Makes: 40 to 50

CHOCOLATE DIPPED BISCOTTI [D]

2 cups unblanched almonds or	1 Tbsp hazelnut or almond liqueur
1 cup almonds and	1/2 tsp almond extract (optional)
1 cup whole hazelnuts	1 cup sugar
3 cups flour	2 tsp orange zest
2 tsp baking powder	2 tsp lemon zest
1 tsp baking soda	1/2 cup butter, melted
1/2 tsp salt	1/2 pound bittersweet or
1/2 tsp ground mace (optional)	semi sweet chocolate and
3 large eggs plus 1 egg yolk	1 Tbsp margarine or butter
(reserve egg white, beaten slightly)	

Spread nuts on ungreased baking sheet and toast in 350 degree oven about 10 minutes. Remove and cool. Increase oven to 375 degrees. Chop nuts coarsely in food processor. In small bowl, sift flour, baking powder, baking soda, salt and mace. In large bowl, beat eggs until frothy. Beat in liqueur, extract and sugar until smooth. Add orange and lemon zest. Add melted butter and mix until smooth. Add dry ingredients. Stir in nuts. Knead a few strokes in bowl until dough is firm. Shape dough into 2 (14 inch) logs and place on greased and floured baking sheet. Press tops of logs to flatten slightly. Brush with reserved egg white. Bake at 375 degrees until golden and firm to touch, 25 to 30 minutes. Remove pan from oven and reduce temperature to 325 degrees. While logs are still warm, cut diagonally into 1/2 inch slices. Return slices to baking sheets, placing on sides and spreading apart. Return to oven and bake until cookies are golden and dry to touch about 20 minutes. Cool. Cut chocolate into 1/2 inch chunks. Melt in microwave with 1 tablespoon margarine. Dip 1/2 of each cookie in chocolate. Set cookie on wax paper and refrigerate to set chocolate. Store in air tight container. Can be frozen.

Preparation time: 30 minutes
Baking time: 50 to 60 minutes
Makes: 4 dozen

LIME SQUARES [D]

Dough:

1/3 cup sugar	1/2 lb butter or margarine
2 cups flour	1 large egg, beaten

Topping:

4 large eggs	3 Tbsp flour
2 cups sugar	zest of 1 lime
1/2 cup fresh lime juice with pulp	powdered sugar

Preheat oven to 350 degrees.

Combine sugar and flour, add butter and mix with fingers to form dough. Add beaten egg. Toss with a fork. Press dough firmly into bottom of a 9 X 13 inch baking dish. Bake for 15 minutes. **(Continued on Next Page)**

Combine eggs with sugar and flour. Beat for a few minutes before adding lime juice and zest of lime. Spoon mixture over hot crust and bake until custard is set, about 25 to 35 minutes or until tester comes out clean. Cool. Dust top with powdered sugar and sprinkle on lime zest. Cut into squares.

Preparation time: 30 minutes
Baking time: 40 minutes
Makes: 45 squares

These freeze well. Takes a little time but worth it.

CHOCOLATE FILLED SHORTBREAD [D]

2-1/2 cups unbleached flour, sifted
2/3 cup packed light brown sugar
1 cup cold unsalted butter
   cut into 1 inch pieces

1 to 2 Tbsp softened butter for greasing pan
1-1/2 tsp vanilla or almond extract
6 oz bittersweet chocolate

Cut 4 pieces of parchment paper to fit two 8 inch round cake pans. Insert 2 pieces of the paper into buttered pans. Butter paper and sides of pans.

Preheat oven to 325 degrees.

Place flour, sugar and butter in processor with steel blade. Turn on and add vanilla. Process until a ball forms (about 1 minute). Turn dough out onto lightly floured board. Roll into two thick rolls, then cut each in half. On lightly floured waxed paper, with lightly floured rolling pin, roll out dough to exactly fit the four pieces of parchment paper. Transfer to freezer on cookie sheet.

Break chocolate into pieces and melt over hot water in double boiler.

Cool melted chocolate using a paper towel under pot lid to absorb steam. Remove layers from freezer. Fit one layer into each baking pan, spread one half of the melted chocolate on each layer. Top with remaining layers. Let dough soften enough to pinch edges together with floured fingers and crimp as for pie crust.

Bake 50 minutes, until brown. Let stand in pan 1 hour. Slip out of pan on paper and cut while warm into quarters, then into quarters again. Store in airtight tins.

Preparation time: 30 to 40 minutes
Baking time: 50 minutes
Makes: 32 cookies

Elegant, a 5 star presentation and is simpler than it reads.

HUNGARIAN CHOCOLATE NUT BAR [D]

Dough:
1-1/2 cups flour
5-1/2 oz unsalted butter
   (1 stick plus 3 Tbsp)
1/4 tsp salt
1 egg yolk (save white for filling)
3 Tbsp cold water

Filling:
5 egg yolks
1 cup sugar
2 oz melted sweet chocolate
1-1/2 cups ground walnuts
6 egg whites, stiffly beaten

Preheat oven to 350 degrees.

Mix dough ingredients and knead lightly. Wrap in wax paper and refrigerate overnight.

Combine egg yolks, sugar, melted chocolate and ground walnuts. Fold in beaten egg whites.

Roll out 1/2 of the dough and place in a 9 X 12 inch baking pan. Pour filling on top of dough. Roll other portion of dough and fit on top of filling. Puncture top with a fork.

Bake for 40 to 45 minutes, or until it tests done. Cool and cut into bars.

Preparation time: 30 minutes
Baking time: 40 to 45 minutes
Makes: 30 to 40 bars

NUTTY FRUIT BARS [P]

1/4 cup glacé lemon, diced
1 cup dark raisins
1 cup golden raisins
1 cup dried apricot halves
1 cup orange marmalade
1/2 cup stem ginger drained, sliced
2 large eggs
1/2 cup light brown sugar, packed
1 cup unblanched whole almonds
1 cup walnuts
1 cup pine nuts
2 cups sifted unbleached flour
1 cup powdered sugar

Preheat oven to 400 degrees. Grease 13 X 9 X 2 baking pan.

Steam lemon, raisins, apricots in strainer over boiling water for about 8 minutes. Put fruit into paper towels to drain. Stir marmalade and ginger slices together. In a small bowl beat eggs and sugar. In a large bowl, combine fruit, nuts and jam mixture. Mix well and add flour. Place dough in bottom of pan. Cover with plastic wrap and with hands press into an even layer. Remove plastic. Bake for 30 to 35 minutes until top is golden brown. Remove from oven. Let stand 5 minutes. Remove from pan. Turn right side up on cooling rack to cool. Put on cutting board and slice. Place bars on wax paper and sift powdered sugar over them, turning to coat each side. Wrap each piece in plastic wrap. Store in air tight container. Will keep several weeks.

Preparation time: 1 hour
Baking time: 30 to 35 minutes
Makes: 40

A non-fat cookie.

FRUITED HONEY SPICE BARS [D]

1/2 cup butter
1-1/4 cups brown sugar, packed
1 large egg
1/2 cup honey
2 cups sifted all-purpose flour
1 tsp baking powder
1 tsp salt
1 tsp ground cinnamon
1/2 tsp ground nutmeg
1/4 tsp ground cloves
1/4 tsp baking soda
3/4 cup chopped candied cherries
3/4 cup candied pineapple
1 cup chopped walnuts or almonds
apricot jam

Preheat oven to 350 degrees. Grease and flour 15 X 10 jellyroll pan.

In large mixing bowl, cream butter and brown sugar until mixture is light and fluffy. Beat in egg and honey. Resift flour into another bowl with baking powder, salt, spices and baking soda. Add candied fruit and nuts, tossing to coat fruit. Add fruit-flour mixture to batter and mix well. Spread onto jellyroll pan. Bake 25 to 30 minutes. Cool in pan. Spread with glaze, then cut into squares or diamonds. Decorate with extra candied fruit or nuts, if desired. For glaze, melt apricot jam, strain through a sieve. Spread over cake before cutting.

Preparation time: 20 minutes
Baking time: 30 minutes
Makes: 32 bars

BUTTERSCOTCH OAT CRISPS [D/P]

1-1/2 cups sifted flour
1/2 tsp salt
1-1/2 cups oatmeal, regular
1/2 cup sweet butter or pareve margarine
1/2 cup vegetable shortening
1 cup light brown sugar, packed
2 large eggs
2 tsp vanilla

Preheat oven to 350 degrees.

In small bowl, sift together flour and salt. Stir in oatmeal. In large bowl, cream butter and shortening. Add brown sugar and combine well. Add eggs and vanilla. Beat until fluffy. Add dry ingredients and blend well. Shape into two 9 inch rolls. Wrap in wax paper and chill in refrigerator several hours. Slice 1/4 inch thick. Place on ungreased cookie sheet. Bake 10 to 12 minutes or until browned.

Preparation time: 15 minutes, plus refrigeration
Baking time: 10 to 12 minutes
Makes: 4 dozen

CHOCOLATE MERINGUES [P]

6 large egg whites (room temperature)
3/4 cup sugar
1 tsp vanilla or almond flavoring
1 cup chopped semi-sweet chocolate

Preheat oven to 275 degrees. Use non-stick cookie sheets or sheets covered with parchment paper.

Beat egg whites, adding sugar 2 Tbsp at a time until all sugar is incorporated. Keep beating on "high" until stiff and shiny. Add flavoring and fold in chocolate.

Drop on cookie sheets. Bake for 1 hour or until crisp to the touch. Let cool and remove from pans.

Preparation time: 15 minutes
Baking time: 1 hour
Makes: 24

Good any time, but a Passover favorite, using up egg whites. Do not attempt this on a humid day.

BRUNELI [P]

12 oz ground walnuts
12 oz ground pecans
1/2 cup unsweetened cocoa
1/2 cup sugar

3 large eggs whites (room temperature)
1/2 tsp instant coffee
2 cups sugar
sugar for board

Preheat oven to 185 degrees. Grease baking sheets.

In a large bowl, mix nuts, cocoa and 1/2 cup sugar. In another bowl, beat egg whites with instant coffee until peaks form. Continue beating until stiff, gradually adding 2 cups sugar. Mix with nut mixture, gently. Refrigerate 1 hour. Gently shape into rolls on a sugared board. Cut slices 1/4 inch thick. Place on baking sheets. Sprinkle with sugar. Bake 50 minutes.

Preparation time: 25 minutes plus 1 hour refrigeration
Baking time: 50 minutes
Makes: 70

HAZELNUT COOKIES [P]

9 oz hazelnuts
3 oz Dutch bitter chocolate
8 oz sugar

juice of 1/2 lemon
4 large egg whites

Preheat oven to 325 degrees. Grease baking sheet.

Grind hazelnuts with chocolate and combine with sugar and lemon juice. Beat egg whites and fold into mixture.

Moisten hands with cold water and form into 1 inch balls. Place cookies on cookie sheet and bake 20 to 25 minutes or until they are hard on the outside and soft on the inside.

Preparation time: 10 minutes
Baking time: 20 to 25 minutes
Makes: 2 dozen

This is a treasured recipe from Holland, popular for Passover.

WALNUT COOKIES (MUSTACHUDOS) [P]

3 cups ground walnuts
1 cup sugar
1/4 tsp cinnamon

2 large eggs, beaten
powdered sugar

Preheat oven to 350 degrees.

Mix dry ingredients. Add eggs forming a thick paste. Drop with spoon in mounds approximately 1-1/2 inch in diameter with peaked tops and about 1 inch apart on floured cookie sheet.

Bake for 18 minutes. Remove from oven and carefully loosen each cookie with spatula before cooling. If they flatten while cooking, shape into mounds again while hot. Sprinkle with powdered sugar.

If making these cookies for Passover use cake meal instead of flour. Line cookie sheet with parchment paper. Do not sprinkle with powdered sugar.

Preparation time: 10 minutes
Baking time: 18 minutes
Makes: 40

Traditional Sephardic recipe perfect for Passover or anytime.

ALMOND BRITTLE   [D]

1 lb butter
2 cups sugar
6 oz honey

6 oz whipping cream
2 lbs sliced blanched almonds
4 oz bittersweet chocolate, melted

Preheat oven to 375 degrees.

In a saucepan, bring to a boil first four ingredients and stir 5 to 6 minutes. Add almonds. Divide mixture among six 9 inch round aluminum foil pans. Dampen fingers with cold water and press mixture into pan until it is flat and covers the bottom of the pan. Bake until golden brown 10 to 12 minutes. Cool slightly then quickly remove from pan and break into pieces. Coat one side with a thin layer of melted chocolate.

Preparation time: 10 minutes
Baking time: 10 to 12 minutes
Makes: 60

NUT BRITTLE   [D]

1 cup sugar
1/2 cup light corn syrup
1 Tbsp butter
1 tsp vanilla

pinch of salt
1-1/2 cups mixed nuts (unsalted)
1 tsp baking soda

Combine sugar, syrup, butter, vanilla and salt in a microwaveable bowl. Microwave on high for 6 to 8 minutes until bubbly and brown.

Mix in nuts and microwave for additional 1 to 2 minutes.

Mix in baking soda. Pour onto greased cookie sheet. Cool at least 15 minutes. Break up and seal in airtight container.

Preparation time: 5 minutes
Cooking time: 8 to 10 minutes

DROP KICHLACH   [P]

3 large eggs
1/2 cup salad oil
2 Tbsp sugar

1 cup sifted flour
1/4 tsp salt (optional)

Preheat oven to 325 degrees. Lightly grease cookie sheet.

Beat eggs with oil and add sugar. Gradually add flour with salt. Drop by teaspoon on cookie sheet at least 3 inches apart to permit spreading. Bake for 15 to 20 minutes until lightly browned at edges and puffed.

Preparation time: 30 minutes
Baking time: 15 to 20 minnutes
Makes: 40

ALMOND SESAME SWEETS [P]

2-1/2 cups sesame seeds
1-1/2 cups coarsely chopped almonds
1/4 tsp salt

1 cup honey
1 Tbsp grated citron or lemon zest
cold water

Grease a medium-sized rectangular baking dish and set aside. In a bowl, mix sesame seeds, almonds and salt. Boil honey in a saucepan, stirring frequently, until a drop forms a firm ball when dripped in a cup of cold water. Quickly stir in sesame almond mixture and citron or lemon zest. Mix well. Layer about 1/2 inch thick in a baking dish and cool slightly, until mixture is somewhat firm. Using a sharp knife, cut in half and remove one half at a time to a cutting board. Slice each half into 1 inch squares. Refrigerate until firm.

Preparation time: 15 minutes
Makes: 40 squares

ESPRESSO TRUFFLES [D]

12 oz semi-sweet chocolate
4 oz sweet butter, softened
2 large egg yolks
4 Tbsp rum

1/2 cup heavy cream
40 espresso coffee beans
1/2 cup ground espresso beans
1/4 cup cocoa powder

In top of double boiler, melt chocolate over low heat, then beat in butter a tablespoon at a time. Add egg yolks, rum and cream. Beat until smooth. Cover and refrigerate until firm. Remove. Using a teaspoon, make mounds of chocolate. Place on waxed paper. With hands, roll into 1 inch balls. Press coffee bean into center and seal.

Sift ground espresso and cocoa powder onto a plate. Roll each truffle in this mixture. Place in tiny fluted paper cups. Store in refrigerator.

Preparation time: 20 minutes
Makes: 40

CHOCOLATE TRUFFLES [P]

8 oz semi-sweet chocolate
1/2 cup unsalted pareve margarine
1/4 cup liquid non-dairy pareve creamer
2 Tbsp almond liqueur or dark rum

2 egg yolks
1/2 cup ground chocolate or
    unsweetened cocoa powder

In a double boiler over low heat, melt chocolate. Add margarine, creamer, liqueur and egg yolks, whisking until well blended. Refrigerate mixture until thick enough to hold its shape. Pipe with a pastry bag fitted with 1/2 inch tip into small mounds, or drop by teaspoonfuls onto baking sheet lined with waxed paper. Refrigerate 20 to 30 minutes, until fairly firm. Dust fingertips with ground chocolate and shape chocolates into irregular balls. Roll them in ground chocolate and place them in paper bonbon cases.

Preparation time: 15 minutes
Makes: about 36 pieces

May be stored in refrigerator one week. May freeze up to four months.

Chocolate Bonbons:

Melt 7 oz semi-sweet chocolate and 1-1/2 tsp vegetable shortening in double boiler over hot water. With brush, paint inside of about 3 dozen bonbon cases with an even coating of chocolate 1/8 inch thick. Avoid painting top edge of case. It makes it difficult to peel off the paper later. Refrigerate while you make filling. Follow recipe above, omitting ground chocolate, and fill chocolate cups with truffle mixture.

BITTERSWEET CHOCOLATE CANDY [D]

2 bars unsweetened chocolate
2/3 cup semi-sweet chocolate chips
May also use almonds or walnuts

2/3 cup crushed cornflakes or
    2/3 cup raisins and peanuts

Melt the two chocolates slowly over low heat or in microwave. Add cornflakes and other ingredients. Drop by teaspoon on wax paper on a cookie sheet. Refrigerate for one hour. Store in refrigerator.

Preparation time: 30 minutes
Cooking time: 3 minutes in microwave to melt chocolate

DESSERT

"THE ENTERTAINERS," BRONZE, DAVID ARONSON

TU B'SHVAT—Desserts Show Off the Talents of Jewish Cooks at Festive Occasions.

CAKE
Janet Salter

In the Jewish tradition, the "sweetness of life" is observed at the slightest opportunity. There are wedding cakes, bar and bat mitzvah cakes, anniversary cakes, and, even when paying a condolence call, an offering of cake or something sweet is brought to comfort the bereaved family. "Cake" includes everything from Strudel to Chocolate-chocolate Fudge Brownies.

When Methuselah celebrated his 900th birthday, there was a tremendous gathering of senior citizens...until the candles on his cake almost burned down the tent. Therefore, when baking the delicious cakes in this chapter, please pay attention to the oven temperature, the proper baking time and the number of candles placed on the cake.

HAZELNUT TORTE [P]

1/2 cup sifted flour
1/2 tsp instant coffee
1/2 tsp cocoa
3 cups coarsely ground hazelnuts
6 large eggs, separated

1 cup sugar
1 tsp lemon juice
1 tsp rum
1/2 tsp vanilla

Frosting:
3 whole eggs
9 Tbsp sugar

3/4 cup chocolate chips
1-1/2 sticks unsalted, pareve margarine

Preheat oven to 350 degrees.

Grease two 9 inch round cake pans and line with waxed paper.

Sift together flour, instant coffee and cocoa. Add nuts. Set aside. Combine and beat 6 eggs yolks and 1/2 cup sugar until very thick and lemon colored. Add lemon juice, rum and vanilla. Set aside. Using a clean beater, beat egg whites until frothy. Gradually add 1/2 cup sugar. Beat until peaks are formed. Gently spread egg-yolk mixture over beaten egg whites. Spoon 1/4 of flour hazelnut mixture over surface and gently fold until batter is partially blended. Repeat until flour is just blended. Fill pans equally with batter and bake 25 to 30 minutes. Cool. Remove from pans. Cut one of the torte layers into halves. Fill and frost all three torte layers. For frosting: In top of double boiler, cook eggs, sugar and chocolate chips until thickened. Remove from heat and beat in margarine. Cover and cool before using.

Preparation time: 20 to 30 minutes
Baking time: 30 minutes
Serves: 8

HUNGARIAN TORTE [D]

7 large eggs, separated
1 cup sugar
2 cups ground nuts
1 Tbsp powdered coffee
1/4 tsp salt

3-4 Tbsp apricot jam
kiwi slices (optional)
1 pt whipping cream
4 Tbsp sugar
6 Tbsp sifted cocoa

Preheat oven to 325 degrees.

Beat yolks and sugar until thick and lemon colored. Mix nuts, coffee and salt together. Then add to yolk mixture. Beat egg whites until stiff with clean dry beaters. Fold whites into yolk mixture. Rinse 10 inch springform pan with cold water. Tap out excess water and pour mixture into pan. Bake 45 to 60 minutes until cake tester comes out clean. Invert after baking.

Whip cream until soft peaks form. Add sugar and cocoa and beat until stiff. Slice cake through middle and spread with apricot jam and chocolate whipped cream mixture. Decorate with remaining whipped cream. Chill.

Preparation time: 20 minutes
Baking time: 45 to 60 minutes
Serves: 8 to 10

PECAN TORTE WITH RASPBERRIES AND LEMON [P]

5 large eggs
1-1/2 cups pecans
1 cup sugar
1 tsp vanilla
3 Tbsp flour

1 tsp baking powder
1/2 cup seedless raspberry jam
2 Tbsps lemon juice, divided
1/2 cup powdered sugar

Preheat oven to 350 degrees. Grease 10 inch springform pan.

In food processor, combine eggs, pecans, sugar, vanilla, flour and baking powder. Process until nuts are finely chopped. Pour into pan. Bake 30 minutes or until cake tester inserted in center comes out clean. Do not overbake. Cool in pan.

Combine jam with 1 Tbsp lemon juice. Make a frosting of powdered sugar and remaining lemon juice. Remove sides of pan. Spread cake with jam, then drizzle frosting over cake.

Preparation time: 10 minutes
Baking time: 30 to 35 minutes
Serves: 6

"LITE" CHOCOLATE CHEESECAKE [D]

12 ginger snaps, finely crushed
1 lb light process cream cheese
1-1/4 cup sugar
1 cup non-fat cottage cheese
1/4 cup plus 2 Tbsp unsweetened cocoa
1/4 cup all-purpose flour

1/4 cup Creme de Cacao
1 tsp vanilla
1/4 tsp salt
1 large egg
1/4 cup semi-sweet chocolate morsels
2 Tbsp chocolate chips for topping

Preheat oven to 300 degrees.

Sprinkle and press ginger snap crumbs in bottom of an 8 inch springform pan. Set aside. In food processor with metal blade, add cream cheese and next 7 ingredients, processing until smooth. Add egg and process just until blended. Fold in chocolate morsels.

Pour mixture over crumbs in pan. Add 2 Tbsp chocolate chips on top. Bake 60 to 70 minutes or until cheesecake is set. Let cool in pan on wire rack. Cover and chill at least 8 hours. Remove sides of pan, and transfer cheesecake to a serving platter.

Preparation time: 20 minutes
Baking time: 60 to 70 minutes
Serves: 12

CHERRY PECAN CHEESE CAKE   [D]

8 oz cream cheese
1 cup margarine
1-1/2 cup sugar
1-1/2 tsp vanilla
4 large eggs

2-1/4 cups cake flour
1-1/2 tsp baking powder
3/4 cups chopped candied cherries
1/2 cup chopped pecans

Preheat oven to 325 degrees. Grease a bundt pan.

Using large bowl and electric mixer, blend cream cheese, margarine, sugar and vanilla. Add eggs one at a time. Sift together 2 cups of flour and baking powder. Gradually add to cream cheese mixture using low speed. Combine remaining flour with cherries and nuts. Fold into batter. Pour into pan. Bake 1 hour 10 minutes.

Preparation time: 20 minutes
Baking time: 1 hour 20 minutes
Serves: 10 to 12

ITALIAN CHEESECAKE PUFF   [D]

Filling:
2 Tbsp yellow raisins, soaked in
    1 Tbsp cognac
1 cup cream cheese
1/4 cup sugar

1 Tbsp flour
1 egg yolk
1 Tbsp sour cream
1 Tbsp grated lemon zest
1/2 Tbsp vanilla

Topping:
1 tart apple, peeled, cored, sliced thin
1 Tbsp sugar

1 tsp cinnamon
1/4 cup almonds, blanched, sliced
1 Tbsp powdered sugar

Classic Choux pastry:
3/4 cup water
1/4 cup milk
1/8 tsp salt

1-1/2 cups unsalted butter
1-1/2 cups flour
4 large eggs

Glaze:
1 egg yolk
1 tsp cream

Preheat oven to 375 degrees. Grease and flour cookie sheet.

Place an 8 inch round pan on top. Draw a circle around the pan with tip of knife. Remove pan.

Prepare filling: Stir together raisins, cognac and lemon zest. In a mixer or food processor, add rest of filling ingredients, folding in raisin mixture last. Set aside.

Topping: Mix apples with cinnamon and sugar. Set aside.

(Continued on Next Page)

Choux Pastry: In a heavy pot, on high heat, add water, milk and salt. Add butter. Cook to a rolling boil. Add flour all at once and cook and stir constantly until mixture comes away from side of pot about 1 minute. Remove from heat. Cool to lukewarm. Add eggs one at a time, with a wooden spoon. Beat well after each egg is added. Keep beating until all eggs are blended.

Assembling cake: Place half of dough on circle, patting it flat with damp hands. Around the edge, drop spoonfuls of dough, using up all the dough. Pour filling into center. Top with apples, neatly arranging them and using all the apples. Sprinkle the nuts on top. Mix egg yolk and cream and brush over edge of dough.

Place on middle rack of oven. Bake 1 hour. Remove from oven, cool. Sprinkle with powdered sugar and place on attractive serving tray.

Preparation time: 45 minutes
Baking time: 1 hour
Serves: 8

Choux pastry is good for making cream puffs, eclairs or miniature puffs.

This is a show piece worth the effort. It is easy to do by following the steps in order.

OLD KENTUCKY FRUITCAKE   [D]

1 egg, well beaten
1/2 cup butter (do not use margarine)
1 cup sugar
1-3/4 cup flour, sifted
1 tsp baking soda
1-1/2 tsp cinnamon
1/2 tsp cloves, ground

1 cup applesauce
1 tsp vanilla
1/4 cup dried cherries
1 cup raisins
1 cup chopped dates
1 cup chopped pecans
1/2 cup sherry or bourbon (optional)

Preheat oven to 250 degrees. Grease and line with buttered waxed paper 10 inch bundt pan.

Remove 1/4 cup flour and mix dried fruits and nuts with flour.

Heat applesauce until it is very hot but not boiling. Add soda, stir, cool. Using an electric mixer with large bowl on medium speed, cream butter and sugar. Add eggs, spices and vanilla. Add applesauce using low speed. Add remaining flour to moist ingredients, then fold in fruits and nuts. Pour batter into pan. Bake 2-1/2 to 3 hours. If desired, sprinkle 1/2 cup sherry wine or bourbon over cake after it is baked. When cool, wrap in waxed paper and foil. Freeze. Slice thinly to serve.

Preparation time: 30 minutes
Baking time: 2-1/2 to 3 hours
Serves: 20

PEAR HONEY CAKE [P]

2/3 cup shortening
2/3 cup brown sugar, packed
4 eggs
2/3 cup honey
2-1/2 cups flour
1 tsp salt
1 tsp baking soda

1 tsp cinnamon
1/4 tsp ground allspice
1/4 tsp ground cloves
3 cups pears, cored, chopped
1-1/4 cups pitted, chopped dates
1 tsp finely grated orange zest

Glaze:
1 cup powdered sugar

2 tsp brandy
1 to 2 tsp orange juice

Preheat oven to 350 degrees. Grease and flour 10 inch tube or bundt pan.

Using an electric mixer, in a large bowl, on medium speed, cream shortening and sugar until light. Add eggs one at a time, beating well. Blend in honey. Sift together dry ingredients and fold into creamed mixture. Blend at low speed till moistened. Beat 3 minutes at medium speed. By hand, stir in pears, dates and orange zest. Pour into pan and bake 60 to 65 minutes or till top springs back at light touch. Cool in pan 30 minutes. Remove and cool on rack. When completely cool drizzle with brandy glaze. Glaze: combine powdered sugar with brandy. Add orange juice to obtain proper consistency.

Preparation time: 20 minutes
Baking time: 60 to 65 minutes
Serves: 8 to 10

OLD WORLD PEAR CAKE [D]

2 cups sugar
1-1/2 tsp vanilla
3 large eggs, beaten
1-1/2 cups oil
3 cups all-purpose flour
1 tsp salt

1 tsp baking soda
1 tsp cinnamon
3 cups thinly sliced, firm, peeled pears
1-1/4 cups powdered sugar
2 to 4 Tbsp milk

Preheat oven to 375 degrees. Grease bundt or tube pan.

In large bowl, using electric mixer, on medium speed, combine sugar, vanilla, eggs and oil. Beat well. Combine flour, salt, soda on low speed and add to sugar mixture 1 cup at a time. Fold in cinnamon and pears. Pour into pan and bake for 1 hour. Cool and remove from pan after 10 minutes. Serve plain or glazed. Blend sugar with milk. Drizzle over cake after it is cooled.

Preparation time: 25 minutes
Baking time: 1 hour
Serves: 12

GERMAN STYLE APPLE TORTE   [D/P]

2 cups flour
1-1/2 cups sugar
1/4 cup cold butter or pareve margarine
1 egg
juice of 1/2 lemon

1 cup water
9-10 large cooking apples
1/2 cup dark raisins, soaked in warm water
1 tsp cinnamon
powdered sugar

Preheat oven to 375 degrees. Lightly grease 9 or 10 inch springform pan.

Mix flour and 2/3 cup sugar. Cut butter or margarine into flour until mixture is mealy. With a fork stir in egg until well blended, then work dough with floured hands until it holds a smooth, non-crumbly ball. Divide dough into thirds, wrap 1/3 in plastic wrap and store in refrigerator until ready to roll. Press remaining dough firmly and evenly over bottom and about 2/3 way up side of pan. Set aside. Peel, core and shred apples and place in lemon juice and water. Drain apples, combine with raisins, 2/3 cup sugar and cinnamon. Mix well. Place apple mixture into baking pan. Remove remaining dough from refrigerator, roll out on floured surface. Carefully fit dough over apples. Press dough top and sides together. Prick top of pastry. Bake 1 hour 10 minutes. Cool 10 minutes in pan then loosen sides of pan. When room temperature, sprinkle with powdered sugar. Remove from pan.

Preparation time: 45 minutes
Baking time: 1 hour 10 minutes
Serves: 8 to 10

APPLE CINNAMON BUNDT CAKE   [P]

2-1/2 cups sugar
3 cups unsifted flour
4 large eggs, lightly beaten
1 cup oil
1 Tbsp baking powder

1/2 cup orange juice plus
   1 tsp grated orange zest
1 Tbsp vanilla
1-1/2 cups chopped nuts (optional)
1-1/2 cups chocolate chips (optional)
powdered sugar

Filling:
3 large apples, peeled and sliced thin

1/4 cup sugar
1/2 Tbsp cinnamon

Preheat oven to 350 degrees. Grease and flour 10 inch bundt pan.

In electric mixer combine sugar, flour, eggs, oil, baking powder, orange juice and vanilla. Beat on low speed until well blended. Add nuts if desired. Pour 1/2 batter into pan. Combine apples with sugar and cinnamon. Spread filling evenly over batter. Spread remaining 1/2 batter on top of apple filling. Bake 1-1/2 to 1-3/4 hours. Cool 1 hour. Dust with powdered sugar, after removing from pan.

Preparation time: 20 minutes
Baking time: 1 hour 45 minutes
Serves: 12 to 14

Freezes well.

OLD FASHIONED CHOCOLATE CAKE [D]

1/4 cup butter
2 cups dark brown sugar, packed
3 extra-large eggs
3 oz unsweetened chocolate,
   melted and cooled

2 cups sifted all-purpose flour
1/2 cup buttermilk*
1 tsp vanilla
1 cup boiling water
1 tsp baking soda

Frosting:
3 cups sifted powdered sugar
3 oz unsweetend chocolate, melted
2 oz warm milk

2 Tbsp butter, melted
1 tsp vanilla
1 tsp instant coffee

Preheat oven to 350 degrees. Grease 9 X 13 inch pan.

In large bowl, using electric mixer, cream butter and brown sugar. On medium speed add eggs one at a time, mix well after each. Combine buttermilk and vanilla. On medium-slow speed add chocolate. Starting and ending with flour, alternate adding flour and milk, cleaning sides of bowl with rubber spatula after each addition. Carefully measure 1 cup boiling water, add baking soda and stir. On slow speed add water quickly, use spatula to mix in thoroughly.

Pour into pan. Bake for 50 minutes or until top of cake springs back to touch. Allow cake to cool in pan on rack for 30 minutes. Frost while still warm.

Frosting: On slow speed, combine sugar, chocolate, 1 oz milk, butter, vanilla and coffee. Continue beating at high speed until smooth and of spreading consistency. Add more milk to obtain proper consistency.

Preparation time: 30 minutes
Baking time: 50 minutes
Serves: 8

*To make buttermilk: If real buttermilk is not available, place 1 Tbsp lemon juice or white vinegar into measuring cup and add milk to make 1 cup. Let stand for 10 minutes before using.

COOKIE DOUGH FOR PIES [D/P]
(FOR AN 8 INCH SHELL)

1-1/3 cups all-purpose flour
1/4 cup sugar
1/8 tsp salt
1 tsp grated lemon zest

1/2 cup butter or margarine
1/2 tsp vanilla
1 large egg yolk, beaten with
   2 Tbsp ice water

Preheat oven to 350 degrees.

Weight the shell with raw rice, beans or pie weights for baking.

In a bowl stir together the flour, sugar, salt and lemon zest. Add the butter and blend mixture until it resembles coarse meal. Add vanilla and egg yolk mixture. Toss the mixture until all is incorporated and the dough forms into a ball. Dust the dough with flour and chill it, wrapped in plastic wrap for 1 hour or longer. Roll out dough 1/8 inch thick on a floured surface, fit into a 10 inch tart pan with a removable fluted rim. Cover and chill the shell for at

(Continued on Next Page)

least 30 minutes or overnight. Line shell with foil, fill with rice, beans or pie weights and bake on rack in middle of oven 25 minutes. Remove foil and rice or beans. Bake 5 to 10 minutes more, until pale golden. Cool in pan on a rack. May be frozen before baking.

Preparation time: 10 minutes
Baking time: 35 minutes

May use food processor, using on/off button until ball forms.

9 INCH DOUBLE PIE CRUST [P]

2 cups flour
1 tsp salt
2/3 cups vegetable shortening
6 Tbsp ice water

Preheat oven to 450 degrees.

Sift flour and salt. Cut shortening into flour, work with finger tips until you have flour particles the size of dried split peas. Add ice water, mixing lightly until flour mixture is dampened. Gather into a ball, gently pressing together. Flatten into a 6 inch round. Wrap in waxed paper and chill in refrigerator for 1/2 hour. Divide into 2 portions and roll on lightly floured board to about 11 inch circle and about 1/8 inch thick.

For pre-baked crust, flute edge and prick all over with tines of fork. Bake in hot oven, 450 degrees for 12 to 15 minutes.

Preparation time: 10 minutes
Baking time: For a single pre-baked crust, bake 12 to 15 minutes. Follow baking time for fruit filled pie.

A food processor may be used with on/off button until ball forms.

BLUEBERRY BUTTERMILK TART [D]

For tart, use preceding cookie dough recipe and follow directions.

Filling:
1 cup buttermilk
3 large egg yolks
1/2 cup sugar
1 Tbsp freshly grated lemon zest
1 Tbsp fresh lemon juice
1/2 stick butter, melted and cooled
1 tsp vanilla
1/2 tsp salt
2 Tbsp all-purpose flour
2 cups blueberries, washed well and dried gently
powdered sugar for sprinkling on tart

Preheat oven to 350 degrees.

In a blender or food processor, blend together the buttermilk, yolks, sugar, zest, lemon juice, butter, vanilla, salt and flour until the mixture is smooth. Spread the blueberries evenly over the bottom of the shell and pour the buttermilk mixture over them. Bake the tart in the middle of oven 35 to 45 minutes, or until the filling is just set.

Let the tart cool completely in the pan on wire rack. Sprinkle with powdered sugar.

Frozen blueberries may also be used instead of fresh ones. However, any ice crystals that may have formed on the berries are best removed by rolling blueberries in a towel before being placed in the pie shell.

FRESH FRUIT PIE [P]

2 cups fresh fruit, or
    3 cups peeled and cored apples
1 cup orange sections
1 cup seedless grapes, halved
1 Tbsp lemon juice
3/4 cup sugar
2 Tbsp quick tapioca
1/4 tsp cinnamon
1/4 tsp nutmeg
dash salt
1 unbaked pie shell plus dough for
    lattice top (see recipe page 227)

Preheat oven to 375 degrees.

Combine fruits with lemon juice. Add sugar, tapioca, cinnamon and nutmeg. Let stand 15 minutes. Pour mixture into unbaked pie shell. Make lattice crust cover. To prevent over-browning, cover edge of pastry with foil. Bake 25 minutes. Remove foil and bake 25 to 30 minutes longer.

Preparation time: 30 to 45 minutes
Baking time: 50 to 60 minutes
Serves: 6 to 8

DEEP DISH APPLE AND PEAR PIE [D/P]

4 large tart cooking apples
4 large firm ripe pears
1 cup sugar
1/4 tsp salt
1/2 tsp ground cinnamon
1/4 tsp ground nutmeg
3 Tbsp flour
2 Tbsp butter or pareve margarine
pastry for pie crust
    (use basic pie crust recipe)

Preheat oven to 425 degrees.

Peel, core and slice apples and pears into 1/2 inch slices. Combine sugar, salt, spices and flour and mix with the fruit. Turn into a 2 qt oblong baking dish, lined with one half the pastry dough rolled 1/8 inch thick. Dot fruit with butter or margarine. Roll remaining pastry dough 1/8 inch thick and cut into six 3-1/2 inch squares. Place squares in 2 horizontal rows over fruit. Bake 10 minutes. Reduce heat to 350 degrees and bake 35 minutes longer, or until crust is golden and fruit is tender when knife is inserted. Serve warm or cold.

Preparation time: 45 minutes
Baking time: 45 minutes
Serves: 6 to 8

DESSERT CHEESE BLINTZES [D]

Blintzes:
2 large eggs
1/2 cup sifted all-purpose flour
3/4 cup liquid (half milk, half water)
1 Tbsp melted butter

Cheese filling:
3/4 lb hoop or farmer cheese
2 -3 oz pkg cream cheese
1/4 cup sugar
3/4 tsp vanilla
3/4 tsp cinnamon
butter for frying
strawberry preserves
sour cream

For blintzes: In mixing bowl, beat eggs. Add flour, alternately with liquid to eggs, beating with rotary beater or whisk until smooth. Add melted butter and beat until well blended. Chill 1 to 2 hours. Heat a 7 inch skillet and butter well. Reduce heat and pour batter in thin stream into pan, starting at center and tipping to coat bottom. Cook until underside is set. Turn out on towel. Cool blintzes, stacking layers with waxed paper between each.

For filling: In food processor fitted with metal blade, combine hoop and cream cheeses. Blending well, add sugar, vanilla and cinnamon. Place 2 tablespoons cheese filling on each blintz, brown side up. Fold edge to center, envelope fashion. May be made to this point and refrigerated. Fry in hot butter until lightly browned on both sides. Serve warm with strawberrry preserves and sour cream.

Preparation time: 35 minutes plus 1 hour to chill batter
Cooking time: 10 minutes
Makes: 12 to 16

For a main dish, omit sugar and cinnamon.

CHOCOLATE BREAD PUDDING [D]

1/2 lb French bread, cut into 1/2 inch cubes
2 cups heavy cream
4 oz bittersweet chocolate
2 oz unsweetened chocolate
3/4 cup unsalted butter, room temperature
2/3 cup sugar
6 large eggs, separated
1 cup ground almonds

Preheat oven to 350 degrees. Butter 3 quart souffle dish.

In a large bowl, soak bread with cream. Melt chocolate over a double boiler and keep warm. In a large bowl, cream butter, sugar and egg yolks. Add bread mixture, chocolate and almonds. Whip egg whites to soft peaks and fold into mixture. Pour into baking dish and place into larger pan filled with hot water to within 1 inch level of top of souffle dish. Bake 50 minutes. Serve warm or chilled.

Preparation time: 20 minutes
Baking time: 50 minutes
Serves: 8

BREAD PUDDING WITH WHISKEY SAUCE [D]

1/2 cup raisins	1 cup sugar
3 Tbsp bourbon	2 cups milk
4 slices French bread, cut in 1/2 inch cubes	2 cups whipping cream
	1 Tbsp vanilla
8 large eggs	2 tsp cinnamon

Preheat oven to 350 degrees. Grease 2 quart baking dish.

Plump raisins in bourbon, set aside. Place cubed French bread in baking dish. Sprinkle evenly with raisins. In large mixing bowl, beat eggs, sugar, milk, whipping cream and vanilla. Pour egg mixture over bread and raisins. Poke bread under liquid, saturating all the bread. Sprinkle with cinnamon. Cover with foil. Set in a pan of hot water to within 1 inch of top. Bake about 1-1/4 hours or until knife inserted in center comes out clean. Serve warm or chilled. Cut into squares.

Whiskey Sauce:

1/2 cup unsalted butter	1/4 cup whipping cream
1-1/3 cups brown sugar, packed	1/4 cup bourbon

In a medium saucepan, melt butter, stir in brown sugar, cream and bourbon. Cook over low heat until mixture bubbles. Spoon generously over bread pudding.

Preparation time: 10 minutes
Baking time: 1-1/4 hours.
Serves: 8 to 12

STICKY TOFFEE PUDDING [D]

6 oz dates, sliced	1 cup less 2 Tbsp sugar
1 cup water	2 large eggs
1 tsp baking soda	1 cup plus 2 Tbsp flour
4 Tbsp butter	1/2 tsp vanilla

Preheat oven to 350 degrees. Grease 8 X 8 inch pan.

In saucepan, place dates and water. Bring to a boil. Remove from heat and add baking soda. In a bowl, cream butter and sugar. Add eggs one at a time. Fold in flour, date mixture and vanilla. Pour into pan. Bake 25 to 30 minutes.

Preparation time: 20 minutes
Baking time: 25 to 30 minutes
Serves: 6 to 8

Butterscotch sauce:

3/4 cup brown sugar	1/2 cup butter
1/2 cup whipping cream	1/2 tsp vanilla
	2 Tbsp brandy

Place first four ingredients in a saucepan and boil for 3 minutes. Add brandy. Makes 1-1/2 cups.

CHOCOLATE SOUFFLE [D]

8 large egg whites
6 large egg yolks
4 Tbsp butter, softened
2 Tbsp sugar
1/2 cup flour
3/4 cup unsweetened cocoa
1 cup sugar

1/4 tsp salt
2 cups milk
2 tsp vanilla
1/4 tsp cream of tartar
1 cup heavy cream
1/4 cup powdered sugar

Preheat oven to 350 degrees. Grease 2 quart souffle dish.

Place 8 egg whites in one bowl and yolks in another bowl. Let stand for 1 hour. To form collar fold 26 inch piece waxed paper lengthwise in thirds. Grease paper. Form 2 inch collar around dish, tie, sprinkle dish and paper with 2 Tbsp sugar. Place oven rack on lowest rung in oven. In medium-size heavy saucepan, mix flour, cocoa, 3/4 cup sugar (save 1/4 cup of sugar for egg whites) and salt. Gradually blend in milk. Cook, over medium heat, until mixture comes to boil. Do not overcook. Beat yolks with wire whisk. Beat in some of cocoa mixture. Gradually stir yolk mixture into rest of mixture in saucepan. Add butter and vanilla, stirring until combined. Set aside to cool slightly. With electric mixer at high speed, beat egg whites until soft peaks form. Add cream of tartar and continue beating. Add 1/4 cup granulated sugar, 2 tablespoons at a time, beating well after each addition. Beat just until stiff peaks form when beater is raised. Whites will be shiny and satiny. Turn a third of cocoa mixture over top of egg whites. Using a rubber spatula, gently fold cocoa mixture into whites, just until combined. Fold in remainder, half at a time, being careful not to overfold. Gently turn mixture into souffle dish, set in a large baking pan. Smooth top, place pan and dish in oven on bottom rack. Pour hot water into pan to measure 1 inch. Bake 1-1/4 hours. With rotary beater, beat cream with powdered sugar until stiff. Chill. Serve with souffle.

Preparation time: 30 to 40 minutes
Baking time: 1-1/4 hours.
Serves: 8

Secret of success is to have eggs at room temperature. Serve immediately from oven.

ISRAELI CHOCOLATE MOUSSE CAKE [P]

9 large eggs, separated
2/3 cup sugar
12 oz bittersweet chocolate
   (reserve 2 Tbsp for topping)

1 Tbsp instant coffee powder
4 Tbsp boiling water
6 to 8 Tbsp bread crumbs for pan
pureed raspberries (optional)

Preheat oven to 350 degrees. Grease and crumb 10 inch springform pan.

In a small bowl, beat egg yolks with 1/3 cup sugar. Melt chocolate and coffee with the water. Cool and add to yolks. In another bowl, beat egg whites with 1/3 cup sugar. Fold yolk mixture into the whites. Pour batter into prepared pan. Bake 25 minutes or until cake tester inserted in center comes out clean. Drizzle with melted chocolate, pureed raspberries or both.

Preparation time: 15 minutes
Baking time: 25 minutes
Serves: 10

SPANISH ORANGE FLAN [D]

1/2 cup sugar
2 Tbsp orange marmalade
1 Tbsp orange juice
3 cups milk
6 eggs

2/3 cup sugar
1 tsp orange extract
1 Tbsp grated orange rind
fresh orange slices

Preheat oven to 350 degrees.

In saucepan, blend sugar, marmalade and orange juice. Cook over low heat, stirring occasionally. Cook until a few drops form a soft ball when dropped into cold water. Pour glaze into a souffle dish (1-1/2 qt) and tilt to coat sides and bottom evenly. Refrigerate until glaze is completely firm.

In a small saucepan, scald milk just until bubbles form. In a mixing bowl, beat eggs with sugar until light, then add flavoring, and finally, hot milk. Beat a few seconds. Pour into prepared dish. Place dish in pan of hot water. Bake 50 minutes or until tester comes out clean. Refrigerate at least 3 hours. Unmold onto platter, decorate with orange slices.

Preparation time: 25 minutes
Baking time: 50 minutes
Serves: 4

BAKED STUFFED PEARS [P]

6 pears, firm ripe
1/4 cup light brown sugar, packed
1/4 cup pecans, chopped
1/3 cup dried currants
12 whole cloves

3/4 cup maple syrup
3/4 cup water
1 Tbsp preserved ginger, chopped
1 Tbsp orange marmalade

Preheat oven to 350 degrees.

(Continued on Next Page)

Core pears from the bottom, keeping stems in place. Combine sugar, pecans and currents and fill pears. Place 2 cloves in each pear, one on each side. Place pears upright in an 7 X 11 inch baking dish. In a saucepan, combine maple syrup, water, ginger, orange marmalade and bring to a boil. Cook 5 minutes. Pour mixture over pears. Bake 1 hour or until pears are tender, basting occasionally.

Preparation time: 10 to 15 minutes
Baking time: 1 hour
Serves: 6

COFFEE RUM MOUSSE [P]

- 2 pkg lady fingers
- 1 cup cold liquid coffee
- 2 pts non-dairy whipped topping
- 1/4 cup sugar
- 4 Tbsp powdered coffee
- 4 Tbsp dark rum
- 1 tsp vanilla

Using a 10 inch springform pan, dip lady fingers, quickly into cold coffee. Place around edge of pan, curved side out. Cover bottom of pan also using broken pieces to fit tightly. In a large bowl, mix whipped topping with sugar, powdered coffee, rum and vanilla. Pour into prepared pan. Cover and freeze. At serving time, carefully remove outer rim of pan.

Preparation time: 20 minutes
Serves: 12

FRUIT MELANGE [P]

- 1/2 lb mixed dried fruits
- 2 large tart apples, peeled, cored and sliced
- 1-1/2 pears, peeled, cored and sliced
- 4 peaches, thickly sliced
- 10 Italian plums, halved and pitted
- 2 pts fresh berries (blackberries, boysenberries or cranberries) or
- 2 16 oz pkg frozen berries
- 1 lb pitted cherries or grapes
- 1/2 lemon, sliced
- 1/2 cup sugar or honey
- 1/2 tsp ground cloves
- 1 tsp cinnamon

In a 6 quart pot, place all the fruits and berries. Add lemon, sugar and spices. Add water to 1/3 depth of the fruit mixture. Cover pot, leaving lid slightly ajar. Bring to a boil. Stir with a wooden spoon. Reduce heat and simmer gently for 1 hour, stirring several times. Serve hot or cold.

Preparation time: 20 minutes
Cooking time: 1 hour
Serves: 12 to 15

Be certain to use Italian or other dark plums or berries which give the dark rich color and fruity flavor.

CRANBERRY STRUDEL [D]

3/4 cup sugar plus 1 Tbsp
2 tsp cornstarch
1/4 cup cranberry juice
2 cups cranberries
1/3 cup orange, peeled, seeded, cut in small pieces
1 Tbsp orange zest
1/2 cup chopped dates
1/2 cup chopped pecans
10 filo sheets
1/2 cup butter, or pareve margarine, unsalted and melted
3/4 cup finely ground pecans
sifted powdered sugar

Preheat oven to 375 degrees.

In a medium saucepan, combine sugar and cornstarch blending well. Whisk in cranberry juice. Add cranberries, orange pieces, zest and dates. Cook over medium heat, stirring until cranberries pop, mixture is clear and thick (like jam), about 10 minutes. Remove from heat and let cool to room temperature. Stir in pecans. Place filo on a large sheet of waxed paper. Cover with a lightly dampened towel. Keep filo covered to prevent drying. Working with one sheet of filo at a time, brush lightly with melted butter on both sides, making sure ends and sides are well buttered. Place on baking sheet lined with aluminum foil. Sprinkle with ground pecans. Repeat layering filo with butter and pecans. Spread cranberry mixture lengthwise across bottom third of the filo, fold in about 1 inch of sides. Using foil as a guide, roll up tightly to enclose filling, leaving ends loosely tucked in to allow steam to escape, forming a 3 X 15 inch roll. Place filled strudel, seam side down, diagonally on the baking sheet. Brush with melted butter. Bake for 35 to 40 minutes until golden brown, turning pan halfway through baking to brown evenly. Let cool on pan 5 minutes, then cool on rack 10 minutes or longer. Dust with powdered sugar. Cut into 1-1/2 inch diagonal pieces. Serve warm or at room temperature.

Preparation time: 40 minutes
Baking time: 35 to 40 minutes
Serves: 8 to 10

ITALIAN STRAWBERRY ICE (GRANITA) [P]

3/4 to 1 cup sugar
1/2 cup water
4 cups hulled fresh strawberrys
1/4 cup lemon juice
2 Tbsp orange juice or strawberry liqueur

In small saucepan, combine sugar and water. Bring to a boil and boil rapidly 5 minutes. Cool to room temperature. In food processor with metal blade, coarsely puree strawberries. Combine pureed strawberries, lemon and orange juices, mixing thoroughly. Pour into freezer trays and freeze until firm. Turn into food processor fitted with steel blade and beat until smooth. Return mixture to freezer and freeze until firm. Spoon into serving dishes.

Preparation time: 15 to 20 minutes
Serves: 6

PASSOVER

PASSOVER RITUAL PLATE, ISRAEL, CONTEMPORARY, TREASURES OF JUDAICA

PASSOVER—At Passover, Symbolic Foods, on a Special Platter, Are Explained and Tasted at the Seder. (see Menus for Specifics) Matzo is Served in Place of Bread, in Celebration of the Ancient Hebrews' Deliverance from Bondage.

PASSOVER IN THE KOSHER KITCHEN

WHAT A DIFFERENCE A HOLIDAY MAKES

Miriam Bornstein

The kosher cook faces the ultimate challenge, when the beautiful freedom festival of Pesach (Passover) approaches. That is the time, when we commemorate with various symbolic foods and rituals, the redemption of the ancient Israelites from slavery and their hasty exodus form the land of Egypt.

Because of the biblical injunction not to eat any leavened foods (chamets) during the entire week of Passover (Exodus 12:15-20), the kosher kitchen must be totally overhauled, scrubbed, cleaned and tendered completely free of every last crumb and vestige of chamets. To ensure that this goal of chamets-free kitchen is met, the kosher household comes equipped with two complete sets of Passover dishes, flatware, utensils, pots and pans; one for meat and one for dairy meals. These are pulled out of their annual storage spaces, washed and cleaned, in order to replace all year-round dishes, which in turn are stored away for the duration of Passover, along with all food supplies that are either opened, or not considered or labeled "KOSHER FOR PASSOVER". It should be noted that year-round glassware, flatware, some utensils and pots may be koshered (rendered usable for Pesach) through a special purging process of either soaking and rinsing or boiling, as the case may require. There are also special procedures for koshered appliances, such as ovens, cook tops, micros, refrigerators, freezers, dishwashers, sinks, etc.

A thorough job of spring cleaning completes the task, so that lo and behold: the kosher kitchen not only sparkles and shines, but also takes on a new look and gives the whole household its unique Passover ambience. The pantry, refrigerator and freezer are then filled with an assorted array of Passover foods and products.

All that's left is the preparation of the tasty, tempting and traditional Seder foods. Their scent and aroma permeates the home. The beautifully appointed Seder table, with its candles, flowers, wine decanter, symbolic foods and unusual ritual objects, which quite often are "Objects d' Art" or family heirlooms, becomes the showpiece of the house.

Matzah is, of course, the only bread we are allowed to eat during the Passover festival. It is unleavened, because it has been completely baked within eighteen minutes after the water touched it, reminding us of the hasty preparations for the flight from Egypt so long ago. The only flour substitutes we can use for cooking or baking are: matzah meal, matzah cake flour, potato starch and ground nuts.

The food we serve during the Seder fulfills two goals: some of it must fit symbolically into the Passover story that we read in the Haggadah, like matzah or maror (bitter herb) for instance, or the four cups of wine that we drink. It also should provide for all gathered around the table—family and friends—a sense of sharing a festive meal and an enriching social experience.

You will find special recipes for Passover in this book. Bear in mind that, while many foods are forbidden on Passover, those allowed certainly provide ample opportunity to create, improvise and present varied and unusual culinary experiences. It seems Pesach brings out the best in the imaginative and innovative kosher cook.

CHAROSET [P]

1 cup pitted dates
12-oz pitted prunes
1-1/2 large Granny Smith apples, shredded
1/2 cup walnuts

1/2 medium size lemon, juice and zest
2 Tbsp red sweet wine
1 tsp cinnamon

Grind or chop dates, prunes and nuts. Add shredded apples, wine, lemon and cinnamon. Mix well.

Preparation time: 30 minutes
Makes: 2 cups

A traditional Sephardic recipe.

CHAROSET [P]

2 large apples, chopped or grated
3/4 cup walnuts, chopped or ground
1 tsp cinnamon

2 tsp sugar or honey
4 tsp sweet red wine or to taste

In food processor using "pulse" setting, chop apples. Add other ingredients and pulse 3 to 4 times. Chill.

Preparation time: 10 minutes
Serves: 4

Traditional Ashkenazi recipe. Increase according to number of guests.

BUCHARIAN BROWN EGGS [P]

12 large eggs
water to cover
1 medium red onion, chopped
1/4 cup olive oil

1/2 tsp salt
fresh ground pepper
juice 1 medium lemon

Boil the eggs in water for 10 minutes. Simmer for 2 hours. Remove eggs from water, crack but do not remove shells.

Braise eggs in olive oil, salt and onions for 1-1/2 hours. Remove shells before serving, Serve with lemon juice, salt and pepper.

Preparation time: 5 minutes
Cooking time: 3-1/2 hours
Serves: 12

Traditional recipe from the Mediterranean and the Black Sea countries. Egg yolk will be very dark.

HORSERADISH [P]

1 medium sized horseradish root, peeled
1 cup fresh cooked beets, peeled
3/4 cup white vinegar
1/2 cup sugar

In a food processor, add small pieces horseradish root and beets. Process till desired consistency. Transfer to a bowl and add vinegar and sugar. Adjust to your taste with either more vinegar or more sugar. Store in tightly covered jar.

Preparation time: 15 minutes
Serves: 8 to 12

GEFILTE FISH BALLS [P]

1-1/2 lbs pike, carp and white fish filets,
    cut in 2 inch pieces
1/4 cup matzo meal
2 large eggs, separated
1 medium onion, finely chopped
1 tsp salt
1/4 tsp white pepper
fish stock for cooking balls

In food processor, chop fish a few pieces at a time until all is fine and smooth. Add matzo meal, egg yolks, onion, salt and pepper using "pulse" speed of processor. In separate bowl, whip egg whites until stiff peaks form. Gently fold into fish mixture.
Using wet hand form balls, gently placing them into boiling stock. Cover. Return to boil. Remove cover, reduce heat and simmer for 1 hour, in fish stock (see below).

Preparation time: 30 minutes
Cooking time: 1 hour
Serves: 8

FISH STOCK [P]

2 lbs fish head, bones, skin of white fish
1 large carrot, cut in 1 inch pieces
1 large onion, quartered
3 large sprigs parsley
2 stalks celery
1 Tbsp salt
1/4 tsp white pepper
2 quarts cold water

In large soup pot combine all ingredients. Bring to a boil. Reduce heat and simmer while preparing fish balls.

GOLDEN GEFILTE FISH MOLD [P]

5 to 6 lbs firm-fleshed white fish,
   3 lbs after boned and skinned
3 medium onions
3 medium carrots
2 tsp salt
1 tsp pepper
2-1/2 Tbsp sugar

1 Tbsp oil
4 large eggs
1/4 cup cold water
1/4 cup matzo meal
1 Tbsp lemon juice
oil or spray
horseradish

Preheat oven to 325 degreees.

Place fish into chopping bowl or food processor. Add onions, carrots, eggs, seasonings and blend. Add matzo meal and water, a little at a time, while continuing to process or chop. Mix very well. Spray a 12 cup mold with cooking spray and spoon in fish. Bake uncovered for 1 hour. Fish will start to rise and get crisp around the edges. There will be liquid around the top. Don't overbake. Invert onto serving platter right from oven. Cover loosely and chill. Slice and serve with horseradish.

Preparation time: 20 minutes
Baking time: 1 hour
Serves: 12

SEPHARDIC FISH BALLS (BOULETTES) [P]

1 small raw potato, finely grated
2 lbs ground white fish
1 large egg
1/4 tsp nutmeg

1/4 tsp white pepper
1 Tbsp minced parsley
1/2 grated onion

Tomato Sauce:
3 Tbsp olive oil
6 cloves garlic, chopped
1 red pepper, sliced
2 jalapeno peppers (optional)

2 large tomatoes, peeled and chopped
1/4 cup chopped cilantro
1/2 cup water
1 Tbsp paprika
salt to taste

Put grated raw potato in kitchen towel and squeeze excess liquid. Combine fish, potato, egg, nutmeg, pepper, parsley and onion. Set aside.

For sauce; heat oil. Add garlic, peppers and tomatoes, saute well. Add cilantro, water, paprika and salt. Shape fish mixture into ping pong size balls. Add to sauce, cover and cook 25 minutes until done.

Preparation time: 25 minutes
Cooking time: 40 minutes
Serves: 8

CHICKEN SOUP [M]

1 large chicken,
    4 lbs addtional backs, necks, wings
water to cover
salt (optional)
8 peppercorns
1 bay leaf
1 small piece fresh ginger, peeled
1 carrot, cut in thirds
2 stalks celery with tops, cut in thirds
1 onion
1/2 cup parsley

Clean chicken and chicken parts thoroughly and place in pot. Cover with water. Bring to a boil. Skim off froth that rises to the surface.

Add other ingredients. Bring to a boil, reduce heat and simmer 1 hour or until chicken is tender.

Strain broth and cool. Refrigerate. Remove fat that has solidified on top. Reheat and serve with stuffed matzo balls.

Preparation time: 20 minutes
Cooking time: 1 hour
Serves: 18

NEVER FAIL MATZO BALLS [P]

1/2 cup pareve margarine,
    room temperature
2 large eggs, beaten
1/2 tsp salt
1/2 cup matzo meal
1 Tbsp parsley

Cream margarine and add eggs, salt, matzo meal and parsley. Mix well. Refrigerate several hours. Wet hands and form walnut sized matzo balls. Place on waxed paper. Bring water to boil in large saucepan. Add matzo balls, lower heat to simmer, cover tightly and cook 45 minutes. Drain. To serve, reheat in simmering chicken broth for 5 minutes.

Preparation time: 15 minutes
Cooking time: 45 minutes
Serves: 5 to 6

Can be prepared ahead and frozen after cooking. Defrost in refrigerator and reheat in soup.

STUFFED MATZO BALLS [M]

4 large eggs
3 Tbsp vegetable oil
1 cup unsalted matzo meal

1-1/2 tsp coarse salt
1/3 cup club soda

Stuffing:
1 Tbsp vegetable oil
1/2 cup finely chopped onion,
1/4 cup finely chopped celery
1/3 cup chopped parsley
1 large clove garlic, minced

3/4 cup finely diced cooked chicken
1 large egg
1/4 tsp dried sage (optional)
1/4 tsp salt
1/8 tsp nutmeg, ground
1/8 tsp pepper, ground

In medium bowl, whisk eggs and oil. Mix in matzo meal and salt. Add club soda and blend well. Cover and refrigerate at least 1 hour.

For stuffing: heat oil in small skillet over medium heat, saute onion and celery until softened, about 3 minutes. Add parsley and garlic, saute 1 minute. Transfer to food processor or blender. Add chicken, egg and seasoning. Pulse, to coarse consistency. Transfer to bowl, cover and refrigerate. Using moistened hands, roll matzo ball mixture into twelve 1-1/2 inch balls. Make deep hole in each matzo ball, place 1 Tbsp of filling into each hole. Reform ball enclosing filling. Bring large pot of salted water to a boil, lower heat and drop matzo balls into pot. Cover and cook until matzo balls are tender about 35 minutes. Using slotted spoon, remove matzo balls to bowl.

Preparation time: 25 minutes
Cooking time: 35 minutes
Serves: 12

Can be prepared 1 day ahead. Keep refrigerated.

LEEK AND MEAT PATTIES [M]

2/3 lb leeks, white part
1/2 lb celery root, peeled,
    cut into pieces
1 lb lean ground beef
1 large egg

6 Tbsp matzo meal
1 tsp salt
1/4 tsp pepper
oil for frying
lemon wedges for garnish

Cut off roots and all but one or two inches of green leek tops. Slice leeks in half lengthwise and rinse under cold running water to remove dirt. Cut leeks into 2 inch lengths. Place leeks and celery root in saucepan with water to cover. Bring to a boil, reduce heat, cover and simmer 30 minutes, until very tender. Drain well and turn into food processor to coarsely puree. In large bowl, combine pureed vegetable with ground beef, egg, matzo meal, salt and pepper. Shape into two inch patties, 1/2 inch thick. Dust with matzo meal and fry in hot oil until browned and crisp. Serve with lemon .

Preparation time: 15 minutes
Cooking time: 45
Serves: 4

STUFFED VEAL OR LAMB BREAST [M]

2 large eggs
2/3 cup water, approximately
1/2 cup matzo meal
1 small carrot, shredded
1 Tbsp minced parsley
1 Tbsp melted chicken fat or oil
1 tsp salt
pinch sugar

3 to 4 lb bone-in veal breast with pocket, well trimmed, or lamb breast
garlic salt, pepper, paprika, to taste
1 onion, coarsely chopped or small leek, white part only, thinly sliced
1 stalk celery, thinly sliced
1 carrot, thinly sliced
1/2 cup chicken broth, heated

Stuffing:
In mixing bowl, beat eggs lightly, add 1/2 cup water, matzo meal, carrot, parsley, chicken fat, salt and sugar. Stir to blend. Add water as needed to make a thick batter.

Meat preparation: Preheat oven to 350 degrees.

Spoon stuffing lightly into pocket. Close securely with skewers and string. Flatten with hand to distribute stuffing. Place on rack in deep roasting pan. Sprinkle with garlic salt, pepper and paprika. Arrange celery, onion, and carrot around veal. Add broth. Cover and bake about 2 hours until veal is tender and stuffing is firm. Add more broth from time to time, if needed. Slice veal between bones and serve with vegetables and pan juices.

Preparation time: 15 to 20 minutes
Cooking time: 2 hours approximately
Serves: 4

MATZO LASAGNE [M]

1 lb ground beef
1 large onion, minced
3 cloves garlic, minced
28 oz can Italian tomatoes
8 oz can tomato sauce
1/2 cup dry red wine
1 tsp salt
1/4 tsp pepper
2-1/2 tsp Italian seasoning

1 bay leaf
pinch sugar
3 Tbsp chopped parsley
10 oz pkg frozen spinach, thawed and drained
1/4 cup chopped basil
3 Tbsp olive oil
3 Tbsp matzo meal
3 matzos

In a large skillet, over high heat, brown meat, stirring often. Add onion and garlic and cook until tender. Add tomatoes, tomato sauce, wine, 1-1/2 tsp salt, pepper, Italian seasoning, bay leaf, sugar and parsley. Cook, uncovered, over low heat, stirring occasionally, about 2 hours.

In small bowl, combine spinach with basil and 1/2 tsp salt. Coat 8 inch square or 7 X 11 inch baking pan with 1 Tbsp oil, sprinkle with 1 Tbsp matzo meal. Moisten matzo by placing under running water and placing one in bottom of baking dish, cutting another into pieces to fill pan. Spoon on 1/3 the meat sauce, half the spinach, repeat, ending with sauce. Sprinkle top with remaining matzo meal and drizzle with remaining oil. Bake at 375 degrees 30 to 40 minutes until heated through.

Preparation time: 30 minutes
Baking time: 30 to 40 minutes
Serves: 4 to 5

ROAST CHICKEN WITH MATZO STUFFING [M]

Stuffing:
- 2 to 3 Tbsp chicken fat or oil
- 1/2 cup minced onion
- 1 stalk celery, minced
- 3 matzos, broken
- 1 Tbsp minced parsley
- 1/2 tsp seasoned salt
- 1/8 tsp pepper
- 1/2 tsp sage (optional)
- 1/2 tsp basil or tarragon (optional)
- 1/2 cup chicken broth

- 4 lb broiler-fryer chicken
- 2 Tbsp chicken fat or oil
- seasoned salt
- pepper
- paprika
- 1/2 cup minced onion
- 1 stalk celery, thinly sliced
- 1 large carrot, thinly sliced
- 1/2 cup chicken broth
- 1/2 cup dry white wine

Preheat oven to 450 degrees.

For stuffing: In a large skillet, heat chicken fat, add onion and celery and saute until tender, but not browned. Add matzos and brown lightly. Add seasonings and chicken broth. Set aside to cool.

Wash chicken and pat dry. Sprinkle cavity with seasoned salt. Stuff lightly. Truss chicken. Rub with chicken fat, sprinkle with seasonings. Place in small, shallow roasting pan. Roast 15 minutes, turn and roast 15 minutes longer. Remove chicken from pan, pour off drippings. Reduce heat to 425 degrees. Place minced onion, celery and carrot in bottom of pan. Put chicken on top of the vegetables, breast up. Combine broth and wine and pour over chicken. Roast at 425 degrees about 1 hour longer, basting every 15 minutes with pan liquid, until chicken is tender, leg moves easily and juices run clear.

Remove to warm platter. Reduce pan juices by cooking over high heat until slightly thickened.

Preparation time: 25 minutes
Baking time: 1-1/2 hours

Stuffing variation: Add one green apple, diced, 1/4 cup pecans or walnuts, chopped.

ORANGE AND ALMOND CHICKEN [M]

2 cups orange juice
1/4 cup brandy
grated zest of 1 large orange
1/4 tsp nutmeg
4 boneless, skinless chicken breast halves
salt and pepper
1/2 cup matzo cake meal
2 large eggs, beaten
1 cup matzo meal
1/4 cup oil
1/4 cup slivered almonds, toasted

Combine orange juice, brandy, orange zest and nutmeg. Wash chicken and pat dry with paper towel. Place chicken between 2 sheets of plastic wrap. Pound until 1/8 inch thick. Marinate 30 minutes at room temperature. Drain chicken, season with salt and pepper, dust with matzo cake meal, dip into eggs, then matzo meal. Refrigerate 20 minutes to set coating. In large skillet, heat 2 Tbsp oil add chicken without crowding pan and cook until golden, about 2 minutes, turn and brown. Remove to heated platter. Repeat with remaining chicken. Add marinade to pan and cook over high heat until slightly reduced. Add salt and pepper to taste. Pour sauce over chicken and sprinkle with almonds.

Preparation time: 50 minutes
Cooking time: 5 to 10 minutes
Serves: 4

MATZO-APPLE KUGELAS [P]

1-1/2 cups matzo farfel
1/2 cup chopped, blanched almonds
1/2 cup matzo cake meal
1/2 cup golden raisins,
    plumped in apple juice 1 hour
3 to 4 large tart apples,
    peeled and shredded
1/3 cup dark brown sugar, packed
1/2 tsp cinnamon
1/2 tsp salt
1/4 cup pareve margarine, melted
grated zest of 1 medium orange
6 large eggs

Preheat oven to 375 degrees. Grease 18 muffin cups.

Put farfel in colander, pour boiling water over, toss and squeeze out water, and cool. In a bowl, combine almonds and cake meal. Drain raisins and add with rest of ingredients to the farfel, adding eggs last. Fill muffin cups 3/4 full. Bake 25 to 30 minutes, until browned. Serve warm.

Preparation time: 20 minutes, plus 1 hour for raisins
Baking time: 25 to 30 minutes
Makes: 18 muffins

Can be made ahead of time. Freezes well.

VEGETABLE FARFEL KUGEL [P]

1 Tbsp pareve margarine
1 large green pepper, diced
2 medium onions, diced
2 stalks celery, diced
2 cups coarsely grated carrots
8 oz mushrooms, sliced
10 oz pkg frozen chopped spinach, thawed and drained
4 cups boiling water
6 oz matzo farfel or 3 cups broken matzo
7 large eggs, whites only
1-1/2 tsp salt
dash pepper
1 tsp sugar
1/2 cup toasted pine nuts (optional)
dash paprika

Preheat oven to 375 degrees. Grease 9 X 13 inch oven proof dish.

In large, non-stick skillet, saute fresh vegetables in margarine 3 to 5 minutes. Add drained spinach. Pour boiling water over farfel (in strainer) to moisten. Add farfel, vegetables, salt, pepper, sugar and nuts. Cool. Beat egg whites until stiff and fold into farfel mixture. Sprinkle with paprika.

Bake 45 minutes or longer until browned.

Preparation time: 30 minutes
Baking time: 45 to 60 minutes
Serves: 12 to 14

Freezes and rebakes well.

CARROT KUGEL [P]

6 large eggs, separated
2 cups grated carrots
1/2 cup matzo meal
1 cup chopped walnuts
1/2 cup oil
1 cup sugar
1 small lemon, peeled, seeded, and finely chopped
zest of 1 small lemon
1/8 tsp cinnamon
salt to taste

Preheat oven to 350 degrees.

In large bowl, beat egg yolks. Add remaining ingredients, except egg whites. Using clean, dry beaters, beat egg whites until stiff peaks form. Fold whites into carrot mixture. Pour into 2 quart souffle dish. Bake 45 minutes to 1 hour. Test center. When tester comes out clean, kugel is done. Serve at once.

Preparation time: 20 minutes
Baking time: 45 to 60 minutes
Serves: 8

SPINACH SOUFFLE [M/P]

1 medium onion, chopped
1 Tbsp chicken fat or
   pareve margarine, melted
10 oz pkg frozen spinach,
   thawed and drained
1 Tbsp matzo meal
salt
pepper
2 large eggs, separated

Preheat oven to 350 degrees. Grease 1 quart souffle mold.

In skillet, saute onion in chicken fat until tender. Combine spinach and sauteed onion. Add matzo meal, salt, pepper and beaten egg yolks. Beat egg whites and fold in gently. Pour into souffle mold and bake 35 minutes. Serve at once.

Preparation time: 10 minutes
Baking time: 35 minutes
Serves: 4

PASSOVER "POLENTA" [D]

3 large eggs, separated
1/2 cup water
3/4 cup matzo meal
1 tsp salt
dash pepper
3 Tbsp butter or margarine
1 medium onion, finely sliced
1 tsp butter or margarine
1/2 lb mushrooms cleaned and sliced thin
3 cups fresh tomatoes or
   1 lb can stewed tomatoes
1/2 cup grated Parmesan cheese,
   kosher for Passover

Preheat oven to 325 degrees. Grease 8 X 8 inch baking dish.

Beat egg yolks. Add water and 1/2 cup matzo meal. Beat egg whites until stiff and add to egg yolk mixture with salt, pepper and remaining matzo meal. Heat butter in large skillet. Add egg mixture by heaping tablespoon and fry till light brown. Remove from pan and set aside. Brown onion in same pan adding additional butter as needed. In baking dish, place fried cakes, then layer onions, mushrooms, tomatoes and cheese over fried cakes. Bake 45 minutes.

Preparation time: 20 minutes
Baking time: 45 minutes
Serves: 6

BITE-SIZE LEEK PANCAKES [P]

4 medium leeks
1/2 cup chopped parsley
1/2 cup matzo meal

3 large eggs beaten
salt and pepper to taste
oil for cooking

Wash leeks well under running water. Cut white and pale green part into 1/2 inch pieces. Place in a saucepan, cover with water. Simmer for 20 minutes until tender. Drain.

Chop leeks well and add parsley, eggs, matzo meal, salt and pepper, making a thick batter. Mix well. Add enough hot oil to coat skillet. Drop mixture by tablespoonful and brown on both sides. Drain on paper towels.

Preparation time: 30 minutes
Cooking time: 40 to 45 minutes

Do not use food processor. Greek specialty that's ideal as an appetizer or side dish.

PASSOVER GRANOLA [P]

4 cups matzo farfel
1 cup coarsely chopped nuts
1/4 cup peanut oil

2 cups honey
1/4 cup raisins

Preheat oven to 350 degrees.

Combine farfel, nuts, oil and honey. Spread out on a cookie sheet and bake 20-30 minutes, stirring from time to time. When cool, add raisins and store in an airtight container.

Preparation time: 5 to 10 minutes
Baking time: 20 to 30 minutes
Makes: 5-1/2 cups

Can be eaten as a snack or with milk as a cereal.

MATZO BREI (FRIED MATZO) [P/D]

4 matzos
hot water to cover
4 large eggs

1/8 tsp salt
2 Tbsp butter or pareve margarine

Soak matzos in hot water for 10 minutes. Press out water. Beat eggs well. Add matzos and salt. Melt butter in pan, add mixture. Fry until brown, turn and brown on other side.

Variations: Don't soak matzos. Run hot water over them, shake and add to eggs. Add cinnamon and sugar. Serve with fruit or jelly.

Preparation time: 10 minutes
Cooking time: 10 minutes
Serves: 4

HONEY GRIDDLE CAKES [P]

1/2 cup raisins
1 cup sweet red wine
8 oz matzo farfel
4 large eggs, beaten
1/2 tsp salt
1 Tbsp grated lemon zest
2 Tbsp brandy
1/2 cup chopped walnuts
oil for frying
1/4 cup honey
3 Tbsp water
3 Tbsp lemon juice
nutmeg

Soak raisins in wine at least 30 minutes. Drain well. Soak the matzo in cold water for 20 minutes, drain and squeeze dry. Mix matzo with eggs, salt, lemon zest, brandy, nuts and raisins.

Heat oil in large skillet and drop the mixture by tablespoon. Fry on both sides until golden brown. For syrup: in a saucepan, combine honey, water and lemon juice. Bring to boil, reduce heat and simmer for 4 minutes. Arrange griddle cakes on serving platter, pour on syrup and sprinkle with nutmeg. Can also be served with jam.

Preparation time: 15 minutes
Cooking time: 15 minutes
Serves: 2 to 4

FRUITY NUT COOKIES [P]

2 cups matzo meal
2 cups matzo farfel
1-1/4 cups sugar
1 tsp cinnamon
1/4 tsp powdered ginger
1 tsp salt
1/2 cup mashed banana
1 cup chopped walnuts
1 cup raisins
3 large eggs, well beaten
3/4 cup oil

Preheat oven to 350 degrees. Grease cookie sheets.

In a bowl, combine matzo meal, farfel, sugar, cinnamon, ginger and salt. Stir in nuts and raisins. In a bowl, beat eggs, oil and banana together. Add to dry mixture. Mix well. Drop by teaspoonful onto cookie sheet. Bake 20 minutes or until browned.

Preparation time: 15 to 20 minutes
Baking time: 20 minutes
Makes: 50 cookies

BASIC PASSOVER DOUGH   [P]

1 cup water
1/2 cup oil
1 tsp salt

1-1/2 cups matzo meal
4 large eggs

Preheat oven to 400 degrees

In a medium saucepan, bring water, oil and salt to rapid boil. Remove from heat and add matzo meal all at once. Stir well and return to heat for 2 to 3 minutes. Remove from heat and let stand 3 minutes. Add eggs, one at a time, beating well after each.

Bagels: Oil hands and roll about 2 Tbsp dough into a rope. Shape into bagel. Place on greased cookie sheet. Repeat with remaining dough. Bake about 40 minutes, or until browned. Makes 12.

Cream puffs: Grease cookie sheet. Drop by heaping tablespoon onto sheet. Bake 35 minutes or until brown. Makes 20.

Soup nuts: roll into 1/2 inch balls. Bake 15 minutes

Preparation time: 15 minutes
Baking time: see above

PASSOVER ROCKY ROAD BROWNIES   [P/D]

1 cup pareve margarine
1-1/2 cups sugar
1 cup matzo meal
4 oz unsweetened chocolate
4 large eggs

3 Tbsp instant powdered coffee
1/2 cup walnuts, chopped
7 oz miniature Passover marshmallows
2 tsp grated orange rind (optional)

Glaze:
1 12 oz pkg semisweet chocolate chips
1 Tbsp unsalted pareve margarine

Preheat oven to 325 degrees. Grease 9 X 13 inch baking pan.

Melt chocolate and margarine over very low heat, add instant coffee and cool. Beat eggs, add sugar, chocolate mixture and cake meal. Spread batter in pan and sprinkle with the nuts and rind. Bake for 20 minutes. Remove from oven and immediately add marshmallows to cover brownies. Melt marshmallows by placing pan back in oven, with oven turned off.

For glaze: melt chocolate chips with margarine over very low heat. While hot spread over the marshmallows. If glaze does not spread easily add a little oil. Place in freezer immediately. Remove from freezer 1 hour before serving and cut into squares.

Preparation time: 10 minutes
Baking time: 20 minutes
Makes: 24

ALMOND TORTE [P]

1 cup very finely chopped dried figs
1 cup ground almonds
1/3 cup matzo meal
3/4 tsp cinnamon

6 large eggs, separated
3/4 cup sugar
1/2 tsp almond extract (optional) or
 1 Tbsp apricot brandy (optional)

Preheat oven to 350 degrees. Oil 9 inch springform pan.

In mixing bowl, combine figs, almonds, matzo meal and cinnamon. In separate bowl, beat egg yolks until thick and lemon colored. Add almond extract or apricot brandy. Gradually beat in sugar until mixture is very thick and forms a ribbon. Add fig mixture. Mix well. In large bowl, whip egg whites just until stiff peaks form. Stir 1/4 of the egg whites into fig-yolk mixture to loosen the batter. Gently fold in remaining egg whites until completely combined. Spoon mixture into pan. Bake 45 to 50 minutes or until cake springs back when lightly pressed and cake tester inserted in center comes out clean. Cool on rack 10 minutes. Remove outer rim of pan. Allow to cool completely. Serve plain or topped with sweetened whipped cream when not served with a meat meal.

Preparation time: 30 minutes
Baking time: 45 to 50 minutes
Serves: 8 to 10

APRICOT SQUARES [P]

1 cup sugar
1 cup margarine
2 Tbsp lemon zest
1 tsp vanilla
2 large egg yolks

2 cups matzo meal
2 cups chopped walnuts
18 oz apricot preserves
1/4 cup lemon juice

Preheat oven to 325 degrees. Grease 9 X 13 inch pan.

Mix sugar and margarine. Add lemon zest, vanilla, egg yolks and blend well. Add matzo meal. Blend well. Add 1 cup nuts. Put 3/4 of dough into prepared pan. Bake for 20 minutes. Place 1/4 of unbaked dough in freezer. Combine apricot preserves and lemon juice. Remove baked dough from oven. Spread apricot mixture over hot baked dough. Remove dough from freezer and grate over apricots. Sprinkle with remaining cup of nuts. Bake for 30 to 35 minutes more. Cut into bars when cool.

Preparation time: 10 minutes
Baking time: 50 to 60 minutes
Makes: 40 bars.

CHOCOLATE WINE CAKE   [P]

1/2 cup cocoa, unsweetened
1/4 tsp salt
1/2 cup potato starch

8 large eggs, separated
1-1/2 cups sugar
1/4 cup sweet wine

Preheat oven to 350 degrees.

Sift cocoa, salt and potato starch together 3 times. Beat yolks until lemon colored and thick. Add sugar gradually. Beat well. Add dry ingredients alternately with wine. In separate bowl, beat egg whites with clean and dry beaters until stiff. Fold into yolk mixture. Pour into ungreased 10 inch tube pan. Bake for 50 to 60 minutes. Invert pan over bottle to cool before removing cake.

Preparation time: 25 minutes
Baking time: 50 to 60 minutes
Serves: 8 to 10

PASSOVER BANANA CAKE   [P]

7 large eggs, separated
1 cup sugar
3/4 cup bananas, mashed
1/4 cup orange juice or lemon juice
1 tsp pumpkin spice (optional)
1 tsp vanilla

3/4 cup matzo cake flour
1/4 cup potato starch
1/4 tsp salt
1/2 to 1 cup coarsely chopped nuts,
   walnut or pecans

Preheat oven to 350 degrees.

Beat yolks with sugar till light and creamy, 5 minutes. Fold bananas, juice, vanilla, cake and potato flour into egg yolks. Beat egg whites and salt until stiff. Fold into batter. Fold in nuts. Using an ungreased, tube pan with removeable bottom, bake for 40 to 45 minutes. Invert pan over bottle until cool.

Preparation time: 20 minutes
Baking time: 40 to 45 minutes
Serves: 8

CHOCOLATE NUT CANDY   [P]

12 oz semi-sweet chocolate chips
1 cup matzo farfel
1 cup chopped walnuts

Melt chocolate in double boiler. Add farfel and nuts. Mix thoroughly. Drop onto cookie sheet lined with waxed paper in smaller than walnut size amounts. Refrigerate. Place in fluted paper candy cups to serve. Can be frozen.

Preparation time: 5 minutes

KING'S CAKE [D/P]

2 Tbsp matzo meal
5 large eggs
2 Tbsp sweet butter or pareve margarine
1-1/4 cups sugar
1 tsp vanilla extract
2 tsp almond extract
grated zest of 1 small lemon
2-1/2 cups blanched almonds,
    chopped very fine
sliced or slivered almonds toasted

Preheat oven to 325 degrees.

Grease and sprinkle a 10 inch spring form with matzo meal. Set aside. Beat egg whites with salt till stiff and dry. In a large bowl, beat the yolks until foamy, gradually add sugar and continue beating until lemon colored. Gradually add the finely chopped almonds, the two extracts and lemon zest. It will be a very hard paste. Mix 1/3 of the beaten egg whites with the almond mixture to make it softer. Delicately fold in the remaining egg whites and pour into cake pan. Place in center of the middle rack for 1 hour without opening oven door. Leave the oven door ajar for 10 to 15 minutes. Remove pan from oven and place it upside down on a cooling rack. When cake is thoroughly cool, remove from pan and place it upside down over a cake dish. Sprinkle with toasted sliced almonds.

Preparation time: 30 minutes
Baking time: 1 hour plus 10 to 15 minutes with oven off when done.
Serves: 6

10 oz almonds makes 2-1/2 cups finely chopped.

APPLE STRAWBERRY CAKE [P]

6 large eggs
1-1/2 cups sugar
1/2 tsp salt
1 cup oil
3/4 cup potato starch
1 1/2 cups matzo cake meal
5 medium, Granny Smith apples,
    peeled and sliced
1/2 cup sugar
1 Tbsp cinnamon
1/2 cup strawberry preserves

Preheat oven to 350 degrees. Grease a 9 X 13 inch pan.

In a mixing bowl, beat eggs, sugar and salt. Add oil, continue beating. Sift starch and meal. Add to eggs. Put 1/2 of the batter into pan. Mix apples, sugar, cinnamon, and preserves. Place on batter. Top with remaining batter. Bake 1 hour.

Preparation time: 35 minutes
Baking time: 1 hour
Serves: 12

STRAWBERRY SPONGE ROLL [D]

6 large eggs, separated
1 cup sugar
1/2 cup potato starch
1/2 cup matzo cake meal
pinch salt

1/2 cup orange juice
zest of 1 orange, grated
1 pint heavy cream, whipped
sliced strawberries
matzo cake meal
Pareve margarine

Preheat oven to 375 degrees.

Beat egg yolks with 1/2 cup sugar till thick and lemon colored, about 3 minutes. Add orange juice and grated zest to the yolks. Beat egg whites till foamy. Slowly add remaining 1/2 cup sugar until stiff peaks form. Fold 1/3 of meringue into the yolk mixture. Fold the remaining meringue into the yolks. Combine potato starch, cake meal and salt. Using a strainer, sift mixture over the top of the egg mixture. Fold it in thoroughly but gently.

To make a roll: dust a jelly roll pan with matzo cake meal. Grease and line with waxed paper and regrease. Pour batter into pan. Smooth to outer edges. Bake for 12 to 15 minutes. Sprinkle a clean, dry towel liberally with cake meal. Invert baked cake onto towel. Remove pan and strip off paper. Cut brown edges off hot cake and using the towel, roll the cake into a cylinder. When cooled, unroll cake. Fill with whipped cream and sliced strawberries sweetened to taste. Reroll. Decorate with strawberries and/or whipped cream.

Preparation time: 30 minutes
Baking time:
Serves: 6

LEMON CAKE [P]

9 large eggs, separated
6 Tbsp water
2 cups sugar
2-1/2 tsp lemon zest

1/4 cup lemon juice
1/2 tsp salt
3/4 cup matzo cake flour
3/4 cup potato starch

Preheat oven to 350 degrees.

Beat egg yolks with water until light and fluffy. Add lemon juice and sugar. Beat 5 minutes. Add lemon zest, beat 2 minutes. Sift together matzo cake flour and potato starch. Fold into yolk mixture. In separate bowl, with clean and dry beaters, beat egg whites with salt until stiff peaks form. Fold into egg yolk batter. Rinse 10 inch ungreased tube pan with water, shake out, and add batter. Bake for 1 hour and 10 minutes. Invert pan over a bottle and cool.

Preparation time: 30 minutes
Baking time: 70 minutes
Serves: 12

OUR THANKS TO THE CONTRIBUTORS:

Abehsera, Melissa
Altura, Florence
Atkins, Sylvia
Balonoff, Edith
Barak, Roz
Beezy, Annette
Behn, Ruth
Benair, Maguy
Berger, Helen
Berinstein, Gladys
Bieber, Geri
Bienenfeld, Dodie
Blahd, Mitzi
Blumenthal, Shirley
Breslow, Bea
Bronsen, Claire
Brott, June
Buchsbaum, Mary
Carmona, Betty
Chester, Ida
Cohen, Arlene
Cohen, Bert
Cooper, Gillian
Collins, Boyd Ward
Comparti, Myrna
Diamant, Bunny
Dortort, Rose
Elinson, Katie
Erlichman, Gussie
Esrich, Dorothy
Feldman, Jackie
Fiske, Ruth
Freedman, Pat
Freeman, Beverly
Freeman, Tamar
Fried, Millie
Friedland, Vi
Friedman, Ruth
Garr, Myne
Geller, Kate
Gerard, Franco
Gerber, Anne
Getzkin, Benita
Glasser, Marie
Glazer, Phyllis
Goldberg, Joyce
Goldenson, Ann
Goldfarb, Blanche
Goldfinger, Marsha
Goldich, Esther
Goldman, Jill
Goldman, Lillian
Goldstine, Roz
Goldwasser, Lottie
Gordon, Ruth
Gorman, Joy
Gould, Dorothy

Greenfield, Pauline
Greenwold, Ruth Jubelier
Greinetz, Toba
Grotsky, Esther
Guefin, Karel
Heeger, Eleanor
Hellman, Lois
Hersch, Millie
Hirsch, Nita
Hirth, Ruth
Josephson, Marion
Kabaker, Betty
Kamenir, Charlotte
Kamenir, Dr. Edward
Kanner, Lucy
Kaplan, Bella
Kaplan, Marjorie
Kaplan, Sylvia
Karosen, Honey
Katz, Aundrea
Katz, Lillian
Kaye, Helen
Kory, Shirley
Kramer, Ruth
Kriegel, Sara
Lamm, Judy
Landres, Mimi
Lavender, Shelley
Lazar, Serene
Lawson, Sylvia
Lee, Sadie
Leff, Ada
Levich, Susan
Levy, Peachy
Lewitt, Marilyn
Leytus, Joyce
Lieber, Esther
Liebross, Lillian
Lincoff, Miriam
Loeb, Eve
Manzi, Barbara Bakal
Marks, Penny
Maron, Bunny
Maurer, Roz
Miller, Anna
Miller, Diane
Miller, Irma
Miller, Jan
Miller, Judith
Mittleman, Ruth
Molmud, Arline
Mornaghan, Lili
Nimmer, Gloria Dee
Ostrow, Bel
Ostrow, Mona
Otchis, Ethel
Pennish, Evelyn

Powell, Jean
Pressman, Marjorie
Rabinovitch, Dr. Babbette
Rainey, Helen
Raskin, Livia
Ratner, Mildred
Ravin, Muriel
Rembaum, Fredi
Reznick, Janice Kamenir
Rips, Raasche
Rubin, Bobie
Rubin, Esther
Sadan, Edmond
Salter, Janet
Salzberg, Ruth
Satnick, Diana
Schindel, Lois
Schnur, Denise
Shapiro, Lorraine
Shapiro, Rita
Schott, Daisy
Schweitzer, Claire
Shulman, Tommie
Silvers, Hilda
Sklansky, Berta
Slaten, Lila
Smolens, Ruth
Sommers, Barbara
Stogel, Adele
Straker, Sybil
Suplin, Adelaide
Szlapak-Abbema, Eliana
Tidus, Barbara
Thornton, Lolo
Tobman, Ann
Tolman, Ann
Troy, Marian
Tynan, Millie
Unger, Virginia
Vorspan, Bonnie
Wachtel, Marsha
Wacker, Ellen
Wagman, Miriam
Walter, Peggy
Ward, Susan
Ward, Sylvia
Wartik, Natalie
Weisman, Lydia
Weiss, Mark
Weiss, Trudi
Wexler, Miriam
White, Harriet
Winkler, Renee
Whizin, Shirley
Wilkin, Judy
Wincelberg, Anita
Yuster, Rose

MENUS

SABBATH

Wine, Whole Wheat Chalah, Vodka Herring, Fresh Garden Salad with Oregano and Basil Dressing, Chicken Okra Soup, Basic Roast Chicken, Broccoli, Wild Rice with Peas, Coffee Rum Mousse.

ROSH HASHANAH

Wine, Challah (made round), Apple with Honey, "Nouvelle" Chopped Liver on Lettuce with Garnish, Ginger Chicken Soup, Turkey with Fruit Stuffing, Farfel, Liqueur Glazed Baby Carrots, Warm Vinigrette of Green Beans, Pear Honey Cake, Melon and Grapes.

YOM KIPPUR AND TISHA B'AV (BREAK THE FAST)

No. 1:

Taramasalata (Greek Cod Roe Dip) with Crackers, Gefilte Fish Balls with Horseradish, German Herring Salad, Pickled Salmon, Buttermilk Noodle Pudding, Vegetable Cholent or Tabouli, Bialys and Bagels, Kosher Dill Pickles, Old Fashioned Chocolate Cake, Fresh Fruit Platter.

No. 2:

Poached Salmon with Caper Sauce, Minted Yogurt Salad, Classic Noodle Pudding, Tabouli Salad, Israeli Chocolate Mousse Cake, Sticky Cinnamon Buns.

SUKKOT/SIMCHAT TORAH PARTY

No. 1: Yomtov Dinner

Wine, Challah, Assorted Raw Vegetables With Classic Humous, Hot Beet Borscht with Boiled Baby New Potatoes, Israeli Pomegranate Chicken or Sweet and Sour Stuffed Cabbage, Barley Casserole, Fresh Snow Peas, Pecan Torte with Raspberries and Lemon, Old World Pear Cake, Cranberry Strudel.

SUKKOT DINNER DURING THE WEEK

No. 2: Vegetarian

Dolmathes, Olives, Radishes and Carrot Sticks, Stuffed Mushrooms, Vegetarian Barley Soup, Vegetarian Moussaka, Stuffed Onions, Santa Fe Cheese Bread, Baked Stuffed Pears.

HANUKKAH

Caponata with Crackers, Moroccan Pepper and Tomato Salad, Brisket with Coffee and Wine, Latke Potpourri:
 Lacy Potato Pancakes with Apple Pear Chutney, Mushroom Latkas, Zucchini Latkas, Zucchini and Potato Latkas.
Israeli Doughnuts (*Soofganiot*), Italian Strawberry Ice, Bruneli, Drop Kichlach.

LAG B'OMER PICNIC

Eggplant Relish Italian Style, Tapanade with Crackers, Smoked Turkey or Barbeque Brisket, Assorted Breads for Sandwiches, Pasta Garden Salad, Cauliflower and Olive Salad, French White Bean Salad, Chocolate Dipped Biscotti, Nutty Fruit Bars.

PURIM PARTY

Fresh Garden Bruschetta, Israeli Chopped Liver, Spanakopita, Smoked Salmon With Endive, Assorted Quiches: Green Chili Quiche, Vegetarian Quiche, Quiche Provencale, Almond Brittle, Nut Brittle, Hamantaschen, Italian Hamantaschen, Fresh Fruit.

PASSOVER

Seder Plate

Greens (Parsley, Green Onion or Romaine), Roasted Egg, Salt Water, Shank Bone (Roasted), Bitter Herbs (Horseradish), Charoset.
Matzo on Separate Plate.

No. 1 Seder Dinner

Wine, Charoset, Hard Boiled Egg, Golden Gefilte Mold with Horseradish, Chicken Soup with Never-Fail Matzo Balls, Roast Chicken with Matzo Stuffing, Bite-Sized Leek Pancakes, Chocolate Wine Cake, Strawberry Sponge Roll with Fresh Strawberries.

No. 2 Seder Dinner

Wine, Charoset, Boiled Baby New Potatoes, Bucharian Brown Eggs, Sephardic Fish Balls, Chicken Soup with Stuffed Matzo Balls, Stuffed Veal Breast, Carrot Kugel, Fresh Asparagus, Apple Strawberry Cake, Fruity Nut Cookies or Hazelnut Cookies, Lemon Cake.

SHAVUOT—INTERNATIONAL STYLE

Wine, "Polish" Houska Challah, "Greek" Tzatziki, "French" Potato Leek Soup, Herbed French Crepes or Russian Blintzes, "California" Summer Squash Cheesies, Artichokes of the Italian Jews, Spanish Orange Flan, Israeli Chocolate/Orange Liqueur.

TU B'SHVAT PICNIC

Cold Rhubarb Soup, Apples Stuffed With Chicken, Swiss Green Pea Salad, Greek Flatbread, Fruit Melange, Chocolate Meringues.

ISRAEL INDEPENDENCE DAY LUNCH

Spinach Filled Challah, Onion Pletzl, Israeli Carrot Salad, Israeli Tuna Salad, Persian Chopped Salad, Baklava, Hungarian Pull-Apart Coffee Cake, Fresh Fruit.

INDEX

BREADS
Brioche for Bread Machine – 23
Challah – 22
Cinnamon Walnut Coffee Cake – 28
English Scones – 29
Glazed Dark Bran Muffins – 32
Greek Flatbread – 36
Houska Challah with Milk – 24
Hungarian Pull Apart Coffee Cake – 28
Hungarian Horns – 29
Israeli Doughnuts Soofganiot – 33
New Method Popovers – 36
Onion Pletzl – 36
Orange Hazelnut Buns – 31
Pecan Alligator – 27
Pecan Lemon Bread – 34
Raisin Challah – 25
Raisin Walnut Wheat Bread – 25
Santa Fe Cheese Bread – 33
Sour Cream Coffee Cake – 30
Spinach Herb Filling for Challah – 22
Sticky Cinnamon Buns – 30
Strawberry Ambrosia Muffins – 32
Sweet & Easy Cornbread – 34
Thin Crust Pizza – 35
Water Bagels – 26
Whole Wheat Challah – 23
Whole Wheat Citrus Bread; Electric Bread Machine Method – 26

APPETIZERS
Caponata – 43
Caviar Dip in Pumpernickel Bowl – 40
Chilied Bean Dip – 40
Classic Humous – 44
Crannberry Meatballs – 53
Dipsy Daisy – 40
Dolmathes – 45
Eggplant Relish Italian Style – 42
Feta Stuffed Tomatos – 42
Fresh Garden Bruschetta – 41
Golden Cheese and Onion Crackers – 51
German Herring Salad – 46
Horseradish and Chive Dip – 41
Horseradish Meatballs, Hot Marmalade Sauce – 54
Israeli Secret Chopped Liver – 49
Knish Roll-Ups – 53
Kosher Dill Pickles or Tomatoes – 44
Kreplach – 52
Lachmajene Middle Eastern Pizza – 52
Miso Seasoned Fish – 48
"Nouvelle" Chopped Liver – 49
Roast Peppers Israeli Style – 43
Salmon Gravlox, Dill Sauce – 48
Smoked Salmon with Endive – 47
Smoked Whitefish Spread – 46
Spanakopita – 51
Spicy Marinated Mushrooms – 42
Stuffed Mushrooms – 50
Tapanade – 45
Tarmasalata Greek Cod Roe Dip – 41
Tiropetes – 50
Traditional Chopped Liver – 49
Tzatziki Greek Cucumber and Yogurt Spread – 46
Vodka Herring – 47

SOUPS
Asparagus Soup – 67
Carrot and Leek Soup – 66
Chicken Okra Soup – 68
Cold Rhubarb Soup – 61
Corn Chowder – 63
Cucumber Soup – 60
Easy Beet Borscht – 62
Gazpacho – 58
Ginger Chicken Soup – 68
Golden Carrot and Corn Soup – 66
Hearty Herb Lentil Soup – 65
Hot and Sour Soup – 69
Hot Beet Borscht – 70
Lemon Chicken Soup – 67
Minestrone – 63
Mushroom Soup – 64
Oxtail Soup – 70
Peach and Apple Gazpacho – 59
Peach Soup – 59
Potage D'Agneau Provencale – 72
Potato Leek Soup – 60
Red Snapper Chowder – 72
Sorrell Soup Schav – 61
Spanish Fish Soup – 71
Split Pea Soup – 65
Squash Soup – 64
Sweet and Sour Cabbage Borscht with Short Ribs – 69
Vegetarian Barley Soup – 62
Vegetable Beef Soup – 71
Watercress Soup – 58

SALADS AND DRESSINGS
Alsatian Cheese Salad – 89
Balsamic Vinegar Dijon Dressing with a Simple Salad – 90
Cauliflower and Olive Salad – 79
Chinese Chicken Salad – 83
Couscous and Orange Salad – 85
Curried Rice Salad – 84
Eggplant Salad – 78
Far Eastern Chicken Salad – 83
French White Bean Salad – 77
Israeli Carrot Salad – 77
Israeli Tuna Salad – 81
Minted Yogurt Salad – 76
Moroccan Pepper and Tomato Salad – 79
Oil Free Vinaigrette Dressing – 90
Old Fashioned New Potato Salad – 86
Oregano and Basil Dressing – 90
Oriental Vegetable Salad – 80
Pasta Garden Salad – 87
Persian Chopped Salad – 81
Rye Apple Salad – 84
Salad Tosca – 82
Salad with Chicken Livers – 82
Smoked Pasta Salad – 88
Smoked Salmon Potato Salad – 86
Spinach Salad with Mandarin Oranges – 76
Swiss Green Pea Salad – 78
Sumi Salad – 80
Tabouli Salad – 85
Turkey Rice Salad – 89
Zesty Chicken Salad – 82

PICKLES AND SAUCES
Apple-Pear Chutney – 97
Authentic Dill Pickles – 103

Chinese Cucumbers – 102
Chinese Cranapple – 99
Cranberry Relish – 99
Curried Fruit – 98
Curry Sauce – 108
Dill Sauce – 108
Fig-Orange Jam – 100
Ginger Mustard Marinade and Glaze – 106
Glaze for Lamb Roast – 105
Herb Vinegar Marinated Red Onions – 101
Hot Cranberry Wine Cup – 104
Marinade for Meat or Chicken – 106
Marinated Red Onions – 94
Moroccan Tomatoes Chuchuka – 96
Onion Marmelade – 95
Papaya-Apple Chutney – 97
Peach Chutney – 98
Pepper Mosaic Relish – 96
Pesto – 104
Pickled Beets – 103
Quick Classic Brown Sauce – 105
Red Onion Relish – 94
Roasted Yellow Tomatoes – 95
Summer Plum Salsa – 100
Sweet and Sour Cucumbers – 102
Sweet Pickle Chips – 101
Vin Chaud – 107
Very Tomatoes Sauce – 104

VEGETABLES
Artichokes of the Italian Jews – 112
Asparagus Tarragon – 113
Brussels Sprouts with Verve – 112
B'tampt Potatoes – 120
Cheese Potato Bake – 120
Citrus Squash – 126
Cranberry Glazed Sweet Potatoes – 124
Creamed Spinach – 124
Curried Eggplant – 115
Flaumen-Potato Tzimmes – 121
Ginger Beans – 126
Jerusalem Artichokes – 112
Lacy Potato Pancakes – 121
Leeks Victoire – 116
Lima Beans, Creole Style – 116
Liqueur Glazed Baby Carrots – 113
Mediterranean Zucchini Bake – 125
Moroccan Carrots – 114
Mushroom Latkes – 122
Mustard Glazed Carrots – 114
Mushroom Moussaka – 117
North African Stuffed Tomatoes – 125
Orange and Yam Casserole – 124
Stuffed Onions – 119
Summer Squash Cheesies – 126
Sun Dried Tomatoes – 125
Sweet and Sour Baby Onions – 119
Sweet Potato Pudding – 123
Tomato, Onion, Potato Melange – 123
Vegetarian Moussaka – 118
Vegetable Tempura – 118
Warm Vinaigrette of Green Beans – 115
Zucchini and Potato Latkes – 122
Zucchini Pancakes – 122

CASSEROLES
Bakharian Pilaf – 138
Barley Casserole – 135
Bean Casserole – 141
Black Bean Chili – 142
Blintzes – 143
Brown Rice with Black Beans – 137
Buttermilk Noodle Pudding – 130
Carmelized Kugel – 130
Classic Noodle Pudding – 131
Confetti Rice, Microwavable – 137
Cornmeal Pudding – 133
Farfel – 139
Fried Rice – 138
Garden Lasagna – 134
Greek Stuffed Tomatoes – 134
Green Chili Quiche – 131
Herbed French Crepes – 144
Indian Fruit and Vegetable Curry – 142
Israeli Chamin or Cholent – 140
Mamaliga Baked with Cheese and Tomato Sauce – 133
Onion Souffle – 144
Quiche Provencale – 132
Risi Bisi with Pine Nuts – 136
Spiced Rice – 136
Vegetable Cholent – 139
Vegetarian Quiche – 132
Wild Rice with Peas – 135
Zucchini Frittata – 141

FISH
Baked Stuffed Gefilte Fish – 148
Bass Poached with Fennel and Oranges – 160
Bass with Tomatoes and Black Olives – 162
Fish Espanol – 157
French Fish Stew – 149
Gefilte Fish Loaf – 159
Halibut Creole – 158
Halibut in Dijon Vinaigrette – 158
Italian Fish Stew – 149
Microwave Poached Salmon – 153
Moroccan Fish – 156
Onion Marmalade and Tomato Butter for Fish – 160
Orange Roughy En Ramequin – 156
Papaya Relish for Fish – 160
Pecan Lemon Halibut – 159
Pickled Salmon – 153
Poached Salmon with Caper Sauce – 152
Salmon with Red Currants – 155
Sherried Salmon – 155
Sicilian Fresh Tuna – 150
Smoked Peppered Salmon – 154
Stuffed Fish in Lettuce Packets – 150
Walnut Stuffed Trout – 151

MEAT RECIPES
Austro-Hungarian Beef – 171
Bar-B-Q Brisket – 170
Beef with Chinese Peas – 174
Braised Veal Roast – 179
Brisket with Coffee and Wine – 168
Creole Chili – 174
Essig Fleisch (Sweet and Sour) – 171
French Mustard Pot Roast – 172
Glazed Beef Brisket – 170
Indian Lamb Curry – 177
Indonesian Bar B.Q. Beef Ribs – 173
Israeli Steak Sandwich – 169
Italian-Style Pot Roast – 172
Lamb Stew and Couscous – 176
Lamb with Plum Sauce – 175
Marinade for Meat or Chicken – 106

INDEX **259**

Osso Bucco (Veal Shanks) – 178
Rib Roast with Mushroom Sauce – 180
Sherried Veal – 178
Short Rib Tzimmes – 173
Stuffed Cabbage with Apricots – 168
Stuffed Cabbage Hungarian Style – 167
Stuffed Lamb Shoulder – 175
Sweet and Sour Stuffed Cabbage – 166
Tahini Dressing – 169
Veal Stew with Green Olives – 179

POULTRY

Apples stuffed with Curried Chicken – 192
Apricot Cornish Hens – 192
Artichoke Chicken – 185
Basic Roast Chicken – 184
Cherry Stuffing – 198
Chicken Fideo, Fideo – 188
Chicken in Filo Bastilla – 184
Chicken Puerto Vallarta – 189
Chicken Stir-Fry – 191
Chicken with Dried Fruit – 190
Cranberry Chestnut Stuffing – 196
Different Ways with Duckling – 197
Do Ahead Turkey Roast – 194
Fruit Stuffing for Turkey – 197
Greek Style Cornish Game Hens – 193
Green Pepper Sauce – 198
Ground Turkey or Chicken Loaf – 193
Honey Glazed Chicken with Apples – 187
Honey Nutty Chicken – 190
Israeli Pomegranate Chicken – 188
Jamaican Chicken – 186
Kabuki Chicken – 189
Mango Sauce – 198
Middle Eastern Chicken – 186
Orange Ginger Chicken – 190
Sesame Chicken – 187
Smoked Turkey – 194
Turkey Breast Champagne – 195
Turkey Chili – 195
Turkey Molé – 196

COOKIES

Almond Brittle – 214
Almond Sesame Sweets – 215
Bittersweet Chocolate Candy – 216
Bruneli – 212
Butterscotch Oat Crisps – 211
Chocolate Biscotti – 207
Chocolate Chip Mandelbrodt – 205
Chocolate Dipped Biscotti – 208
Chocolate Filled Shortbread – 209
Chocolate Meringues – 212
Chocolate Truffles – 216
Cinnamon Mandelbrodt – 204
Drop Kichlach – 214
Espresso Truffles – 215
Fruited Honey Spice Bars – 211
Hamantaschen – 202, 203
Hazelnut Cookies – 213
Hungarian Chocolate Nut Bar – 210
Italian Hamantaschen – 204
Lebkuchen – 207
Lime Squares – 208
Mock Strudel – 206
Nut Brittle – 214
Nutty Fruit Bars – 210
Rugelach – 205
Traditional Pfeffernuesse – 206
Walnut Cookies – 213

DESSERTS

Apple Cinnamon Bundt Cake – 225
Baked Stuffed Pears – 232
Blueberry Buttermilk Tart – 227
Bread Pudding with Whiskey Sauce – 230
Cherry Pecan Cheesecake – 222
Chocolate Bread Pudding – 229
Chocolate Souffle – 231
Coffee Rum Mousse – 233
Cookie Dough for Pies – 226
Cranberry Strudel – 234
Deep Dish Apple and Pear Pie – 228
Dessert Cheese Blintzes – 229
Fresh Fruit Pie – 228
Fruit Melange – 233
German Style Apple Torte – 225
Hazelnut Torte – 220
Hungarian Torte – 220
Israeli Chocolate Mousse Cake – 232
Italian Cheese Cake Puff – 222
Italian Strawberry Ice – 234
"Lite" Chocolate Cheesecake – 221
Nine Inch Pie Crust – 229
Old Fashioned Chocolate Cake – 226
Old Kentucky Fruitcake – 223
Old World Pear Cake – 224
Pear Honey Cake – 224
Pecan Torte with Raspberries and Lemon – 221
Spanish Orange Flan – 232
Sticky Toffee Pudding – 230

PASSOVER RECIPES

Almond Torte – 251
Apple Strawberry Cake – 253
Apricot Squares – 251
Basic Passover Dough – 250
Bite-size Leek Pancakes – 248
Bucharian Brown Eggs – 238
Carrot Kugel – 246
Charoset – 238
Charoset – 238
Chicken Soup – 241
Chocolate Nut Candy – 252
Chocolate Wine Cake – 252
Fish Stock – 239
Fruity Nut Cookies – 249
Gefilte Fish Balls – 239
Golden Gefilte Fish Mold – 240
Honey Griddle Cakes – 249
Horseradish – 239
King's Cake – 253
Leek and Meat Patties – 242
Lemon Cake – 254
Matzo Apple Kugelas – 245
Matzo Brei or Fried Matzo – 248
Matzo Lasagne – 243
Never Fail Matzo Balls – 241
Orange and Almond Chicken – 245
Passover Banana Cake – 252
Passover Granola – 248
Passover "Polenta" – 247
Passover Rocky Road Brownies – 250
Roast Chicken with Matzo Stuffing – 244
Sephardic Fish Balls, Boulettes – 240
Spinach Souffle – 247
Strawberry Sponge Roll – 254
Stuffed Matzo Balls – 242
Stuffed Veal Breast – 243
Vegetable Farfel Kugel – 246